The Airline Pilots

A Study in Elite Unionization

The Airline Pilots
A Study in Elite Unionization

George E. Hopkins

Harvard University Press
Cambridge, Massachusetts
1971

© 1971 by the President and Fellows of Harvard College
All rights reserved
Distributed in Great Britain by Oxford University Press, London
Printed in the United States of America
Library of Congress Catalog Card Number 71-152699
SBN 674-01275-5

For Elaine
and Ginger

Acknowledgments

This study would have been impossible without the cooperation of the staff and officers of the Air Line Pilots Association. President Charles Ruby graciously allowed me full access to the union's noncurrent archival material, placing neither restrictions on my research nor censorship on the final copy. The members of the Chicago staff of the union were polite, and their thoughtful descriptions of ALPA's functions benefited me enormously. Mr. Wallace W. Anderson, Executive Assistant to the President, was particularly helpful in pointing out the location of important correspondence files, long-forgotten boxes of memorabilia relating to the union's origin, and the stenographic records of conventions and formal meetings. In addition, he patiently endured, frequently on his own time, hours of my questions about the union's nature, its early leaders, and its present condition. As a final burden, he read the finished manuscript and kept me from error on several occasions, although of course its shortcomings are my responsibility alone.

I must credit Professor Paul F. Boller of the University of Massachusetts at Boston for inspiring me, while I was an undergraduate, to pursue a career of scholarship. I owe an enormous debt to Professor Robert A. Divine of the University of Texas at Austin and Professor David D.

Van Tassel of Case Western Reserve University, both of whom read the manuscript, for their help and guidance in initiating me to the professional study of history. Professor Robert W. McAhren of Washington and Lee University befriended me in this task, listening long and patiently to my ideas. In addition, Professors Joe B. Frantz, Phillip L. White, and Forest G. Hill of the University of Texas at Austin read the preliminary manuscript and offered valuable advice. My colleagues at Western Illinois University, particularly Professors William Burton, George Shadwick, and Larry Balsamo, provided an atmosphere of wit and scholarship in which to work while I wrote the final draft. Miss Kathryn Kallweit, a student at Western Illinois University, typed the final draft and rendered valuable editorial assistance as a complement to her unfailing good humor.

I must thank David and Phylis Ekleberry and Robert and Priscilla Borgstrom for opening their homes to my family during a portion of my research. Edgar and Patsy Sneed, Mike and Lynne McMahon, Charles and Sue Gouaux, and Nicholas and Susan Bocher deserve special thanks for offering their friendship and encouragement. Finally, I must acknowledge the help of my wife, Elaine Bridges Hopkins, who was my constant critic and companion.

Macomb, Illinois
November, 1970

Contents

Illustrations

The Airline Pilots
A Study in Elite Unionization

Abbreviations

AA	American Airways (American Airlines)
ALPA	Air Line Pilots Association
A.S.B.	Aviation Safety Board
ATA	Air Transport Association
ATC	Air Transport Command
BAT	Boeing Air Transport
C.A.A.	Civil Aeronautics Authority
CAB	Civil Aeronautics Board
EAL	Eastern Air Lines
EAT	Eastern Air Transport
I.C.C.	Interstate Commerce Commission
IFALPA	International Federation of Air Line Pilots
NAPA	National Air Pilots Association
NAT	National Air Transport
N.A.T.A.B.	National Air Transportation Adjustment Board
N.I.R.A.	National Industrial Recovery Act
N.L.B.	National Labor Board
N.M.B.	National Mediation Board
NPA	National Parks Airways
N.R.A.	National Recovery Administration
NWA	Northwest Airways
PAA	Pan American Airways
PPA	Professional Pilots Association
TAT	Transcontinental Air Transport
TWA	Trans World Airlines
T&WA	Transcontinental and Western Air
UAL	United Air Lines
WAE	Western Air Express

Introduction

The men who fly the nation's airliners have achieved such
unparalleled prosperity that they are perhaps the best
symbols of the good life in our affluent, technocratic society.
Although skeptics sometimes say that they are little more
than glorified bus drivers, their customary three-day work
week and salaries which can go as high as $40,000 annually
give them the kind of prestige which acquisitive civilizations
rarely bestow on bus drivers. Despite what the public and
many pilots themselves think however, today's incredibly
high pilot salaries result less from the responsibility pilots
bear or the technical skill they possess than from the protected position they have achieved through a union. That
union is the Air Line Pilots Association (ALPA) of the
AFL–CIO, which restricts its membership to professional
pilots who are employed on U.S. airlines. Owing to air
transportation's ever increasing dominance of the passenger
travel system, ALPA currently ranks as one of the most
influential and powerful labor organizations in the country.
Over 30,000 of the men who work in the cockpits of the
nation's airliners are members of the union, and the minority
who are not members usually belong to one of its derivative
splinters. Speaking through ALPA, the pilots have exerted
influence on almost every aspect of the development of

1

commercial aviation, and on matters as diverse as aircraft technology and the current epidemic of "skyjacking." As America enters the age of "jumbo jets," such as the Boeing 747, it seems likely that the importance of the union, speaking for the workers located at the industry's critical apex, will continue to grow.

This study focuses on the evolution of the profession, the process of unionization, and the subsequent techniques through which the union secured enough federal protective legislation to make the professional airline pilot practically a ward of the state. Under the leadership of a rambunctious United Air Lines pilot named David L. Behncke, the pilots entered actively into the maelstrom of Washington politics during the New Deal and won almost every battle they engaged in. Even when they lost they managed, as in the air-mail cancellations controversy of 1934, to make it seem as if they had won. By shamelessly manipulating the masculinity symbols which were so blatantly a part of aviation, by assiduously exploiting anxiety over air safety at a time when Congressmen were flying more and enjoying it less, and by loyally lining up behind the Roosevelt Administration when almost every prominent aviator in the country (including Charles A. Lindbergh) opposed it, Behncke and his pilots provided a point of departure for comparing the effectiveness of special-interest, pressure groups in Washington. By 1938 the union's position was so secure and the economic future of its members was so certain that not until the early 1960s, when the introduction of jets created considerable temporary technological unemployment, did it have any major external problems.

The metamorphosis of the pilots from outspoken rugged individualists into close-lipped advocates of union solidarity was a complicated process, involving a straightforward rejection of some ancient and ingrained notions about "professionalism." The pilots initially responded to the mystique of the aviator, which during the 1920s and 1930s depicted them as supermen, by thinking of themselves as "professionals." But when the depression revealed that they were as hopelessly dependent on the good will of their employers as any other group of salaried workers, they acted to protect themselves. Ironically, only through unionization and formal identification with the major institutions of the labor movement could they give substance to their cherished ideal. In addition, their resort to collective action has provided both a bench mark for comparison and a model for emulation in the movement to unionize elite "professional" groups which has followed.

1 | The Pilot Mystique

For I dipt into the future, far as human eye
  could see,
Saw the vision of the world, and all the wonder
  that would be;

Saw the heavens fill with commerce, argosies of
  magic sails,
Pilots of the purple twilight, dropping down
  with costly bales;

Heard the heavens fill with shouting, and there
  rain'd a ghastly dew,
From the nations' airy navies grappling in the
  central blue.

Tennyson, "Locksley Hall"

Tennyson's prophetic verse has been a favorite of aviation enthusiasts since the dawn of manned flight, and American lawmakers have inserted it in *The Congressional Record* with monotonous regularity as a preface to their speeches on matters relating to aviation. While the poet placed primary emphasis on the peaceful use of flight, and only secondarily conjured up the specter of war in the skies, the bulk of early progress in aviation lay in the military sphere. World War I spurred the development of warplanes and

created a climate of military opinion which tended to per-
vade aviation thought. However, a businessman could
readily see that an airplane capable of dropping bombs on
a distant city might as easily transport a commercial cargo.
The technology of aviation proved to be too primitive for
air transportation to be competitive with surface transportation in the beginning, but this fact was not immediately
apparent to most businessmen. At the end of World War I,
several schemes blossomed simultaneously in the United
States and Europe for transporting passengers and cargo by
air. In the absence of governmental subsidies, all of them
failed within a few months, after the novelty wore off.[1]

Where public money was available to support it, however,
the transportation of mail by air proved to be remarkably
efficient. Germany established the first regular mail service
during World War I, using military aircraft on the route
between Berlin and Vienna. After the Armistice, neither
Germany nor Austria could afford the service and it lapsed.
England and France agreed to establish a joint civilian
London-to-Paris mail service to replace the military service
operating during the war, but before they could do so, the
United States began what eventually turned out to be the
oldest continuous air-mail service in the world. Using
Army aircraft and pilots temporarily assigned to the Post
Office Department, regular mail flights between Washington
and New York began in May 1918. Congress clearly intended
to encourage the development of commercial aviation when
it agreed to sponsor this experiment, and aviation enthusiasts
predicted that private entrepreneurs would quickly learn
to operate it without government subsidy.[2]

The success of the air mail in the early 1920s encouraged
businessmen to try again. Their schemes generally focused
on carrying passengers, since human beings were relatively
light, and in many cases they were willing to pay handsomely
for rapid transportation. In Europe, heavily subsidized com-

mercial airlines carried passengers on a regular schedule, but in the United States unsubsidized operations were unprofitable, and consequently there was no significant development in the technology of commercial aviation until Congress passed the Kelly Act, in 1925, authorizing private contractors to take over the transport of mail by air.[3]

The government mail subsidy guaranteed profits and lured a substantial private investment into the air transportation business. After Charles A. Lindbergh's flight created mass enthusiasm among bankers and investors for aviation enterprises, the flow of private money became a torrent. No major breakthrough in technology accompanied the "Lindbergh boom," and it seems apparent that ostensibly practical men of business were simply swept away by the drama and excitement of the moment. Their rapid investment of over $500,000,000 far exceeded the practical potential for a sound return. After a few years of depression, less than $200,000,000 of the total investment remained, thus indicating that businessmen had completely misjudged the situation. But the debacle proved that the lure of commercial aviation was a strong one.[4]

But while businessmen sought early to harvest the heavens' reward, and warriors at first regarded the frail craft of wood and fabric skeptically, they shared a common belief that the man who flew was somehow special. The first fliers were inventor-builders such as the Wrights, Glenn Curtiss, Louis Bleriot, and others. Dixon Wecter has described the rustic "inventor-tinkerer" as an authentic type of American hero, and, in addition, airmanship benefited from the association with "science."[5] The self-taught ingenuity of the Wrights seemed to fit the heroic mold of Thomas A. Edison, and their exploits at Kitty Hawk seemed sufficient proof of the superiority of native American practicality over the formal systems and theoretical knowledge of the Old World.

A generation of fliers who were little more than circus performers replaced the pioneer inventors. Famous pre-World War I "birdmen" such as Lincoln Beachey, John Moissant, and Arch Hoxey, to name but a few, lived by giving public exhibitions. Consequently they cultivated the flamboyant and colorful quirks of character and dress common to show-business people. As one might expect of showmen, their backgrounds were diverse, their temperaments erratic, and their personal lives bordered on the psychotic. They shared a common tendency to die young, however, and it was this certain expectation of imminent death, combined with a visible scorn for personal safety, which added another ingredient to the curious mixture of attitudes and ideas which was gradually coalescing into the aviator's special mystique. Largely to increase attendance at their exhibitions at county fairs and the like, the birdmen and their press agents encouraged the notion that flying was fitted only for a special man of nearly mystical talents. Popular writers spread an awareness of the mystique to the general public by describing fliers as men of "strange temperament," who were "more indifferent to death than ever were the swarthy soldiers of Mohammed."[6] This view of pilots proved to be enduring, lasting long after the birdmen had folded their wings and flying had become little more than a practical exercise.

Thus flying was, in the beginning, pure romance, nearly an art form, and the man who dared the heavens could indulge in peculiarities usually conceded only to artists in our society. The flying machine was in some respects the perfect blending of idea and technology, and the man who sat at its controls personified untold centuries of human wonderment at the concept of flight. A few of the pre-World War I birdmen dreaded the day when flying would become an ordinary means of transportation. A highly off-beat view, challenging Tennyson's poetic vision, begged the world to "hold back the trappings of war and the bales of commerce, and give over the sky for a season, while it is yet clean and sweet, to art's fair uses, for in a little while it will be stained with advertisements, and with blood."[7] It was a hopeless plea.

Blood stained the heavens first and, in the process, bequeathed a spate of air heroes who added the ingredients of glamour and dash to the aviator's developing mystique. History's most hideous blood-letting had little that was either glamourous or dashing in it aside from aerial combat, and the "ace," whose battles in the sky seemed to resurrect the medieval code of chivalry, provided the perfect foil for the cynicism, mud, and brutality of the trenches. While the machine gun eliminated courage as the determinant of victory on the ground, the blending of the technology of flight and weapons in aerial combat seemed to give new dimension to the ancient notions of bravery, camaraderie, and adventure, which so curiously merge in war. But the horror of the war in the trenches begged for some diverting sideshow, literally shrieked to be hidden from public view. Mankind would have had to invent something like the hero aviator if he had not emerged. For this reason alone, since aerial warfare really did nothing toward determining the eventual victor, "warbirds" became popular heroes whose names were household words on both sides of the conflict. Manfred van Richthofen, the "Red Baron," and Edward V. Rickenbacker were more famous, despite their relatively low military ranks, than many general officers who commanded entire armies.

After the war, many of these fliers wished to continue making a living in aviation, but the competition for the few available jobs was very keen. Literally thousands of young Americans had learned to fly in the Curtiss JN4D2 "Jenny" during the war, and they were willing to work for practically nothing. The "traditional surplus" of pilot labor, which has generally characterized aviation,[8] complicated life for pilots from the very beginning. The vast majority of former military pilots who wished to remain in aviation had no alternative but to purchase a surplus "Jenny," available for under $2,000, and enter the precarious field of "barnstorming." The barnstormer, or "gypsy flier," traveled from town to town selling rides and flight instruction. In the early 1920s barnstorming could be a lucrative business, and energetic pilots frequently earned enough in the summer months alone to last through the remainder of the year. Despite frequent crashes and occasional hostility from local law-enforcement officers, the barnstormers succeeded in popularizing flying in America in the half-decade after World War I. As federal regulation of aviation tightened during the late 1920s, the barnstormers faded away, either becoming employees of the new airlines after 1926 or, as in many cases, becoming fixed-base operators, local entrepreneurs engaged in selling a variety of aviation services.[9]

Celebrity fliers, both civilian and military, occupied a large place in the public consciousness during the second decade of manned flight. The exploits of famous long-distance and speed fliers such as Roscoe Turner, Clarence Chamberlain, Captain Frank Hawks, and Major "Jimmy" Doolittle, to name but a few, continued the swashbuckling tradition of the warbirds, and added a new dimension of sophistication as well. Popular books, magazines, and even movies pictured them as hard-living, hard-drinking playboys. Advertisers found celebrity fliers useful in selling everything from underwear to cigarettes. A full-page spread in the *New York Times* in 1933 showed Roscoe Turner, attired in flying togs and wearing the thin mustache of the worldly sophisticate, emerging from an open-cockpit aircraft with a cigarette in his mouth, declaring: "Like most pilots I smoke a lot . . . But I watch my nerves as carefully as I do my plane. I smoke Camels for the sake of healthy nerves." [10] Obviously, an expert was speaking, for ironically a whole generation of Americans had come to regard fliers as the very epitome of physical perfection, despite their supposed life of excess. The *Literary Digest* rhapsodized on professional aviators: "sleek in mind and body as the streamlined machines they pilot through the skies, these modern day mercuries are sorted out of the common run of humanity by a selfless elimination process which tolerates no flaw of body, nerve, or character." [11] *Fortune* magazine eventually described the flier as an "evolutionary type of man" who could defy the normal physiological process of aging. "The devotee of the more abundant life—excess in all things— can glance over a roomful of veteran . . . fliers and take heart," an article appearing in 1941 stated. "Something has kept these chaps young, and it isn't asceticism either. When they play poker they play all night. When they smoke they smoke too much. When they drink their glasses leak, and when they make love complaints are rare." [12] Piece by piece, the pilot mystique grew and flourished in the public mind.

The pilots who began flying regularly scheduled passenger trips for the new private airlines after 1926 fell heir to this mystique and, in addition, to a tradition of technical expertise which the public had previously associated with locomotive engineers, steamboat captains, and the masters of ocean vessels. They could also call upon the reputation for efficiency, skill, and courage which the pilots of the Post Office Department's Air Mail Service had established in the years before the private contractors assumed the routes. Indeed, such things as pay practices, piloting tech niques, and work rules applicable to the airline pilots stemmed in direct line from the Air Mail Service experience. Prior to 1926 the Post Office Department's pilots were almost the only fliers working regularly at their trade, and their exploits were the fancy of hero-worshipping boys of all ages. The Post Office recruited its own pilots, but for the most part they had military backgrounds. Nevertheless, they were highly individualistic, self-consciously proud of their skill at "contour" or "terrain" flying in bad weather, and impatient of the bureaucratic restrictions and procedures which the Post Office Department imposed upon them. They never numbered more than about fifty at any one time, but their prestige and fame were such that they exercised a considerable influence on the airline pilots who came after them.

After the experimental service between New York and Washington proved successful, the mail routes rapidly expanded westward to Chicago and Omaha by the end of 1919, and across the continent by the end of 1920. The Air Mail Service began night flying on certain routes as early as 1922, and by 1924 it was moving the mail continuously from coast to coast without benefit of railroad relays. It was a dangerous job and there were continuous fatalities among the pilots, but there was never any shortage of applicants for the available positions. As early as 1923 these intrepid pilots were regularly spanning the continent in under thirty hours, a dramatic improvement over Calbraith P. Rogers' first transcontinental flight in 1912, which took fifty days. Given the American worship of improvement in the technology of transportation for its own sake, it was small wonder that the pilots of the Air Mail Service rapidly became demigods.[13]

Opportunities for pilot employment expanded somewhat after 1927, when private operators began to offer regular service between major cities in trimotored Fords and Fokkers. Most of the former Air Mail Service pilots found jobs with the new airlines, and ex-military fliers filled the remaining positions. The private contractors tended to pay their pilots on the old Post Office Department scale, which started at $100 per week and could go as high as $250 a week in rare instances.[14] Needless to say, an airline pilot's job was enormously desirable to the country's air-struck youth, and largely as a publicity gimmick Transcontinental Air Transport (TAT), the predecessor of Trans World Airlines (TWA), hired Lindbergh to test the swarm of pilot applicants.[15]

There was ostensibly a slight shortage, for a brief interval in the late 1920s, of pilots who were qualified to fly the new trimotors. Major Thomas Lanphier, the Operations Manager of TAT, frequently lamented that there were very few "trained" pilots in the country.[16] But this shortage was largely a matter of semantics, for there were many experienced pilots eager to work who could be "qualified" or "checked out" in the new aircraft with very little effort. The Department of Commerce announced that while there were nearly 7,000 men with commercial pilot licenses in 1928, only 2,000 of them were actually employed in aviation.[17] In fact, aviation trade journals, airline officials, and even government spokesmen tended to overstate the need for pilots because it benefited the industry to have young men paying to learn to fly at the commercial pilot-training schools. Most of the operating companies ran auxiliary pilot-training schools, but company spokesmen candidly admitted that they hired pilots with military training whenever possible.[18] The dozens of commercial schools purporting to turn out airline pilots were mostly sham. A typical advertising foldout in *Aviation* magazine in the late 1920s solicited students for "Walter Hinton's Aviation Institute of America." Urging "men of action" to hurry, the advertisement declared that "TODAY there is a tremendous growth, tremendous profits in the air. This is no time for doubting or hesitation.

Thousands of jobs—big pay jobs—are open." The art work suggestively beckoned to the romantic neophyte; it showed rosy-cheeked young men clad in flight suits, helmets, and goggles, looking at folding maps as if they were planning a long journey.[19]

Aviation magazine, although it never rejected such advertising, eventually had to admit, indirectly, that most of the students who graduated from such schools could not secure an airline piloting job immediately.[20] Indeed, a staff writer criticized the "false propaganda that there is a crying need for air line pilots" as early as 1926. "The youth of the nation—the sucker list—poor fellows," he said, "will . . . emerge from the main gates of their alma mammys with diplomas suitably framed, all eager to slip on the helmet and goggles." Only a few of them, he knew from experience, would ever persevere long enough in the grubby, second-rate jobs that were available to gain the skill "requisite for an air line pilot."[21] A survey of the classified section of *Aviation* from 1927 to 1929 proves his point—for every notice asking for applicants there are dozens of notices from experienced pilots asking for work.

Since there was an abundant supply of pilot labor, and since dozens of minimally qualified schools purported to train airline pilots, how did the notion of "professionalism" emerge? While the majority of airline pilots had military backgrounds, and while military officers have traditionally regarded themselves as professional men, service fliers generally laid scant claim to such status. In fact, the majority of World War I warbirds tended to be from the officer candidate schools rather than from West Point or Annapolis, and many of them were not even college graduates. "Cap'n Eddie" Rickenbacker, a racing-car driver before the war, for instance, failed to finish the seventh grade. It was common knowledge that senior career officers frowned on the idea of commissioning aviators in the first place. In short, much of the aviator's mystique stemmed from sources which were distinctly nonprofessional. Self-taught inventors, daredevil birdmen, and hard-living celebrity fliers were in many respects the antithesis of the formally educated man with a college degree. Even the great "Slim" Lindbergh was a college dropout.[22]

One of the few scholars who has addressed himself to the question of whether or not piloting is a profession believes that the long apprenticeship a pilot undergoes substitutes for the formal education which has been one of the traditional predicates of professional status.[23] Today airline pilots frequently spend a decade or more as co-pilots before obtaining a captaincy, but when the notion of professionalism evolved in the early 1920s, no such lengthy period of apprenticeship was necessary. Yet by the end of the third decade of manned flight, most observers simply accepted the airline pilot as a professional in the classical sense. *Fortune* magazine expressed a typical view of the airline pilot when it called him "as high a type of man as can be found in any profession."[24] This view has won wide acceptance today, for a recent article in the *Chicago Sun-Times* describing an airline pilot's work and life style placed him in the same class as doctors, lawyers, and engineers.[25]

The basic dichotomy between a "profession" and a mere job is archaic, and probably irrelevant in the modern world because no precise definition of terms is possible. Nevertheless, there is an explanation for the growth of the notion that airline piloting constitutes a profession. In the 1920s, the airline companies conducted a conscious campaign to depict their pilots as professionals in order to instill public confidence in flying. The airline pilots believed this publicity and conducted a campaign of their own which helped to influence the public to concede them professional status.

While the government subsidy after 1926 insured that the new airlines would be lucrative, it was immediately obvious to most operators that they could substantially increase their earnings if they could haul passengers as well as mail. National Air Transport (NAT) began a regular passenger service over the relatively safe route between Chicago and Kansas City in 1927,[26] and before long most of the airlines were trying to lure paying customers by offering the in-flight meals, the pretty uniformed hostesses, and in one instance even the movies with which airline patrons are familiar today.[27] But customer resistance was strong, and in order to foster a sense of security and safety, airline managers boasted of the high salaries their pilots received, pointing to these salaries as a sure indication of caution and conservatism.[28] As early as 1926, *Aviation* advised the public: "there is one place where the new air lines cannot afford to economize, and that is in respect to pilots. The very best is none too good."[29] Toward the end of 1928, several airlines seem to have hit simultaneously on the idea of uniforming their pilots in the manner of sea officers, and even giving them titles, such as "Captain" and "First Mate," in order to borrow the reputation for solid dependability which those terms suggested.[30]

The operations manager for Maddux Air Lines, which eventually merged with TAT, declared that his company forced its pilots to wear uniforms, sometimes against their will, in order to increase their "authority" and enable passengers to distinguish them from "hangers on" about the flying field. "No longer do we speak of pilot so-and-so," he said, "but rather of Captain so-and-so." In addition, Maddux installed a loudspeaker in the passenger cabin so that the pilot might address his riders in the same fashion as the captain of an ocean liner.[31] *Aviation* consistently lauded the operators' conscious decision to build prestige for the pilots as an important step in "selling flying to the public."[32] It repeatedly warned that if the pilots and field men dressed in "grease-stained or rough and tumble clothing," customers would stay away.[33] By the time Pan American's huge seaplanes began to fly the oceans, with full replacement crews of flying officers aboard, the connection between the professional sea officer and the professional air-sea officer seemed self-evident to the public.[34]

It was therefore small wonder that airline pilots came to think of themselves as true professionals, a cut above and apart from ordinary working men. Yet in the economic crisis of the depression, they found that their real power was quite limited. They could not readily transfer their piloting skills to another industry, and they were therefore as terribly dependent on the good will of their employers as other salaried workers. Ironically, they found that the only way they could convert their theoretical "professionalism" into concrete reality was by forming a union and affiliating with the American Federation of Labor. Acting under the leadership of David L. Behncke, a United Air Lines pilot, the pilots organized a union which over the years helped to define the occupation's standards, made enormous contributions to the industry, and acted decisively to protect its members through federal legislation. Behncke exaggerated only slightly when he told the Second Annual Convention of the Air Line Pilots Association International (AFL–CIO):

Before we organized there was no such thing as an air line pilot. It was a commercial pilot. It has all been created by publicity. They confused you . . . with those other 18,000 pilots [a piece of rhetorical hyperbole], and they are still trying to do it . . . What we have done, we have taken the air transport pilots that fly on the lines, we have given them their real names, we have given them their birth right, they are air line pilots. That has been blazed over the papers so much that if you would have to buy it it would cost you a figure that would be absolutely astonishing. Cartoons setting forth the air line pilot and hundreds of . . . words blazing across the papers . . . have set you up separate and distinct with high qualifications and high in the economic set up of this country. That is worth plenty.[35]

Because of the activities of Behncke and the union he and his fellow pilots created, the airline pilots are among the highest salaried workers in the world, whether they are truly "professionals" or not.[36] As Behncke said, that is worth plenty.

2 | Early Pilot Organizations

Homer F. Cole, a Northwest Airlines pilot who served as the first Secretary of the Air Line Pilots Association (ALPA), once flamboyantly declared that the union became a reality because "Dave Behncke became pregnant with an idea. He nurtured it, cobbled it, argued with it, ate, drank, and slept with it until finally a proper day arrived and he gave birth to it."[1] Behncke had been discussing the idea of a national organization of airline pilots with any pilot who would listen to him for several years prior to the onset of the depression. But until the pilots of the larger airlines actually became convinced that their employers were contemplating a pay reduction, he gained only a handful of converts to the idea of a union. Behncke was ideally located for the task of becoming a pilot union leader, since his home base, Chicago, was then the nation's air transportation hub, and he used the Chicago air field, located on the site of present-day Midway Airport, as a contact point to talk to pilots coming into Chicago. He gradually gained the confidence of the pilots, and he frequently entertained them in his South Side Chicago bungalow; indeed, his wife Gladys was famous among bachelor aviators for her home-cooked meals.[2]

Behncke had precedents for his pilots' organization. In the early 1920s, the government air-mail pilots formed a union, and they did so under the spectacular circumstances of a full-fledged strike against the Post Office Department itself. The U.S. air-mail pilot was the darling of the aviation world in the early 1920s and the hero of countless thousands of boys. Popular magazines serialized his exploits, and he bore many of the hallmarks of hero worship which a later generation would transfer to astronauts.

From its beginning in 1918, the Post Office Department's air-mail service proved surprisingly efficient. The early months of operation indicated that the mail flights could be completed 93 percent of the time.[3] But as the air-mail service expanded, flying conditions tended to vary more from region to region. The efficiency norms established for the northeast, principally on the runs from Washington, D.C., to Philadelphia to New York, were impossible to maintain over a larger area. Also, while a 93 percent completion rate might be possible over an extended period of time, an interval of extremely bad weather lasting for a month or more might eliminate air-mail operations altogether, since all-weather operations were only a distant dream in 1920.

Nevertheless, in the second year of air-mail operations, government officials came to expect and demand a high percentage of completed flights. President Wilson's Postmaster General, Albert Burleson of Texas, declared in his annual message to Congress that after one year of operation "the high standard of daily perfect flight which the Army succeeded in gradually establishing is being maintained by the Post Office Department, *regardless of weather conditions.*"[4] The Assistant Postmaster General, Otto Praeger, boasted in May 1919 that the Post Office had actually bettered the Army's record in flying the mail.[5] Eventually, the Post Office Department established an efficiency rating system for its pilots, based on the percentage of flights they completed. In fact, quite early the pilots of the government air-mail service began to realize that the nonflying bureaucrats of the Post Office Department in Washington were ignoring weather altogether.

In mid-summer of 1919, the east coast experienced a period of extremely bad weather, with fog and rain and low visibility. The Post Office supervisors, in an effort to maintain a high operating record, insisted that the pilots fly despite the poor flying conditions. As a result, there were fifteen crashes and two deaths in a period of two weeks. The pilots, based mainly at Bellefonte, Pennsylvania, and Mineola, New York, held a series of secret meetings and decided to assert the traditional pilot's prerogative of determining whether or not to fly when the weather was bad. They agreed that if one pilot should refuse to fly, then all would refuse to fly.[6]

On July 22, pilot Leon D. Smith reported to the Belmont, New York, flying field, surveyed the weather, which was foggy with visibility measuring only 100 yards, and declared that he would not fly. The field manager summoned the next pilot on the waiting list, E. Hamilton Lee, and ordered him to fly, but he also refused.[7] Both pilots were veterans who had been with the air-mail service since its inception. Both had been rated pilots prior to World War I and because of it they served as instructors during the war. Smith, in fact, was the senior Army instructor. He had learned to fly at the Curtiss Flying School in 1913, where his teachers had been the famous "birdmen" Frances Wildman and Lansing Callahan. Lee was the current world record holder of several aviation records.[8]

Officials of the air-mail service knew that there was discontent among the pilots, chiefly owing to problems with the aircraft. Because Post Office officials expected them to fly in bad weather, the pilots had requested "stabilators," a primitive blind-flying device then on the market, for their aircraft.

The devices cost about $75 each, but the Post Office deemed them too expensive and refused to purchase them. Furthermore, the pilots wished to fly the lighter and smaller "Jenny," which was equipped with the Hispano-Suiza 150-horsepower engine, because it could fly slower and lower, prerequisites for bad-weather flying in the days when pilots necessarily had to keep the earth in sight. The problem was that the Post Office Department had decided to standardize its operations with the larger and faster De Haviland 4 biplane, which, as modified by the Curtiss Company, was equipped with the larger and more powerful Liberty engine, which had been mass-produced during World War I. The government found itself with a considerable surplus of Liberty engines, and the Post Office insisted on their use in the mail service.[9] This friction between the Post Office Department and the pilots over equipment set the stage for a showdown.

When Assistant Postmaster General Praeger learned that Smith and Lee had refused to fly, he immediately dismissed them from the service, citing postal regulations as his authority in doing so! Acting in unison, the pilots at Belmont field and Bellefonte, Pennsylvania, wired Praeger that unless he promptly reinstated the two pilots, they would all refuse to fly. Praeger refused to accept the telegram from the pilots because it was signed only "air pilots" and hence, in his mind, was anonymous. In addition, Praeger warned the pilots that they were "putting themselves in a position of conspiring against the government." But the pilots replied in an open letter that it was not conspiracy "to avoid killing oneself for the sake of a two-cent stamp."[10]

When the unusual spectacle of a strike by the aviators broke into the daily press, Praeger attempted to exonerate the Post Office Department by claiming that it was merely following "sound" employment practices. Government employees, he declared, must either do their jobs and obey orders or resign. The pilots replied that even the Army did not require its pilots to fly under extremely bad weather conditions, and hence the orders to fly were clearly unreasonable. No pilot in his right mind, they maintained, would have flown under such weather conditions as Smith and Lee faced. Aware by now that the Post Office Department was getting bad publicity, Praeger huffily informed a press conference in Washington that the pilots "came into the service as every other pilot, with the knowledge that they must comply with Departmental orders . . . and where flying conditions are such that they cannot operate have the option to resign. If they refuse . . . and fail to tender their resignations, removal must be made!" Flustered and angered by hostile questions from the reporters, Praeger admitted that there had been a series of crashes in the weeks preceding the strike, but he insisted that such crashes were normal and occurred "all the time." He pompously informed the newsmen that the Post Office Department would be the master of its own house and declared that even a general strike would not seriously curtail air-mail operations since there were "other pilots aplenty." [11]

Praeger was apparently resolute in his intention to break the pilot strike, and only the frantic efforts of the Superintendent of Air Mail, Charles I. Stanton, who was himself a pilot, averted an immediate showdown. Stanton promised the pilots that either Praeger or perhaps even the Postmaster General himself would meet with a committee of pilots to discuss grievances, and he promised to do his best to reinstate the two pilots. But Praeger carried the dispute a step farther by seeking to arouse patriotic resentment against the pilots for criticizing the DH 4 airplane, saying that such remarks were a "calumny on our aeroplane industry." [12] Such remarks indicated Praeger's general ignorance of aviation, for the DH 4 was a British design. In response, the pilots based at Bellefonte held a meeting at which most of the pilots from Mineola, New York, were present, and voted to strike. During the meeting they received telegrammed assurances of support from nearly all the air-mail pilots in the country.[13]

Public opinion almost immediately forced Praeger to alter his hard line. The pilots were popular and glamorous figures, and most people assumed that the Civil Service regulations protected them from arbitrary dismissal. The public criticism of Praeger quickly translated itself into Congressional dissatisfaction. Representative C. R. Ramseyer of Iowa asked for a full Congressional investigation of the air-mail service in view of the Post Office Department's dispute with its pilots.[14] Representative Halvor Steenerson, Chairman of the House Post Office Committee, declared that he would personally investigate the situation. Furthermore, Steenerson said that to the best of his knowledge the pilots were due the protection of Civil Service laws and procedures in their dealings with the Post Office Department.[15] The Congressmen were undoubtedly reacting to the newspaper accounts of the spectacular dispute, which was front-page material in most newspapers. The papers seemed to favor the pilots in the conflict, if not editorially, then because the reporters who covered the story could not hide their pro-pilot bias.

Praeger belatedly realized that his pomposity had generated a reaction and he adopted a more reasonable tone. He informed Ramseyer by letter that "this represents one of those cases where the newspapers mislead the public by printing only one side of a case"[16] (a lament which has a curiously modern ring). But the combined criticism of the public and Congress had shaken Praeger, and he agreed to meet with the pilots' committee—provided it did not have any pilots on it who were personally involved in the controversy. The pilots, considerably nettled by Praeger's earlier combativeness, refused to accept this limitation and sent Lee, who had been fired, and T. H. Anglin, who was almost as deeply implicated as Lee and Smith in the strike since he also had refused to fly the same morning Lee and Smith were fired for not doing so. The pilots declared in the press, which seems to have been the principal means of communication between the Post Office Department and themselves during this affair, that their first demand was the reinstatement of Smith and Lee. But they also adamantly insisted on the right of the pilot to judge the weather for himself. As the pilots put it: "We will insist that the man who risks his own life be the judge—not somebody who stands on the ground and risks other peoples' lives." [17]

One extraordinary aspect of this dispute was the obvious conflict between the reporters who covered the event, and who generally favored the pilots, and their editors, who generally favored the Post Office Department. The reporters seemed to identify with the pilots, and they colored their accounts of the strike to depict the pilots' side favorably. Even editorials relatively critical of the pilots could not offset the effect of reportorial admiration. On July 26, the *New York Times* editorialized that while ship captains do not ordinarily leave port during a heavy fog, they must do so if the owner of the ship so directs them. Presenting the analogy of the Post Office Department as the ship owner, the editorial declared that "the men who voluntarily undertake the performance of a task that has incidental dangers must not recoil from facing them." [18] Amazingly, the same issue of the *New York Times,* in what was ostensibly a straight news story, described Praeger as being either a deliberate liar or woefully misinformed when he said "stabilators" were not commercially available. A reporter investigated Praeger's statement, found that, as the pilots had insisted all along, "stabilators" were on the market for $75 each, and noted that "today they [the Post Office] agreed to buy some."[19]

The pilots also received unexpected support from another source when J. Laurence Driggs, President of the American Flying Club, which was actually a manufacturers' front group, came to their support. Driggs maintained that since the DH 4 had originally been designed for military purposes, the pilots were quite right in their reluctance to fly it in mail operations. The Manufacturers' Aircraft Association, of course, had a great deal to gain from government contracts for new air-mail planes. "If the pilots themselves have found them unfit and unsafe . . . ," Driggs intoned, "then their word should be taken in preference to that of the engineers who supervised the alterations."[20]

When Praeger and the pilots' committee met in Washington on July 27, the pilots gained only a half victory, despite the wide public and Congressional support for them. Praeger agreed in advance to discuss pay rates, although pay was not an original point in dispute, perhaps because he wished to employ the psychological technique of the carrot and stick. Pilot T. H. Anglin acted as spokesman for the pilots' committee, although he was assisted by an attorney specially hired for the occasion. The eventual settlement agreement encompassed the rehiring of Lee, but not of Smith. Anglin said that Smith was not rehired because of "complications which require separate action," but that his case would be the subject of further discussion between the pilots and the Post Office Department.[21] (Smith was never rehired, and years later he was still making a living in aviation as an itinerant barnstormer.)[22] On the question of weather, the pilots agreed that the field manager, who was normally a pilot, would have to agree that conditions were unsafe before a pilot could cancel his flight. In case of a disagreement between the pilot and the field manager, the manager would go aloft to demonstrate that the weather was flyable—a novel arrangement. Both sides ended the conference praising each other publicly. The pilots received a per-diem rate of $3 for each day spent away from their home base, perhaps in return for their not insisting on the rehiring of Smith. In any case, the per diem actually constituted a considerable pay raise, since most pilots spent about half their time away from home.[23]

So while the strike of the air-mail pilots was spectacular, and resulted in some improvement in the pilots' pay and working conditions, they were really not much better off than they were before the strike. They won only half their "essential" demands, and they still did not have total control over whether or not they would fly when the weather was bad. In fact, after the dispute disappeared from the newspapers, the air-mail pilots were faced with the same old problem of official decisions which showed no understanding of the most basic necessities of flying.

By 1920, the government mail service was very nearly transcontinental in scope. The pilots were domiciled at a number of bases along the way between New York and Cleveland, in Chicago, and even beyond. Pay was not one of the pilots' chief complaints, since most pilots made over $100 per week, and a few enterprising fliers eventually made as much as $12,000 a year.[24] By flying at night, pilots could increase their earnings considerably over the Post Office Department base pay, which began at $2,000 per year and, with annual increments of $200, rose to a maximum of $3,600 a year. In addition, the pilots could receive special raises and promotions on the basis of "special qualities revealed in the pilot's service, such as unusually meritorious work or executive ability."[25] But, like most workers, the pilots viewed promotions based on "executive ability" rather skeptically, and they insisted that favoritism was responsible for such promotions. The pilots wanted a higher and standardized base pay, with seniority as the sole determining factor.

Increasing pilot complaints led the Post Office Department to institute an efficiency rating system with monetary incentives for the pilots. The pilots of a "division," that is, the pilots who lived at a particular base and who regularly flew a segment of the transcontinental run, were offered a chance to increase their pay by being more efficient. This plan entailed no revision of the basic pay structure because it substituted a series of bonuses instead. The pilots of a division qualified for a bonus if their division as a whole had fewer accidents and a higher percentage of completed flights than any other division. Apart from the bonus, the pilots could individually receive more pay by making a ground speed of eighty miles per hour. The pilots grumbled about this system because it injected an element of competition which they considered dangerous to flight safety, and also because the requirement for eighty miles per hour did not allow for wind factor or for flight-path deviations to avoid areas of bad weather. In short, the pilots found among bureaucrats the same lack of understanding of the weather factor in aviation which had caused the strike in the first place. The pilots could not understand why Post Office officials would not take into consideration the technical aspects of flying. Many pilots began to suspect the bureaucrats of total indifference to the personal safety of airmen.[26]

The strike had been only partially successful, but there did exist a nucleus for a pilot organization. The air-mail pilots reasoned that if they formally organized an "association," they could communicate with the Postmaster General on a regular basis. In November 1920, the air-mail pilots formally created the "Air Mail Pilots of America," claiming "practically" 100 percent membership among the Post Office Department's pilots. The pilots denied that the organization was in any way a union, insisting that its purpose was simply "to enable pilots to keep in touch with each other and help them, through cooperation, to solve their problems." To this end, the group desultorily issued a newsletter, *The Air Mail Pilot of America.* The organization never had a formal office or any paid employees, and the president, vice-president, and secretary-treasurer were elected annually and rotated in office.[27] The pilots simply formed the organization and then allowed it to lie dormant. Dues collection was sporadic, and since its membership was restricted to government air-mail pilots, who never numbered more than about fifty at any one time, the financial power of the organization was almost certainly negligible. In fact, the creation of the Air Mail Pilots of America seems to have been nothing more than an exercise in contingency planning. In the event of renewed conflict with the Post Office Department, the organization would serve as the formal vehicle for pilot protest. As long as relations between the pilots and their employer were generally good, the organization would do nothing. But it did exist, and nearly all pilots—whether they worked for the air-mail service or not—were aware of it.

As the date neared for the Post Office Department to turn over all of its air-mail operations to the private contractors, the pilots of the air-mail service began to seek other employment, and most of them eventually secured jobs with one or another of the new airlines. Many of the pilots working for the new airlines had not been Post Office Department employees, and hence were never eligible for membership in the Air Mail Pilots of America. But by and large they agreed with the old government air-mail pilots in their ranks that there ought to be an organization similar to it which would be broadly enough based to encompass all professional fliers. Indeed, the old government pilots seem to have been active missionaries in the cause of a new organization.

During 1926 several pilot organizations emerged seeking support from aviators. The Professional Pilots Association (PPA), a California-based group, was typical of these generally unsuccessful, usually local attempts to create a national pilots' organization. Since one could claim "professional" status as a pilot in 1926 if one were engaged in any of a variety of aviation activities, PPA attracted a sizeable membership. But the nature of the "pilots" in PPA made it an amorphous and unwieldy group which was generally ineffective, even though it maintained a separate existence until the early 1930s.[28]

The semantic confusion in the effort to found a "pilots'" organization was such that many enthusiastic supporters of such schemes were fixed-base operators, really employers, rather than working pilots. But briefly in 1926, PPA looked like a viable group, and it enlisted the support of many authentic professional pilots. PPA was very weak, however, having no salaried officers, a very limited staff, and thus no machinery for enforcing membership standards. Almost anybody willing to pay the $5 initiation fee and the $1.50 monthly dues could become a member, and it seems that no one ever enforced the requirement that prospective members have four years of flying experience. In fact, some pilots suspected that the membership requirements were left purposely vague in order to attract a large membership. Most pilots lost interest in PPA when they became skeptical of the tenuous connections with aviation that some members cited as proving that they derived "at least a portion of their livelihood therefrom." [29]

A further indication that PPA could not fill any real need for pilots was the resignation of the President of PPA, Waldo D. Waterman, a California fixed-base operator, to work as a lobbyist for a group of capitalists interested in contract airmail operations.[30] One of Waterman's associates in founding

PPA, Gilbert H. Budwig, also a California fixed-base operator, traded in the presidency of PPA after a short term in
office to become Director of Air Regulations in the U.S. Department of Commerce. In retrospect, it appears that one of
PPA's real functions was to provide a pipeline for many of
its officials to highly desirable government jobs.[31] And so it
must have seemed to many working airline pilots at the time.

While most pilots refused to take PPA seriously once they
discovered its shortcomings, the National Air Pilots Association (NAPA) was another matter. NAPA was by far the most
impressive and successful of the pilot organizations preceding ALPA. In a conscious effort to transform the old Air
Mail Pilots of America into a broader organization, several
air-mail pilots approached the General Superintendent of the
Air Mail, Carl F. Egge, as government air-mail operations
neared their end, to see if he would agree to lead the reorganization effort. Egge was nearing retirement after many
years with the Post Office Department; he had been continually associated with the air-mail service since August
1918, eventually rising to the office of Second Assistant
Postmaster General.[32] He served as Superintendent of the
Air Mail from July 1921[33] until he resigned because of ill
health in 1925.[34] After a brief retirement, Egge's health improved, and the Post Office Department reemployed him in
the less strenuous office of Superintendent of the Eastern
Division of the Air Mail in 1927. He apparently had the respect and confidence of the fliers,[35] and he played a leading
role in the air-mail pilots' unsuccessful effort to organize
their own company in order to bid on a portion of the transcontinental air-mail route when it was let out to private
contractors.[36]

In 1928 Egge permanently retired from the Post Office
Department and agreed to oversee the reorganization of the
old Air Mail Pilots of America. He established a head-

quarters at Cleveland and presided over the creation of a new set of membership qualifications. There were three classes of members in NAPA. Class A members were defined as those pilots holding a "Master or Transport" license and employed either as a regular airline pilot or in a "commercial" flying activity such as advertising, air taxiing, or instructing. Also, pilots employed by the government, other than military pilots, were eligible for Class A membership. Thus Class A membership included not only the airline pilots, but also a broad category of other pilots who somehow made a living in aviation. But there was a clear distinction between real working pilots and employers who happened to be pilots. It was supposedly impossible for a pilot who was a part of the owner-operator-employer group to become a member. Class B members were pilots who held a "commercial" license and who made a living in some phase of aviation. Ex-members of the Air Mail Pilots of America were also Class B members, regardless of whether or not they were employed. At the time, a few ex-air-mail pilots were still unemployed and seeking airline jobs. Class C was reserved for honorary members.[37]

After doing the initial organizational work, Egge became Executive Secretary of NAPA. The presidency was a rotating office filled annually by an elected member. The first President of NAPA was Earnest M. Allison of Bellevue, Nebraska, and the first Vice-President was R. L. Wagner of Omaha, Nebraska. Significantly, neither was an airline pilot. The organization had a national structure, with the nation divided regionally into five zones, with a "governor" in charge of each zone. The membership of each zone elected its own governor, and he reported directly to the president. The president was supposedly the leader of NAPA, but since the office rotated annually and the president could not succeed himself, real control of the organization gravitated to

Egge, the Executive Secretary. Egge was the only salaried official of NAPA.[38]

The great flaw in NAPA, so far as the airline pilots were concerned, was its relatively open membership. The airline pilots were lumped together with all other pilots holding a transport license, and they held no distinct status within the organization. There were fewer airline pilots in Class A than pilots in other types of flying work, and they were consistently outvoted on measures they considered crucial to making NAPA into an effective organization. Furthermore, membership was permanent and a man could retain full voting rights even after leaving the flying profession. The governor of each district, moreover, was for all practical purposes in charge of membership qualifications, although in theory the National Executive Committee, consisting of the governors of the five districts, the president, the vice-president, and Egge, passed final judgment on membership applications. The purpose of NAPA, as stated in the preamble of its constitution, was to "provide close relationships among pilots to enable them to perfect any movement that may benefit them as a class." [39]

At first glance, NAPA seemed to offer possibilities of growth into an organization which might effectively represent pilot laborers in their dealings with employers, particularly if internal reforms could give the line pilots the separate and distinct status within the organization they desired. As a matter of fact, most airline pilots belonged to NAPA, and they made efforts to have NAPA represent them in talks with their employers in the late 1920s. Homer F. Cole declared: "We wanted Egge, who was the only spokesman for the NAPA, to get together with the few air carriers who were operating in the middle and late 1920s, to have them set a higher standard rate of pay and less flying hours . . . Mr. Egge, to our knowledge . . . never did offer us any proof or indicate that he had ever forwarded these requests to the various air line companies. And several of us thought that Mr. Egge went along more with management ideas then with pilot ideas." [40] Behncke was once elected Governor of NAPA's Central District,[41] and in 1928 he ran for president. He narrowly lost the election, significantly, to a nonairline pilot, and from then on he seems to have given up on restructuring NAPA.[42] Most airline pilots shared Behncke's dissatisfaction with NAPA, and although they tended to remain dues-paying members, they were increasingly receptive to arguments in favor of a completely new organization for airline pilots only. As soon as ALPA began to function, most airline pilots rather quickly transferred financial allegiance to it from NAPA. Since the airline pilots paid most of NAPA's dues, their withdrawal doomed the organization, and it collapsed in 1932, chiefly because of lack of support from what was left of the membership.[43] But the record is clear; the airline pilots did make an effort to convert NAPA into an effective labor-representing organization before they deserted it. Egge tried to play a part in ALPA in its early days, but the pilots did not trust him by then, and, as Walter Bullock put it, "he was cold-shouldered out of it." [44]

The record of attempts to organize pilots' associations in the 1920s indicates that, although the pilots prided themselves on their individuality, they were at best gregarious individualists. They tended to join organizations which returned relatively little to them for the dues they paid. There was, nevertheless, a clear pattern of organizational activity among the pilots during the pre-ALPA period, and Behncke found his task of forming a union of airline pilots considerably easier because of it.

3 | The Impact of the Depression

By the late 1920s, the aviation business had gained a measure of public acceptance and was on its way to becoming a major industry. Aviation stocks were popular on Wall Street, and many people who had never seen the inside of an airplane could speak knowledgeably of Transcontinental Air Transport's or Western Air Express's previous quarter earnings. The pilots had benefited enormously from the growth of the regularly scheduled airlines, and their pay was high. Some gypsy fliers still plied their trade in remote cow pastures where federal aviation regulations had not yet reached, but by and large the foot-loose barnstormers tended, by the late 1920s, to settle into fixed-base operations, giving lessons and engaging in occasional charter work. The celebrity flier still caught the public's eye, but none of them could hope to match Lindbergh's achievement, so the genre tended to become less important as a focal point for public interest in aviation. The pilot who flew a regularly scheduled airliner, such as the magnificent and complex Ford and Fokker trimotors, rapidly displaced all other pilots in the public mind as *the* professional aviator.

While the pilots were very satisfied with themselves and were rapidly attaining the "professional" status they desired, low profit margins relative to the capital invested in the airlines created concern in managerial ranks. The airlines were not alone in this problem, for general aviation too suffered from low earnings. Much of the furious activity in the industry was deceptive, for too often operating expenses were met by capital raised in the sale of stock rather than by revenues from the sale of goods and services. There was a nagging backlog of aircraft which the public refused to buy after late 1928, and the airlines' regularly scheduled flights were seldom full, despite celebrity flights and other gimmicks. As with many other sectors of the American economy, the hectic activity in aviation issues on Wall Street bore little relation to actual earnings per share, and even in the best of times profit margins never lived up to their touted possibilities.

By early 1929, normally optimistic trade journals such as *Aviation* magazine began to worry editorially about the state of the industry. The concern was valid, of course, for, as the Federal Aviation Commission later revealed, much of the $550,000,000 invested in aviation companies prior to the depression was hasty. An alarming percentage of the total investment came only after Lindbergh's flight, and although the industry was quite willing to capitalize on this windfall of public interest, it was simply not prepared to make proper use of the money.[1] The vast financial input merely spurred the development of shaky concerns and caused undue expansion in companies that were basically sound.[2]

By February 1929, *Aviation* was attempting to restrain participants in the business by criticizing "the refinancing of the aeronautical industry which has been going on at such a rapid pace during the past year." The frenzied bidding-up of aviation stocks led "old-timers" to gasp at the money available to an industry which only a short while before had been operating on a shoestring. Many observers worried that the public's enthusiasm for aeronautical stocks might generate a "boom and bust" psychology in the industry. But despite these worries, most editorialists remained generally optimistic, largely because they believed that the larger aviation firms would survive a stock market crash owing to their affiliations with "very substantial banking firms."[3] *Aviation* believed that the crash came about because "everybody from the gum-chewing secretary to the portly bank president . . . tried to pick the G.M. or RCA" from among the new stocks, thus forcing a "readjustment." But like most of the trade journals, it was sanguine about the prospects for the industry, preferring to equate the situation with the automobile industry's troubles in 1920–1921, which had proved to be temporary. Optimistic statements such as "no airplanes are built at the corner of Wall and Broad Streets" were typical of editorial responses, and there was even some approval of the crash as a proper way of ridding the industry of "fly-by-night" operators who had entered aviation only because of the Lindbergh boom.[4] Still, there was general uneasiness, and the Guggenheim Foundation's decision to end its support of aviation development, to which it had contributed over $3,000,000 in 1926 and 1927, only added to the dismay.[5]

The new economic conditions accelerated the merger movement which was already in full swing among the airlines before the depression. The McNary-Watres Bill of 1930, which was really an amendment to the Kelly Air Mail Act of 1925, encouraged the development of mergers in air transport by changing the method of paying for air mail from the pound-mile basis to the space-mile basis. Under this arrangement, an airline would receive a Post Office Department subsidy on the basis of the space it made available for the transportation of mail, rather than on the number of pounds of mail it actually carried. This kind of subsidy favored the larger, richer corporations, since only they could afford the multi-engined aircraft which allowed top payment under Post Office pay scales. President Hoover's Postmaster General, Walter Folger Brown, originated the idea of paying for capacity rather than efficiency because he wanted to force the airlines to purchase larger aircraft. Brown reasoned that larger aircraft would encourage the lines to develop their passenger operations on a profitable basis. Lines which geared their operations to passenger carrying would someday become independent of governmental subsidy, he believed, while small lines operating merely as mail carriers would never leave the government dole. Brown's policies would later become the subject of bitter partisan wrangling in Congress when the controversy over air mail broke out in the early New Deal years. In the short run, Brown's program undeniably encouraged mergers among the major and minor air carriers, as each struggled to meet the qualifications for subsidy laid down in the McNary-Watres Act.[6]

By early 1930, *Aviation* estimated that 90 percent of all air transport operations were carried out by only four corporate groupings. Transcontinental Air Transport had merged with Maddux Air Lines and then had joined with Western Air Express to form Transcontinental and Western Air (T&WA), the precursor of Trans World Airlines, which dominated the central transcontinental route from New York to Los Angeles. National Air Transport had been swallowed by United Air Lines, and Stout and Varney Air Lines, after first becoming part of Boeing Air Transport, subsequently became part of United. Robertson and Standard Airways had merged with American Airways to dominate the southern transcontinental route, and later such pioneer lines as Alaska, Colonial, Interstate, Southern, and Universal Air Lines fell into American's corporate orbit.[7]

The number of individual operating companies involved in air transportation fell from a high of thirty-eight in 1930–1931 to only sixteen by the end of the decade. The largest part of this decrease resulted from mergers rather than bankruptcies. So while the number of operating companies fell drastically, the decrease in the number of miles flown on a regularly scheduled basis was not nearly so drastic. The airlines had already ordered new multi-engined equipment prior to the crash, and while the total number of aircraft in service dropped from a high of 497 in 1928 to 265 by the end of the decade, the new aircraft were so much more efficient that they could easily handle the old route structure.[8] But there was, nevertheless, a decline in passenger travel. Faced with decreasing passenger revenues, the airlines began a period of intense economic competition among themselves. The fabulous "era of rate cutting" saw the price of a transcontinental airplane-train combination trip drop to less than the regular price of rail transportation alone. While there were fewer passengers than there had been in late 1928 and early 1929, the lines managed to attract just enough to avert bankruptcy. The reduction in rates was general, and it actually began before the crash, thus reflecting the creeping malaise which affected all American business. In the early months of 1930, not a single airline managed a profit, but the rate cutting did at least allow them to stabilize their relative positions, explore new methods of retrenchment, and barely eke out an existence—with the aid of the Post Office subsidy.[9]

One of the striking facts of the period of economic adversity after 1930 is that it did not really affect the pilots. Only in a few cases were wage cuts actually instituted, and even then the pilots' relative economic condition seems to have remained about the same as it had been, largely owing to the deflationary cycle the country was in at the time. Most of the operating companies were loath to incur the ill will of the pilots for the very sensible reason that the pilots were essential employees. When a laborer has complete control of a large portion of a corporation's net worth, in the form of a very expensive airplane, it is not wise to give him a grudge against the company.[10] The companies were reluctant to fire a pilot after he had been with the company for even a short while, because his training was expensive and a sudden business upturn, if no pilots were available to meet it, might mean lost revenues. In fact, the total number of airline pilots, employed full-time, did not drop at all during the depression. Indeed, there is a straight-line progression upward in the total number of pilots employed from 1928 to 1940, with even the depression year of 1931 showing an increase from 580 to 621 pilots regularly employed on scheduled airlines.[11] Military leaders worried because their qualified pilots were leaving the service for more lucrative and less strenuous airline jobs.[12]

But while there were jobs for some pilots, there were not jobs for all pilots. The airlines have always been able to pick and choose from an abundant supply of pilots, and frequently the man who got the job had only the slenderest margin in qualifications over the man who did not.[13] Many pioneer fliers who had previously flown with the smaller airlines found themselves unemployed, either because the airlines preferred to fill available pilot positions with younger men or because they lacked certain technical qualifications. The flying fraternity was fairly close-knit, and all pilots knew of brother fliers who were down on their luck. Thus there was widespread job insecurity among the pilots, despite the fact that there were no wholesale layoffs. The older pilots, who had been barnstormers and who frequently lacked military training in heavy aircraft, were especially anxious. The coming of all-weather operations, involving radio-instrument flying under "blind" conditions in the clouds, was a significant factor in this widespread uneasiness. In the early days, radio instruments did not exist because there were no radio aids to navigation, and most pilots would not fly when they could not see the ground. Even after aircraft began to come from the manufacturer already equipped with "blind" flying instruments, there were many pilots who did not know how to use them. Recent graduates of Army and Navy flying schools had usually been exposed to the new instrument-flying techniques, and hence, in an unstructured job market, might be more desirable employees, even as "new hires," than the old hands, for all their experience.[14]

Aviation, which had been in the vanguard of those lauding the airline pilots as neo-pioneers, became more critical of them as the depression deepened. Calling for a reduction in pilot authority in order to curb "up-and-at-'em" daredevils, *Aviation* advocated tighter control over pilots, with rigid discipline on the order of the military's. The magazine declared that the company manager should have a veto over any flight the pilot contemplated making into adverse weather. "If he vetoes a pilot twice," *Aviation* said, "there should be an opening for a new pilot."[15]

The coming of modern flying techniques, involving skills many of the older pilots did not have, made the pilots realize that they held their jobs only at the pleasure of their employers, and it aggravated their emotional insecurity. As the depression worsened in the winter of 1930–31, *Aviation* openly speculated that not only pilot salaries but pilot status should be cut. With the coming of blind flying, *Aviation* reasoned that pilots would merely follow electronic beams through the sky while down below operations managers would make all critical decisions and then transmit them to the pilot by radio. The pilot would become, in short, a chauffeur, and the pay of a chauffeur would logically be lower than that of a sea captain—the analogy which *Aviation* had most frequently applied to the pilots before.[16] Since *Aviation* was the principal trade journal of the industry, the pilots correctly assumed that it reflected the thinking of airline management.

The year 1931 was critical in the growing insecurity of the country's airline pilots. The early optimism which had characterized the aviation industry at the beginning of the depression disappeared, and the airlines began to seek new economies in their operations. The number of passenger boardings dropped in 1931, even though the lines concentrated on luring passengers with a variety of special services.[17] The pilots were aware that the airlines were considering some reduction either in pilot pay or in the pilot force, because labor costs were one of the largest items in their budgets. There was a bread-line mentality among all workers, and the pilots were as susceptible to it as were bricklayers. After enjoying the security and status which regular airline flying brought, most pilots did not wish to turn to rum-running or stunt-flying in order to make a living. Pilot F. F. Frakes of Nashville provided an example of a rather undesirable way to pay the rent when he got 10,000 people to pay 75¢ each to watch him crash an airplane.[18] Undoubtedly this exhibition left the country's line pilots with the feeling that their present occupations offered better chances of longevity.

In late 1930, rumors of an impending "pay adjustment" began to circulate in the pilot ready rooms of T&WA and United, two of the largest airlines. Most airlines paid their pilots on the same basis and scale that the Post Office Department had used with its pilots when the Post Office flew the mail itself. When private operators took over from the Post Office, they simply continued to pay their pilots on the same mileage, terrain, and day-or-night basis. That is, a pilot's monthly salary would depend on the number of miles he had flown, with increases for such things as hazardous or mountainous terrain and night flying. The problem with this method of pay was that it gave the pilots too big a share of the productivity gains associated with improved aircraft. The operators felt that such productivity gains should accrue to management. Rather than press for an outright reduction of pay, the operators sought to change the basis of pay from so many cents per mile to a flat monthly salary. This change would not only effectively cut pilot salaries *in the future,* as new aircraft were introduced, but it would simplify bookkeeping procedures.

In early 1931, after months of hesitation, T&WA changed from the mileage to the hourly basis of pay. Management argued that the hourly basis of pay was a compromise between the mileage basis and a flat monthly salary and, hence, should satisfy the pilots. Management insisted that the hourly rate on T&WA would not reduce present pay. While the pilots admitted this was true, they feared the end result would be a pay cut, and, in fact, pilot salaries tended to decrease slightly under the hourly basis of pay. Pilots could fly more hours and earn the same amount as they had previously earned, but T&WA would not allow them to slow down their flights. T&WA had averaged the times of all the runs and would pay a pilot only on the basis of the flight's average duration, regardless of the time the flight actually took.[19]

The pilots were already insecure, worried about a possible loss of status, and concerned about the potentially tenuous nature of their jobs. The talk of a pay cut forced them to take action in self-defense, and they began to contemplate some kind of union. The pilots had been trying to reform NAPA for some time, but up to 1930 nothing substantial had been accomplished in organizing a union. There was a group of pilots, however, largely from United Air Lines, who began to plot actively some kind of pilots' union in late 1930.[20]

The leader of this effort was David L. Behncke, a pilot for United whose regular route ran from Chicago to Omaha. A hulking six-footer with prematurely gray hair and the thin mustache aviators affected in the 1920s, he seemed an unlikely leader of unionization effort. A man of severely limited formal education, Behncke ran away from his father's Wisconsin farm in 1913 when he was sixteen.[21] Airplane exhibits at county fairs had fascinated him, and he idolized the famous "birdmen" of the pre-World War I era. Without financial resources but longing to fly, he joined the Army prior to World War I because there was a remote possibility that he could become an enlisted pilot in the Signal Corps. Behncke participated in Pershing's expedition into Mexico in search of Pancho Villa in 1916, but the closest he got to an airplane was peeling potatoes in an aviation unit.

World War I gave Behncke an opportunity to qualify as an enlisted pilot, and he subsequently earned a second lieutenant's commission. After the Armistice, he tried to find work in flying but like thousands of others he could not find a suitable job. So he went into business for himself; he purchased a surplus Jenny and joined with other former service fliers to form a flying circus, which demonstrated wing-walking, parachute-jumping, and other acts of derring-do at county fairs and the like.

Behncke wanted to make the Army a career, but his lack of formal education hampered him in the highly selective competition for a regular commission. He frequently requested active duty in the interval between 1919 and 1925, without success. Unable to remain in the Army, Behncke attempted to become a business operator. After barnstorming for a season, he opened a primitive freight express service at Chicago's Checkerboard field. Using two nickel-plated Jennies, he offered to carry freight, give rides, and teach flying. He even tried sky advertising, painting the sides of his aircraft with the names of various businesses and then flying low over Chicago. Behncke got a loan in 1921, purchased Checkerboard field, and began to establish a name for himself in commercial aviation. In September 1921, he won the Chicago Air Derby, taking forty-nine minutes to cover the fifty-five mile course in a Jenny he owned.[22] But the competition for the aviation dollar was fierce. The price of rides plummeted as public interest wore off, and in 1925, nearly bankrupt, he was forced to sell out, losing both his field and his airplanes.

Just in time, the Army accepted him for active duty and granted him a six-month tour. But despite his best efforts, the Army again rejected his application for a regular commission and he reluctantly returned to civilian life.

Through the remainder of 1926 and early 1927, Behncke worked for Charles Dickenson, one of the first private airmail contractors, who had the route from Chicago to the Twin Cities. A group of Minneapolis bankers later reorganized Dickenson's operation, christening it Northwest Airways (NWA), and thus Behncke became the first pilot of that line. Behncke flew for NWA throughout most of 1927, but after a dispute with the operations manager he was fired.

Still enamored of the military life and hopeful of an Army career, Behncke jumped at the chance to go back on active duty when it was offered to him in late 1927. He joined the Second Bombardment Group at Langley Field, Virginia, but, much to his dismay, he filled a bombardier's billet. Although he won promotions to first lieutenant and subsequently captain, the Army again denied Behncke a regular commission. At the end of his one-year tour, he returned to civilian life again.

As luck would have it, the Post Office was in the process of turning over its operations to private contractors, and the new airlines were hiring pilots with heavy multi-engine experience. Behncke had managed to get in some pilot time in large aircraft in his most recent tour, and he used it to gain employment with Boeing Air Transport, which through merger eventually became part of United.[23]

When news of the T&WA pay changes reached the United pilots, they resolved to fight, and Behncke emerged as the pilots' spokesman. After consulting with as many United pilots as he could find at the Chicago Air Terminal, Behncke decided to pledge only the trustworthy ones to a joint effort to prevent any change in pay. He rented a room in the Morrison Hotel in Chicago, and on June 19, 1931, a group of United Air Lines pilots gathered there in secrecy, even going so far as to stop up the keyhole with tissue paper. Although such precautions were probably overly dramatic, some kind of secrecy was necessary, since management might have attempted a reprisal against the pilots participating in the meeting, had it been aware of their identities. By acting as the ringleader, Behncke was definitely placing himself in jeopardy, but the mystique of brotherhood among the pilots was such that he knew he could rely on his fellow pilots to protect him—once they agreed to do so. Behncke's major problem was to get the United pilots together so they could agree on some combined course of action before management became aware of their activities.[24]

Behncke began the meeting by asserting the need for solidarity among the pilots. "A man in my position in doing this, and he assures you it will damn well be done," he said, "must have your absolute loyalty." In definite terms and pungent language Behncke informed the pilots that unless they stuck together and brought pressure on all the pilots of United to join them, they might all lose their jobs. It seems likely that Behncke arranged to have a professional stenographer present to take a verbatim transcript of the meeting in order to discourage backsliders. Secrecy and loyalty were essential ingredients in such an undertaking, and Behncke instinctively knew that he must commit the pilots in advance to forming a coherent and unified front. Behncke pled his cause in emotional terms, reminding the pilots that "we must stand together and in case I am shot at, or knocked down, why that is a cause for immediate support from you." [25]

The pilots immediately and unanimously endorsed Behncke's proposals. One pilot called for a special "escrow" agreement by which the pilots would submit their undated resignations in advance to a "central figure." Smith declared that such a written agreement would relieve Behncke of any worries he might have about the pilots supporting him in the event that management attempted to intimidate them. Behncke enthusiastically endorsed Smith's proposal and also favored an amendment to the "escrow" agreement that no United pilot would work for another airline at a "less rate of pay" than he received previously. The pilots balked at this step but did agree that none of them would work for United if it carried out reprisals against Behncke. As a final step, the pilots decided to call themselves the Emergency Council, agreed that Behncke should hire a lawyer, and contributed $20 each to cover legal fees.[26]

In early July 1931, Behncke headed a committee of United pilots which requested direct talks with management. The pilots had given Behncke the "escrow" agreements he had requested, and many had included power-of-attorney agreements as well. United's management was unaware that their pilots had been organizing, and they were flabbergasted when Behncke solemnly presented his collection of presigned, undated letters of resignation from nearly all the

Chicago-based United pilots. Confronted with what appeared to be a united front among the pilots, United's management agreed to talk and proved conciliatory during the discussion. After a tough all-day bargaining session, United agreed to maintain the old pay rates and methods of computation for the time being, but it reserved the right to alter them in the future. One important concession the pilots won, however, was United's agreement to consult fully with the pilot council prior to initiating any changes.[27]

T&WA's pilots met an entirely different fate, largely because they had no Behncke to oversee the organization of a united front. In addition, T&WA's management proved openly hostile inasmuch as senior pilots had refused to cooperate with the pilots' committee. T&WA had already arbitrarily initiated the hourly basis of pay before the pilots attempted to organize, and it flatly refused to talk with the committee. Rather than talk, T&WA officials read the pilots a curt message that they could either accept the payroll procedures of T&WA or seek employment elsewhere.[28] Later, after ALPA became a reality, T&WA proved to be its toughest opponent, the first to form a company union in an effort to thwart ALPA and among the last to accept it as the bargaining agent for its pilots.

The pilots' limited success with United contrasted sharply with the total failure at T&WA, assuring Behncke's leadership in any eventual pilot union. At the time, most pilots had been thinking only in general terms of a pilot union, but the lack of success at T&WA made many of them realize that they must either form a national organization which could cut across company lines, or their victories would be limited and local. The pilots reasoned that management would pay little attention to them if they organized only on a company-by-company basis.[29]

The aviation trade journals had been rife with rumors of

pilots' unions for months, but the operators were not seriously worried that their pilots would form a national union. *Aviation* declared that a pilots' union could only waste the members' money, since "air plane pilots . . . especially those who have attained the dignity of positions with transport lines, are far too intelligent" to join a union. *Aviation* approved of "professional" organizations, but it contended that any organization concerned solely with wages and working conditions would be a disaster for air transportation, since it would lower the status of the pilots. "The pilot is not merely a hired man in a virtually fixed status. He is a vital part of the organization. Its success is his success, and in many cases he is an executive in the making."[30]

Behncke later declared that the United bargaining session brought him to the realization that the airline pilots of the nation must function as a unit—regardless of the particular line they worked for. Shortly after the United and T&WA bargaining sessions, pilot leaders from both lines held a meeting in Chicago to explore the possibility of a national union. Declaring that a national union was a matter of self-preservation, Behncke later told the 1932 convention: "When this wage fight was over, everybody realized that something had to be done and that the pilots would have to organize or our leaders of the movement . . . would be singled out and fired." The conference of United and T&WA pilots decided that the new union should be narrowly based, consisting only of airline pilots who were regularly employed. Crop-dusters, barnstormers, and most "commercial" pilots would not be eligible for membership.[31] The pilot conferees selected Behncke to act as the "central figure" in the organizational effort, partly because he wanted it and partly because he had demonstrated at United that he could handle such an undertaking.

It is difficult to explain Behncke's Motivation in accepting the leadership of a project which was potentially so dangerous for his continuance in his chosen profession. His own standard explanation was that he formed the union because the lines were cutting wages and increasing flying hours per month.[32] While it was true that there were some wage cuts and occasionally there were increases in flying time per month on a few lines, such conditions were not general. Behncke's line had not been one of those to institute more rigorous working conditions, and so he was not operating under any immediate personal threat. The depression-bred uneasiness among the pilots was general, and there were many pilots with a greater personal stake than Behncke in forming a union, and they might have as easily accepted the leading role.

Probably, Behncke exposed himself to danger because of his personal and psychological needs. He lacked formal education but he was intelligent and educated men impressed him. He attached considerable importance to having a college degree, and in later years he liked to boast that ALPA had more college-trained men working in its administrative positions than many airlines.[33] Behncke painfully educated himself, and for years he carried a dictionary with him, frequently enraging opposition bargainers during union contract talks by meticulously looking up every word he did not understand.[34] Furthermore, he developed a certain literary taste, particularly for dramatic historical narrative, and he was always very conscious of the historical importance of his own activities.[35] Over the years he carefully collected historical mementoes of his role in securing aviation legislation for his pilots, and he was particularly interested in preserving letters from persons of prominence in politics. He was a New Deal Democrat and an open admirer of Franklin D. Roosevelt at a time when most of his pilots were becoming increasingly conservative.

Behncke was the product of self-help in the classic American mold. He had worked hard, he had overcome severe handicaps, and he had developed, as most pilots did, an inordinate sense of his own self-worth. But he had come to realize that despite his accomplishments, he was clearly expendable. The Army had rebuffed him, and the Army was at the time a relatively patrician organization, with West Pointers constituting an established elite of educated insiders. Behncke was unable to crack this establishment despite his best efforts. He knew from personal and bitter experience that the Horatio Alger syndrome was pure myth. The depression affected Behncke like it did most pilots—transforming them from men who were certain of their economic worth and secure in their personal accomplishments into men who lived under conditions of great economic uncertainty.

It seems that Behncke and the pilots who followed his leadership were driven by a desire to assert their own worth as much as they were driven by a desire to secure and maintain high wages. The propaganda and mystique of the time had posited the aviator as a special kind of man—superior in talent, nerve, physique, and intellect. When it became apparent that their real powers, despite the myths of the time, were very limited, they acted to protect themselves.

4 | Creating a National Union

A small group of T&WA and United pilots met in Chicago in late May of 1931 and approved Behncke's plan to form a new national organization of airline pilots. In Behncke's estimation, pilot support on two airlines was enough to give him the trappings of legitimacy he desired. Even before Behncke received this formal authorization, however, he had been engaged in organizing the pilots. Most airline pilots in the country knew that the T&WA and United pilots had organized committees to discuss wages and working conditions with their employers, and they waited for the results of the conferences with interest. Behncke took care to see that pilots were aware that a movement was underway to create a new pilot group. In April 1931, he mailed a mimeographed "Information Sheet" to every pilot for whom he had an address. Behncke had addresses for most of the pilots in the old Central District of NAPA, and he had added to this list by his personal contacts among the pilots who flew in and out of Chicago.

Behncke cleverly made the organizational movement seem widespread and active. "There have been a number of meetings held throughout the U.S. in the last few months," he said, "all with the view of organizing some sort of national air pilots association . . . but to date things do not seem to have reached every pilot." (To those pilots who had no idea of organizing prior to receiving the "Information Sheet," Behncke very wisely offered an excuse.) He warned the pilots not to delay participating in the new scheme, which "everyone is vitally interested in," to see what would develop in the old NAPA. NAPA, Behncke declared, was useless because it had shown "little or no consideration for the air line pilots or about their wishes concerning certain matters." With deliberate vagueness, Behncke went on: "It is understood that pilots working on the western air lines have recently organized themselves into a group, although we do not have definite information . . . We believe that they . . . have organized to such an extent that they would be in a position to . . . join with similar groups from other lines."[1]

Perhaps to confuse any member of management who might come into possession of this document, Behncke used innuendo and rumor to suggest that the "western" lines were the center of organizational activity when in fact the midwestern lines were more organized. Perhaps Behncke calculated the effect of this approach on the pilots themselves, for when news began to circulate that the United pilots were organized in Chicago, it would lend the organizational effort psychological momentum. Behncke suggested that a series of meetings had already been held "in hotels along the air mail routes," but he specifically cited only the meetings held at Oakland and Salt Lake City in early April by pilots from the Pacific Air Transport, Boeing, National Air Transport, and Varney divisions of United. Behncke advised the pilots that despite discussions of a national organization, "little or no thought was given to the details." He speculated that a national organization would be more easily constructed if the pilots formed locals first, and he suggested a structure of nine "divisions." Behncke repeatedly admonished the pilots "not to hold out waiting to know what will eventually happen," and he urged them to an immediate collective effort. Behncke insisted that haste was necessary, and he warned: "if the organization is not started and completely formed this summer, it is our opinion that the pilots might as well forget the idea for all time."[2]

It is not clear if Behncke was at this time in contract with professional labor organizers, but he seems to have studied the Railroad Brotherhoods, the Great Lakes Pilots Association, and the American Federation of Labor for guidance on organizational techniques.[3] At any rate, he adopted a time-tested labor tactic of asking prospective members of the new pilots' union to show faith by signing an "escrow" agreement to cease work at some future unspecified date. In its ordinary form, an escrow is a bond or deed delivered to a third person, to be delivered by him to the grantee when some stipulated condition or circumstance shall have been met.[4] As labor organizations have used the "escrow" agreement, the workers would agree in advance to cease working unless they received a certain wage.[5] Behncke wanted the pilots to sign an undated letter of resignation to their employers, and then deliver it to the key man, or organizer, for the particular line. Behncke hoped this escrow, when coupled with a sizeable mandatory cash donation, would insure that only trustworthy pilots would join.[6]

The process which Behncke used to organize the pilots was a nebulous, word-of-mouth, hint, and rumor campaign —at least in the beginning. Wherever two airlines joined, and their pilots laid over for a night, "then the boys would go out on their beer parties . . . the word got around, the old human telegraph" functioned, as Homer Cole put it. Cole declared he never spoke to a pilot who was not enthusiastic to join, but he admitted that "when we tried to supply presidents for councils, why then these enthusiastic birds would back off and say, 'fine, I'm all for it, here's my check, but you do the work!'"[7]

But from the beginning Behncke received active support from a few pilots on almost every line, and they acted as missionaries to the rest. By May 9, Homer Cole had secured promises of support from fifteen of the seventeen pilots of Northwest Airways, and he expected the two who had not signed up to do so shortly. Enthusiasm for a real airline pilots' union was strong on NWA because the operations manager at the time was Walter Bullock, who favored the movement and was aware that the pilots were organizing. While he could not participate openly because of his managerial status, Bullock made no move to intimidate Cole, who was his brother-in-law.[8] Cole informed Behncke, who used either the code initials "TWB" or the code name "Central Figure" during the period prior to the first organizational meeting: "The company's pilots are one hundred per cent and the other two agreements are with two of our pilots who operate out of Milwaukee and whom I will not see until my next trip takes me through."[9] By May 11, M. D. "Doc" Ator had secured agreements from twelve pilots on the northern section of the Interstate division of American Airways, and afterward he arranged a transfer to the southern division so he could organize it. Ator got $50 each from the twelve pilots and forwarded it to Behncke with a note saying: "you will hear more from me. P.S. Please send more receipts."[10] Owing to Ator's efforts, American began to fall into line nicely, and very quickly Behncke had escrows from all the pilots in the Embry-Riddle division.[11]

Behncke had an easy time of it so long as he had trusted pilots like Ator and Cole working to organize pilots on their own lines. Behncke handled all the Chicago-based pilots of American and United himself, and so he had a respectable nucleus of members in a fairly short time. But before long many pilots began to balk at signing the escrow agreement. While they favored the idea of a national organization, most pilots were leery of signing a letter of resignation and turning it over in escrow to a third party whom they did not know well. In the midwest, where most pilots knew Behncke personally, the escrow was no problem, but farther west there was considerable opposition to it. In fact, Behncke had to concentrate all his efforts on securing organizers for some western airlines, for Behncke was unknown to most of their pilots inasmuch as Omaha was the westernmost extension of his regular run. Many western pilots were willing to contribute money and give verbal assurances of support, but they refused to sign letters of resignation unless every other airline pilot in the country did likewise. In order to overcome this problem, one western key man, R. J. Little of Boeing Air Transport, wrote Behncke urging that "key men of the various groups start cross-fire reports to other key men right away advising how many men are signed up . . . as some are holding back until they are sure that action is being taken by fellows in other sections." Little recommended that Behncke communicate with all key men regularly by means of a newsletter which would inform them of the activities of key men in other parts of the country. Little apologized to Behncke for the extra work this project would entail, but he jokingly concluded: "I am sure that most of the boys will appreciate your work and someday they might decorate you with a pair of rubber wings." [12]

Most of the western airline pilots were interested in specific grievances against their particular airlines, and they were rather skeptical that Behncke, far away in Chicago with his grandiose dreams of a national association, could do anything to help them. Behncke's only real success in organizing western pilots prior to inaugurating his weekly newsletter to key men came on Varney Air Lines, where

George T. Douglass got twelve of the company's thirteen pilots to sign escrows and contribute $50 each. But Douglass warned Behncke that the majority of the pilots, despite signing the escrows, would not quit if it came to a showdown. Furthermore, Douglass made it clear that the pilots opposed his plan to forward the escrows to Chicago, and he expressed fears that any slight untoward pressure might quickly destroy their allegiance.[13]

Behncke explained to Douglass: "Keep them yourself, and under lock and key and turn them over to nobody . . . The point right now is to keep all your resignations intact and do not give any back . . . I feel we should hold them for a year to prevent various leaders from being picked off by some smart brass hat." Behncke stressed to Douglass, and other pilots, that the purpose of the new organization was not to deal with current problems so much as to provide a means of fighting battles which might arise in the future. "The slight standards we have maintained in the past have been maintained only at the expense of a few leaders fighting fearlessly and alone for the good of all," he said, and he adamantly declared: "Personally I am either going to nail this fight up for good and all through the medium of an effective line pilots' organization, or fold up for all time and start selling peanuts—and I don't like peanuts!" Behncke constantly argued that a national airline pilot organization would make it unnecessary for individuals to take risks in the future, and he insisted that a primary function of the new group would be to force pilots to support their brother pilots in a crisis situation. "About half has the guts to stand in line," he wrote, "and the other half must be kept there through the medium of a heavy boot. I feel that the right kind of organization will serve as the boot."[14]

While the organizational work progressed very slowly in the west, Behncke was having considerable success with the pilots he knew personally in the old Central District of NAPA. Behncke made practically no effort to contact the southern pilots of several airlines, principally Eastern Air Lines and American based at Atlanta, because he seemed to fear, correctly as it turned out, that an inherent anti-union streak in them might wreck the whole venture before it got off the ground. He gained a few members among the New Orleans pilots, since most of them flew in and out of Chicago, and he was making some progress in the northeast among the Pan American Airways pilots. But the press of work in the midwest alone was such that Behncke found himself devoting almost every off-duty waking hour to organizational work and getting the newsletter out to key men. In order to alleviate the secretarial load on himself and his wife, Behncke hired an unemployed ex-newspaper reporter named Hugh Barker, whom he had met while he was, as he put it in a typical Behnckeism, "talking alone at the airport." Behncke bestowed the title of "Executive Secretary" of the as yet unnamed organization upon Barker, and paid him $20 a week out of his own pocket. Together, Behncke, his wife Gladys, and Barker performed all the housekeeping chores of the organizational effort from a converted bedroom in Behncke's home.[15]

Behncke's regular newsletter to key men seems to have had a considerable influence on western pilots, and, beginning in June 1931, they began to come into the fold in greater numbers. A small group of pilots from several airlines based at Cheyenne, Wyoming, signed up unanimously and elected their own key man.[16] Hal George, one of the founding members of ALPA, and who would die very shortly in a crash, worked long but with little success at T&WA.[17] George traveled throughout the T&WA system in April and May, seeking to organize the pilots for the ad hoc conference with the employers which was complementary to Behncke's at United. Repeating the process to stir up interest in Behncke's proposed national organization, he found the majority of T&WA pilots to be so intimidated by management that he had difficulty even securing key men for organizational work. T&WA's management had frightened the Los Angeles-based pilots so badly that George had to rely on a pilot in Albuquerque to act as key man for them. Despite the unfavorable results on T&WA's far western routes however, George informed Behncke that he had "one hundred per cent support east of Amarillo and Albuquerque." [18] On American's western routes though, "Doc" Ator had better success. Moving west from St. Louis like some kind of clandestine Comintern agent, Ator used his seniority to arrange transfers from one division to another among the various western runs out of St. Louis, and he quickly had them organized and a key man, W. J. Hunter, in charge.[19]

By late June 1931, Behncke could boast in a newsletter to key men that most United, American, and Northwest Airways pilots were formally committed to the new organization. Behncke had commitments from the pilots of a number of small airlines, but he admitted that T&WA was "coming along but weak in membership." He acknowledged that almost nothing had been accomplished on Eastern, the majority of whose pilots were based at Atlanta. Behncke could not be sure of the Pan American pilots, since their dispersed domiciles throughout Latin America and the Caribbean presented a formidable organizational task. Nevertheless, Behncke felt he had made enough progress to schedule a national organizational meeting, and he set July 27 in Chicago as the date and place for a convention of key men.[20]

As it turned out, Behncke didn't really need to wait for the Pan American pilots, for owing to the efforts of Frank

Ormsbee, the organizational drive there began to show remarkable progress. Ormsbee was one of the pioneer pilots on Pan American, and he had a well-deserved reputation for individualism and pugnacity. He seemed to enjoy fulfilling the public's image of the pilot as a high-living, hard-drinking playboy, and a friend once declared that he was "quite a drinker, given to long, highly technical, and slightly tipsy explanations to passengers."[21] Ormsbee was a close friend of Behncke's until they feuded over control of ALPA later, and he was early and ardent in his support of Behncke's plan to organize the airline pilots. Ormsbee worked under severe handicaps on Pan American because most of the company's senior pilots were hostile to the idea of a new pilots' organization, and he had to keep his activities secret from them. He had good success with the Compania Mexicana de Aviacion subsidiary of Pan American, signing up all the pilots except the senior Mexican pilot, whom he considered untrustworthy. Ormsbee warned Behncke that foremost among the desires of Pan American pilots was a pledge of absolute secrecy, as they feared immediate reprisals if management found them out.[22] After making his regular run from Brownsville, Texas, to Cristobal in the Canal Zone, he reported that most Pan American pilots would join a new organization if they could do so with safety. He got several pilots to act as key men for the various Latin American divisions of Pan American, and he had hopes that the Pan American Grace Airways (Panagra) pilots, all of whom were U.S. citizens, would also be eager to join. Ormsbee declared of the other Pan American bases outside the continental U.S.: "I know practically all these boys, and Crane can contact the rest at San Juan and pass the word on down the line through Dewey."[23] Ormsbee had trouble with the New York City- and Miami-based pilots because the senior pilots were congregated at these locations. After making a trip to

Miami and then New York, Ormsbee reported to Behncke: "you can bank on twenty-six members. There are two of whom are doubtful and three who will have to be taken in, if at all, after the association becomes perfected. The pilots here have an investment association [for] which Captain Swinson handles the funds, and for that reason I felt he would be the logical man to handle our pledges." Ormsbee warned Behncke that Basil L. Rowe and Edwin C. Musick, Sr., the chief pilots in Miami and New York respectively, were either indifferent or hostile toward the new organization, and this hurt recruiting among the younger pilots. But for Rowe and Musick, and the fear and respect they commanded from junior pilots, Ormsbee insisted that most Pan American pilots would join.[24]

By late June of 1931, Behncke had collected enough money to rent office space for his fledgling union. He was desperately eager to have an "office" because he thought it would give his organizational scheme the appearance of solidity. He solved this problem by renting a room in the unpretentious Troy Lane Hotel just off South Kedzie Avenue in Chicago.[25] Behncke also wished to hire a "high-powered" man to help him with the organizational work and the administrative details associated with it. He had grown increasingly unhappy with Barker, his "Executive Secretary," but he was reluctant to fire him because, as he later told the 1932 convention, "he had a complete knowledge of . . . this organization which would be dynamite in the hands of our enemies."[26] Behncke decided that the best way to keep Barker silent was to continue paying him, but meanwhile he began to search for an administrator to take over much of the burdensome detail work. Behncke had a predilection for college-trained men, and on the recommendation of several pilots he hired a Chicago lawyer named Ray Brown to be his "business agent." Brown had some tenuous contacts with organized labor, and Behncke thought he would be the ideal man to direct the organizational drive on the eastern airlines. Behncke believed that it would be necessary to devote a great deal of concentrated time and effort in the east before most pilots there would join, and he feared that he would be unable to direct such a drive while maintaining his full-time job with United. Against his better judgment, Behncke signed a contract agreeing to pay Brown a salary of $5,000 annually. Brown appears to have been an aviation buff who romanticized pilots. He originally wanted $6,000 annually, but he informed Behncke that he would take the position at a lesser salary because he wanted to work in aviation, even though he could make more money elsewhere.[27] In the light of the damage Brown would later do to ALPA, Behncke must have fervently wished he had taken other employment.

By the end of June, Behncke had created a skeleton organization of pilots in the midwest, with some support from pilots in the west. He had an office and a staff, and he was ready to take a momentous step. Before leading the United pilots in their discussions with management, Behncke decided to move decisively toward a formal connection with organized labor, which the pilots would ratify at the convention of key men he had called for July 27. Behncke knew this was a risky step, and he was by no means sure that the pilots, even those who were his close friends, would accept his action. There was a bias among pilots against organized labor, and the decision to formally align with labor meant that they would have to reject the ancient shibboleths which postulated aviators as superior to ordinary working men. The professional image and the labor union image would come clearly into conflict, Behncke knew, and there would be no way to blur the distinction. But Behncke realized what most pilots did not—the new pilots' organization would have to have powerful friends in order to survive in the event that management made a concerted effort to destroy it. Most pilots assumed that the organization could survive by itself. Behncke gingerly brought up the subject in private conversations with pilots he could trust, but he got very few to agree with him that some kind of affiliation would benecessary—even in the beginning. Behncke catered to this attitude by arguing that once the pilots established themselves, they could go their own way, much like the American Medical Association or any other group of "high-class" professionals.[28]

In the beginning, Behncke got support from some of his key men for a working agreement with the Brotherhood of Locomotive Engineers. The prestige of the locomotive engineer was strong, he was the elite of labor, and somehow above the common run of working men in the public mind. Most pilots could readily see the similarity between themselves and the engineers, and they did not feel that the comparison was invidious. With Behncke's approval, five veteran pilots from three different divisions of United approached G. W. Burbank, the Assistant Grand Chief Engineer of the Brotherhood of Locomotive Engineers.[29] There was an opening for aviators in the Brotherhood, for the organization's 1930 convention had established an aviation department which permitted licensed aviators to join. The five pilots, Reuben Wagner, H. A. Collison, Jack O'Brien, R. J. Little, and John C. Johnston, met with Burbank in San Francisco in early May of 1931 to discuss, as Burbank put it, "what our organization has to offer aviation pilots seeking membership."[30] Little, acting as spokesman for the five pilots, was enthusiastic about joining, even though Burbank informed him that there was little likelihood that the pilots could have a separate autonomous organization within the Brotherhood, at least in the beginning.[31]

Behncke immediately discarded any idea of affiliating with

an organization which would not allow the pilots complete internal autonomy and a separate identity. He could not see any advantage in splintering the pilots by merging them into a larger organization where they would essentially be only common members, without a coherent or unified voice. Such a course of action would mean that all his hard work would go for naught. Reluctantly, Behncke turned to the American Federation of Labor. He knew that it would be easier to affiliate with the Brotherhood of Locomotive Engineers than the Federation because the railroad brotherhood's "professional angle" attracted many pilots. For many years Behncke had to stress the close connection between the Brotherhood of Locomotive Engineers and the American Federation of Labor in order to allay residual hostility among the pilots over his actions. His arguments that the Federation included such "professionals" as the Masters and Mates of America and the Great Lakes Pilots Association helped, but never really succeeded in smoothing the rankled feelings of many pilots.[32]

Behncke was determined that his new pilots' organization would not, like the old NAPA, degenerate into "another semi-social club." He had employed a lawyer, Reginald Thorsness, to act as counsel for the United pilots in their ad hoc wage talks. From Thorsness, Behncke secured an introduction to Victor Olander, Secretary of the Illinois State Federation of Labor. Behncke discovered, much to his surprise, that Olander's early association with organized labor was in the Great Lakes Pilots Association, and the similarities were obvious to both men. Olander had originally granted Behncke a thirty-minute interview, but he canceled the remainder of his appointments for the day when Behncke demonstrated that he had the nucleus of a national airline pilots' union which might possibly affiliate with the Federation. Throughout the day, Behncke and

Olander discussed the labor movement, the nature of the American Federation of Labor, and the advantage a numerically small union derived from belonging to it. The more Behncke heard about the Federation, the better he liked the contrast between it and the Brotherhood. In the Federation, the pilots could have a separate union, collect their own dues, and exercise complete internal autonomy. The privilege of having the Federation support them would cost the new union only one cent per member per month.[33]

On Olander's advice, Behncke decided to make immediate application for a charter to the American Federation of Labor's national headquarters, without consulting the other pilots. Olander told Behncke that two other pilot organizations were in the process of applying for Federation charters, and he explained that haste was necessary since, under the by-laws of the Federation, once a group representing a particular type of labor received a charter, then all similar groups would have to affiliate through it, and conceivably the opportunity to secure a primary charter for the airline pilots might be lost forever. Olander pointed out that the Executive Council of the Federation would meet late in June in Atlantic City, at which time it would consider applications for new charters. Olander urged Behncke to write President William Green immediately, and he also suggested that Behncke send a representative to the Washington headquarters to present the pilots' case.[34]

Behncke had grave misgivings about proceeding with the affiliation before consulting other pilots. He contacted Homer Cole, who happened to be in Chicago, and asked for his opinion. When Cole agreed that Behncke should proceed to affiliate, subject to later approval by the pilots, Behncke suggested that he agree to serve as an "officer" so the decision would have some stamp of legitimacy. They decided on the spot to call the new organization the Air

Line Pilots Association, and the following day Cole got John Huber, a pilot on Trans-American Airways, a small feeder line operating between Chicago and Detroit, to serve as an officer. As Cole put it: "We just sort of appointed and elected each other."[35] Behncke then sent a "confidential ballot" to all trustworthy pilots, asking them to temporarily confirm himself as President, Cole as Vice-President, and Huber as Secretary-Treasurer.[36] Behncke knew it would be difficult enough to explain the affiliation, and he did not want the additional burden of defending himself against charges of dictatorial rule.

Behncke could not go to Washington since he was, after all, still a working pilot with a regular run. He decided to send Thorsness, paying all his expenses out of his own pocket. Thorsness's main job was to convince President Green that he ought to delay action on the affiliation requests of the other two pilot groups, one in Kansas City and the other in California, neither of which represented airline pilots. Behncke wanted the Federation to delay action until after the July 27 meeting of key men. Without too much difficulty, Thorsness secured Green's promise to hold the matter open until the airline pilots could present their application. But both Green and Frank Morrison, the Secretary-Treasurer of the Federation, suggested that the optimum time to act on the pilot affiliation requests would be at the next session of the Executive Council, which would meet in Atlantic City in late June—before the July 27 meeting of key men.[37] Furthermore, Green recommended that Behncke come in person to the Executive Council Meeting to present his case.[38]

United Air Lines granted Behncke a leave of absence, and he journeyed to Atlantic City for the meeting with the national leadership of the American Federation of Labor. The labor executives received him warmly and allowed him to address their session. Behncke could be very impressive in certain situations, and his flair for dramatic descriptive narrative won over the labor executives. They asked him to return the same afternoon for their decision on his application for a national charter. Upon his return, Green announced that since he had proof that pilots in more than six states had committed themselves to ALPA, and since Frank Ormsbee had organized pilots in Mexico, the Executive Council of the American Federation of Labor had decided to issue ALPA an international charter. Behncke was visibly moved at the action of the labor magnates, as amid high good humor they christened the new pilots' union the "baby international." [39] There seems little doubt that the labor leaders were impressed with Behncke, and that they were flattered that the glamorous aviators wished to affiliate with them. The pilots had prestige to spare, and the labor executives reckoned that an association with them might prove mutually beneficial. Behncke and Green dined together that night, and Behncke came away from Atlantic City elated and happy, but also a bit apprehensive over the possible reaction of the other pilots to his activities.

After returning to Chicago, Behncke devoted most of his spare time to preparing for the conference of United Air Lines pilots with their employers. The partial victory he won in those talks enhanced his reputation among pilots generally. Prior to the conference, most pilots outside the midwest and the Central District of the old NAPA did not know him. This meeting demonstrated his ability to get things done, and when the pilots compared the modest success he had at United with the dismal failure of the effort at T&WA, they respected him all the more. One of Behncke's main objectives in holding the ad hoc wage talks with management, in fact, may have been to demonstrate and publicize the practicality of a working pilots' organization. Because of his success, Behncke knew the meeting of key men on July 27 would carry more prestige and authority. He would need all the prestige and authority he could command to secure the approval of the key men for his decision to affiliate with organized labor, and subsequently the approval of pilots throughout the nation.

Only a handful of pilots were privy to Behncke's activities in securing a provisional charter from the Federation for ALPA. Behncke worked and planned endlessly to find a way to present the news of the proposed affiliation in as painless a manner as possible. Apparently, only Huber, Cole, Hal George, and Frank Ormsbee knew of the affiliation prior to the convention of key men, and all but Ormsbee had their doubts about it. Basically, they decided to support the affiliation only if Behncke could persuade the rest of the key men to do likewise. Thus Behncke's presence at the meeting would be absolutely essential, as only he had enough information to present the argument in favor of affiliating.[40]

Behncke had to schedule the July 27 meeting at least a month in advance so the key men could make arrangements to attend. Many of them could schedule their flights so they could be in Chicago on July 27, but a few pilots representing western and eastern lines needed to get time off in order to attend. As it turned out, Behncke's personal scheduling problems, complicated by the weather, nearly caused him to miss the meeting. He left on his regular run to Omaha on July 25, expecting to return to Chicago the following day, in plenty of time for the meeting. But as luck would have it, a severe weather front brought low ceilings and visibility into the Omaha area on the morning of July 26, and Behncke had to cancel his return flight. He frantically searched for a replacement pilot (apparently determined to take the train back to Chicago if necessary), but one was not available. In that day of primitive weather forecasting, it was anybody's guess when the weather would improve enough for Behncke to fly his Ford trimotor back to Chicago. Behncke resigned himself to pacing the flight line, alternately cursing the weather and beseeching the helpless weathermen to change it. The other pilots assembled at the room in the Morrison Hotel which Behncke had rented for the meeting on the morning of July 27, and in Behncke's absence Hal George presided, attempting to hold the apprehensive pilots in some kind of session until Behncke could arrive. Fortunately, the weather lifted briefly early on the morning of July 27, and Behncke bolted for Chicago, daring the intervening patches of bad weather. He made Chicago by noon with the aid of a brisk tailwind, and he rushed to the Morrison Hotel, arriving literally out of breath.[41]

There were twelve key men at the meeting. Besides Behncke and the recording secretary Barker, Vice-President Cole and Secretary-Treasurer Huber were present. Behncke held the proxies of two pilots from United's Boeing Air Transport division, Ray Little and Ralph Johnson. "Doc" Ator and John Pricer represented the Interstate division of American, and National Air Transport was represented by Marion Sterling and Byron S. Warner. Walter Bullock represented NWA, having lasted only a few weeks as operations manager, after which he returned as a pilot at the bottom of the seniority list. Frank Ormsbee represented Pan American, Panagra, and Caribbean Air Transport, while James Burns and W. A. Hallgren represented the Southern and Universal divisions of American respectively. Behncke's close friend Hal George represented the badly intimidated T&WA pilots, and Howard Fey represented United's Varney division. For a variety of reasons, eight other key men who had played prominent roles in the organizational effort were unable to attend. They were: Reuben Wagner of Boeing; Glen T. Fields of Embry-Riddle;

Usher Rousch of Interstate; R. L. Dobie of NAT: Ed Garbutt and George Douglass of Varney; and two pilots from Eastern Air Lines, V. E. Treat and G. E. Thomas.[42]

Behncke began the meeting with a plea that the key men accept Air Line Pilots Association (ALPA), which he and Cole had tentatively bestowed upon the organization, as the permanent name. He had already secured the charter from the American Federation of Labor using this name, and it was personally important to him that the pilots confirm it. He encountered immediate opposition, however, because most of the pilots wanted "Air Mail" included somewhere in the name in order to soak up the residual prestige of official status the government pilots used to have. But Behncke won his point by arguing: "we had a lot of discussions on names . . . but we finally decided it would be best if we stuck right to the old fight. We are air line pilots and this is the air line pilots' association and if we deviate from that we generalize the idea and we take a lot of wind out of our sails."[43] Behncke's powers of persuasion were effective, and he survived the first crisis on the road to having the key men accept affiliation with the American Federation of Labor.

Planning to save the crucial affiliation question for last, Behncke first discussed routine matters such as the details of calling the first national convention. The key men were generally in favor of leaving the mechanics of the process up to Behncke, but he shied away from such responsibilities.[44] Behncke knew he must maintain a self-effacing posture in order to protect his real power. He did not wish to appear arbitrary or make the operation seem a "one-man show," although in fact the organizational effort would have failed had not Behncke been a hard driver. The pilots were novices at parliamentary procedures, and most of them had no idea how to run either a meeting or an organization—not unusual traits for pilots. Behncke, however, had immersed himself in organizational techniques, and while there was no guarantee that the key man would confirm his temporary presidency and make it permanent, they never seemed to have had any idea that anybody other than Behncke would be president.

A few of the pilot delegates realized that some kind of incorporation or other effort to legalize their organization would be necessary. But their desultory conversations about "incorporating" revealed that they had no idea of affiliating with organized labor. Behncke moved swiftly to plant the idea of affiliating in general terms when the opportunity arose. "I heard a big fellow in organizational work ['organizational work' was the euphemism Behncke constantly used to describe labor unions] state he was uncertain whether it was a good thing to incorporate," he said, but he added that they could take it up later in the meeting—when Behncke intended to drop his affiliation bombshell.[45]

Partly because of the dominant racism of America in the 1930's, and partly because Behncke wished to forestall possible complaints from pilots in the south, where he was sure the opposition to unionization would be strongest, the key men agreed on a "whites-only" membership clause. There were no Negro airline pilots at the time, and since the Army was segregated and almost lily white in its officer corps, it seemed unlikely that the racial restriction on membership would ever cause any problem. John Pricer of American, perhaps stirred by conscience, reminded the key men during the brief discussion that "a man is capable whether you like him or not." But the other key men were unmoved, and Behncke actively supported inclusion of the restrictive clause, which was not removed from ALPA's by-laws until 1942.[46]

A more immediate matter for the consideration of the key

men was the question of fees and dues. The organizers had been collecting $50 each from prospective members, and many pilots considered this sum excessive. Bristling at the suggestion that the organization should be run cheaply, "Doc" Ator declared: "This organization has to be . . . high class . . . us boys are in here and we can afford to put out this money for future protection . . . This is going to be a damned expensive organization. I might be wrong, but we are going to need . . . real high powered men and they are going to cost us money." Carping about the way other pilots might react to the high dues, Walter Bullock countered: "Personally it is all right with me, but I do not think the boys up there understand it that way." Ator replied that in his opinion the boys "up there" were eager and willing and not afraid of the expense. "I do not think we should . . . be lenient on these dues," he said; "I think right now is a good time because the boys are anxious to get into it." Behncke threw his weight behind the idea of high dues. "The men in the field in this proposition must be financed," he declared, "and not skimped a bit. By God the money will be there!" The pilots agreed that money would be necessary, and they established a standard of $50 for initiation and $60 annually for dues.[47]

At this point, nobody, including Behncke, had any idea how to structure the internal organization of ALPA. The key men agreed that there should be an elected "executive council" to govern the organization, but they wished to delay making a decision on its powers and composition. Behncke was clearly unhappy that his key men were proving so indecisive on this issue. With some exasperation he remarked: "It's all very easy to say there will be an executive council and they will be elected. But how are they elected and what do they do?"[48] Many of the key men wanted the powers of the central council to be minimal, since they preferred to keep real power in the locals. Behncke worried that local autonomy might weaken the voice of the national organization when it spoke for the pilots in Washington, but he was at a loss for an argument to counter the apparently innocent demands for local control. Frank Ormsbee rescued Behncke by pointing out that a powerful central committee would be necessary to keep locals from falling under management control. Since most pilots knew from personal experience that the blandishments of management could be quite alluring, Ormsbee's suggestion that national headquarters have the power to remove "wobbly" pilots from local councils made sense. Upon reading the minutes of a local council's meeting, Ormsbee suggested, the executive council could "see what John Jones says . . . and if he keeps making evasions it will be damn well apparent."[49]

Behncke hammered home Ormsbee's point: "The thing that breaks down organizations is individual groups saying 'well what the hell good is it to us? What the hell do we get out of it?' "[50] This attitude, he maintained, made a strong central executive absolutely necessary. Behncke's preferred method of keeping the local councils from vitiating the authority of the central executive council was to empower the latter to remove local council officials. Grudgingly, the key men accepted the arguments of Behncke and Ormsbee, but there was an undercurrent of dissatisfaction. After a prolonged discussion, the key men agreed that a five-man Central Executive Council, of which the three national officers would be ex-officio members, would have the power to make all decisions and take care of all business for the association. The only exception to this rule would be a strike situation. Before national headquarters could order a strike, the pilots of a local would have to give their consent.[51] Thus Behncke succeeded at the outset in establishing the power of the national to curb unruly locals. Later events would demonstrate that it was a very wise move.

After agreeing that Behncke should be reimbursed for the expenses he had borne in establishing an office, and a desultory discussion of qualifications for membership, the key men turned to a discussion of "incorporating" their association.[52] Behncke still had not thought of an easy way to present the news that he had secured a charter from the AFofL, but he decided he could delay the issue no longer. Behncke took the floor and simply told the pilots, straightforwardly, that he had been to Washington and Atlantic City to talk to the national officers of the Federation, and that he had secured a primary charter from the Federation, subject to their ratification. A stunned silence greeted his announcement, then all the key men began to talk at once. Behncke tried, amid the rising dissension, to point out that the cost of affiliating would be minimal, and that in the event of future trouble they would have the support of an old and established and respectable labor organization. The controversy waxed so hot at this point that the meeting went off the record. After a vigorous discussion, the key men bluntly rejected affiliation. Crestfallen, and for once at a loss for words, Behncke sat down. Frank Ormsbee refused to give up, however, and, with George helping him defend Behncke, he prolonged the debate even after the formal vote. At last, summoning all the eloquence he could command, Behncke asked for permission to make one last statement. He stressed what he called the "hard facts of life," and he pleaded with the key men to reconsider: "While we could still carry this organization forward, it would really mean practically nothing as we would have no recognition whatsoever other than as that of an unaffiliated, semi-social association. And the votes are the thing that largely gets consideration in Washington and don't forget it! No matter who you are, if you are small in number it means nothing. If we went to Congress with an organization like that about all we could get would be 'it's a nice day, how does it seem to fly?'" One by one, Behncke began to win the key men over to his position. He acknowledged that the idea of pilots being associated with common laborers was repugnant, but he pointed out that several other highly professional groups, such as the actors and movie stars, were members of the Federation. But mainly it was a matter of political muscle. The AFofL had muscle in Washington, and Behncke convinced the key men that ALPA would inevitably need it. Behncke later explained the pilots' acceptance of the affiliation by saying: "I concentrated on the seriousness of what I was trying to get across to them and pointed out that the destiny of the organization would rest on what action they took at this time."[54] Behncke finally persuaded the delegates to reconsider and they formally approved the affiliation. But they unanimously insisted that Behncke keep the affiliation a secret from the rest of the membership for the time being. They did not relish the task of explaining an affiliation with the AFofL to their fellow pilots, and they wanted Behncke to do the persuading, cajoling, and education which they knew would be necessary.[55]

The organizational meeting marked the beginning of ALPA as a recognizable entity. In securing the approval of the key men for the affiliation with organized labor, Behncke had successfully concluded the first crisis in the organization's history. It remained to be seen whether or not Behncke could persuade the mass of the nation's airline pilots to abandon the notion of "professionalism" they cherished in favor of an open affiliation with ordinary working men. Of course, Behncke knew he could make an excellent case that the Federation was not a group of ordinary laborers, but in order to do so he would need time and an audience which was willing to listen. The pilots' hostility toward aligning themselves with organized labor, at least in the beginning, was almost overwhelming, and Behncke feared that they would not listen. Although he could not know it then, Behncke's task of selling the airline pilots on the merits of affiliating with the AFofL would never really end. For the remainder of his life, he would have to wrestle periodically with the problem of convincing the pilots that the affiliation was a good idea.

ALPA's initial organization presents a curious mixture of the unique and the ordinary in comparison with the experience of other American labor unions. There was a concrete organizational pattern in ALPA's case, while by and large the actual organizational process for most unions has been lost in the mists of time, and historians have been able to trace only the most general and nebulous outlines.[56] In addition, ALPA was unique because the organizational process very quickly led to the creation of a national union. Of course, the pilots presented an ideal situation, for they were an exceptionally cohesive and stable group. In this respect, their experience resembles that of the railroad engineers, who organized a union under conditions in the 1850s which were similar to those the pilots faced in the 1930s.[57]

While most American labor unions owe their initial organizational impulse either to a spontaneous strike or the activities of an outside group, ALPA sprang from causes which were more complex. Nevertheless, organized labor rendered ALPA substantial help later in its existence, and there was at least the implicit threat of a deteriorating labor situation to spur the pilots onward. In many respects, ALPA reflected and helped to mold the trend toward unionization in occupations which had previously been outside the scope of the labor movement. Musicians and actors had organized before the pilots, but their example was at best indirect. The movement to unionize white-collar occupations, teaching, and even professional sports, which gained momentum in the 1930s and continues unabated today, has always had the ALPA example before it, offering positive proof that articulate and intelligent workers can profit from overt identification with the major institutions of the trade union movement.[58]

5 | Internal Problems of Leadership and Policy

The volatile emotionalism which the affiliation with the American Federation of Labor aroused in the convention of key men temporarily unnerved Behncke, and he dreaded trying to explain it to the bulk of his associates. Consequently, he decided to proceed cautiously with the matter, keeping it secret from all but the most trustworthy and committed of his pilots until he could call a general convention of all airline pilots sometime in 1932. Behncke believed he could make the pilots see the necessity of affiliating if he had time to organize and prepare them psychologically. Accordingly, his major concern after the official birth of ALPA lay in the practical business of organizing Eastern Air Transport and T&WA.

The T&WA effort should have been relatively easy, for Behncke had the support of Hal George, one of the airline's most senior and respected pilots. George had been one of Behncke's early supporters, and he had some early success in organizing the T&WA pilots, particularly on the central portions of the transcontinental route. Behncke had every reason to expect that George's influence with the pilots at the eastern and western extremities of T&WA's domain would bear fruit without much further attention from ALPA. But, as if to illustrate the importance of a trustworthy and respected insider on the airline being organized, when a crash claimed the life of Hal George early in 1932, the T&WA organization effort collapsed.[1]

Behncke had difficulty securing another leading key man for T&WA because of the overt hostility of higher management there. Shortly after George's death, in fact, T&WA embarked on a concerted effort to liquidate the ALPA "infrastructure" where it already existed on the central portions of its route structure. The principal tactic the T&WA managers used was to make as much personal trouble as they could for the pilots who were members or whom they suspected of being members of ALPA. Pilots brave enough to openly declare their affiliation with ALPA found that the company frequently transferred them to new domiciles. Not only did these transfers wreak a considerable hardship on the pilots' families, but often they resulted in loss of rank, since seniority did not automatically transfer from division to division in the pre-ALPA period. The managers greeted pilot complaints with an air of injured innocence, but the situation looked highly suspicious, for when a pilot formally dropped out of ALPA such harassing transfers suddenly ceased.[2]

Before Hal George's death, however, Behncke thought that T&WA would be relatively easy to organize, and he concentrated his efforts on Eastern Air Transport. He was anxious to give his "business agent," Ray Brown, an opportunity to earn his salary, and Eastern looked like the logical place to begin. The predecessor of Eastern Air Lines, Eastern Air Transport was one of the "big four," along with United, American, and T&WA, and it was perhaps the most successful of the nation's airlines in the 1930s. As a subsidiary of North American Aviation, a giant corporate holding company, the line had immense financial resources, and it dominated the very profitable New York to Florida route along the eastern seaboard. The heavy traffic between New York and Florida made winter Eastern's most prosperous season of operation, which was the exact opposite of most other airlines. Eastern made a profit every month of every year up to 1934, when the cancellation of the air-mail contracts caused it to lose money for the only time in its history.[3]

Behncke had obtained two key men for the Eastern pilots, V. E. Treat for the northern segment, and G. E. Thomas for the southern wing.[4] Most Eastern pilots were based at New York City, but there were also sizeable groups at Richmond, Virginia, and Atlanta, Georgia. The attempt to organize the New York City contingent of Eastern pilots failed because of the opposition of the famed World War I ace, Captain Edward V. Rickenbacker. At the time, he was a vice-president in charge of sales for General Motors, which owned Eastern through its North American Aviation Corporation subsidiary. Ostensibly because of his aviation background, but more probably because of the tenuous business of trying to survive in General Motors' hierarchy on a sixth-grade education and a warbird's fading reputation, Rickenbacker increasingly interested himself in the airline's affairs. He was an ardent conservative even then, and his attitude toward labor unions was, to put it mildly, unfavorable.[5]

Almost from the beginning of his connection with Eastern, Rickenbacker exercised considerable personal influence over the pilots, especially those based in New York City where he lived. Treat, therefore, could not interest them in joining ALPA, but more because of Rickenbacker's presence than because labor conditions were especially good for the pilots there. Homer Cole explained the failure to organize the northern end of Eastern solely in terms of Rickenbacker's presence and magnetism. "Due to his . . . exploits, for some reason or another," Cole believed, "these pilots thought they were just the cream of the crop, and didn't need any association to help them along. Eddie Rickenbacker would take care of them."[6]

But G. E. Thomas had more success with the Eastern pilots at Atlanta and Richmond, where Rickenbacker's influence was not so pervasive. Thomas reported that he had a number of pilots interested in ALPA, and early in September 1931 Behncke decided to send Ray Brown to Atlanta to talk to them. Behncke gave Brown specific instructions, however, to avoid discussing the affiliation with the American Federation of Labor.[7]

By a combination of bad luck and an unquestioning acceptance of some of the startling misconceptions which were then prevalent among the general public about the nature and personality of the men who flew airliners, Brown managed to outrage the pilots at Atlanta and set the whole Eastern organizational effort back about two years. He came to Atlanta with a woman who was apparently not his wife, and together they established quarters in the same room in the Piedmont Hotel. He scheduled a meeting of all Eastern pilots in his room on the evening of September 18, but when the pilots arrived they found him intoxicated and dining with his lady friend. Brown apparently believed that such behavior would endear him to the dashing aviators. Thomas, who had been the spearhead of the organizational effort, was flabbergasted and naturally bore the brunt of the pilots' resentments over Brown's actions. He informed Behncke: "Everyone was in favor of me getting the money sent in, refunding all dues, and dropping the matter . . . Dave . . . you cannot blame these fellows for feeling as they do . . . After all, this means their livelihood. They have too much at stake to be fooling around like that."[8]

The meeting between Brown and the Eastern pilots resulted in a flurry of irate letters to ALPA headquarters. "Pete" Brandon, one of Thomas's earliest converts to ALPA, informed Behncke by telegram that he doubted that ALPA officers could even talk to the rest of the pilots, and he threatened to cancel his own membership.[9] Behncke received corroborating evidence of Brown's antics when another pilot, the reliable Usher Roush of American, telegrammed him that Brown, in his drunken ramblings, had informed the pilots about the affiliation with the American Federation of Labor. He told Behncke that the general opinion of the pilots was that there was no place for a drunken playboy in the enterprise: "Everyone feels that a weak spot like that will leave a place for the operators to get a crack at them." [10]

Behncke wired Brandon back immediately: "A thousand thanks for your warning. This is . . . [Brown's] first assignment among the membership. Wire me his stopping place at once so I can recall and dismiss him." [11] Brown had, in the meanwhile, gone on to Jacksonville to talk to the small contingent of pilots based there. To Roush, Behncke telegrammed: "Wire me his stopping place and go no farther with him under any circumstances. Will come down myself." [12]

After sobering up, Brown must have realized that he had erred grievously in supposing that the hard-drinking, playboy image was still in vogue with pilots. In fact, most pilots never lived up to this image, and they were basically a sober, stable group of church-going family men.[13] Brown wired Behncke that the furor was because of Brown's "guarding association secrets too closely." [14] Furthermore, he accused Brandon of being an "operators' informant," and he denounced Thomas as "weak." [15] He insisted that the pilots had found out about the affiliation "without my making a single statement," but he maintained that he had sold them on the affiliation anyway.[16] Brown's story perplexed Behncke, who had already decided he must fire Brown to restore unity, but he concluded he must investigate the situation personally. He telegrammed his fellow officers, Huber and Cole, that he was leaving for Atlanta, and he simultaneously asked Roush, Brandon, and Thomas to advise him of the action he should take to "clear the situation."[17] Thomas wired Behncke that his presence was urgent,[18] and Behncke wired back that he would arrive as soon as he could get a leave of absence from United. He asked Thomas to set up another meeting with all pilots so they could discuss Brown's activities, but Behncke had already made up his mind, for he flatly declared that the conference would "undoubtedly result in his dismissal."[19] Seeking to minimize the damage Brown might have done among southern pilots generally, Behncke persuaded one of his closest associates in founding ALPA, James Burns of American's Interstate division, based at New Orleans, to go to Atlanta in the interim to help Thomas formulate a "plan of action to clarify the situation."[20]

Aside from the alienation of the Eastern pilots at Atlanta, the most serious result of the "Brown affair" was the premature revelation of the affiliation with the American Federation of Labor. Thomas, it turned out, did not know about the affiliation despite the fact that he was the key man for the Eastern pilots at Atlanta, because he had not been present at the Chicago convention of key men. James Burns and Usher Roush, the New Orleans and Atlanta key men respectively for American, knew about the affiliation but were unprepared to explain it to a group of hostile pilots. While Behncke wanted to delay the news of the affiliation as long as possible, Brown's premature revelation made it necessary for him to get somebody to explain the connection with organized labor to the Eastern pilots immediately.[21] Because of Burns' prestige and experience, Behncke urgently requested that he go to Atlanta to "keep the lid on" until he could arrive to give a full explanation. Burns, in the meantime, had already contacted Thomas and Roush on his regular run which took him through Atlanta every five days. He explained to Thomas as best he could the reasoning behind the affiliation, and then he, Thomas, and Roush spent an afternoon in Atlanta contacting the outraged pilots of both Eastern and American. The results of their missionary efforts were not too impressive, and Burns believed that the entire ALPA effort might collapse with the southern pilots if Behncke did not hurry to Atlanta—leave of absence from United notwithstanding. Burns also caught up with Brown at Atlanta and read him Behncke's telegram which forbade him further contact with the pilots.[22]

The demoralized Brown was left with nothing to do but await Behncke's arrival. He was preparing to leave for Richmond when Burns delivered Behncke's injunction. In the three days that intervened before Behncke's arrival, Brown occupied himself with writing a long letter justifying his actions. He insisted that he was "following instructions to the letter and . . . proceeding cautiously, even more so since this pop-off Brandon . . . is just another one of those types you have to learn them before you can handle them [*sic*]." Brown dismissed the significance of the drinking and the woman by saying: "Dave, I expect you to back me to the limit when petty things of this nature develop . . . Let's not be kids!"[23]

Behncke's visit to Atlanta, despite the prompt firing of Brown, was only partially successful. The operations manager at the Eastern Atlanta base had stated he would "cut the heads off his men who belonged to any pilots' association,"[24] and this threat exacerbated the normal fears of the pilots, especially when they considered Brown's bumbling behavior. Behncke talked with most of the Atlanta-based pilots, but he only barely managed to retain the strength ALPA had there, and he did not win any significant number of converts.[25] Eastern joined Western Air Express and T&WA as airlines which would need intensive organizational work and, more importantly, iron-clad assurances that ALPA would not collapse before the majority of its pilots would become members.[26]

After returning to Chicago, Behncke concentrated his attention on the internal apparatus of the ALPA headquarters and flying his regular route for United. He had requested two leaves of absence from United in a little over two months, and although he was granted these leaves, he realized that they might provide an excuse for United to dismiss him—and the company could claim, with some justification, that it was for failure to fly enough, rather than for his ALPA activities. So he stayed close to home, working to create an ALPA newspaper. Behncke hoped a regularly published newspaper would be decisive in convincing wavering pilots that the association was permanent. He hired a newspaperman for technical assistance, and the first issue of *The Air Line Pilot* appeared in April 1932.[27] Behncke distributed free copies to management, partly because he was proud of his handiwork,[28] and partly because there was no use trying to keep the existence of ALPA a secret any longer. Behncke maintained over the years that management did not know of ALPA until accident investigators found an ALPA membership card on the body of a pilot who had been killed in a crash. Like much else connected with ALPA's early history, Behncke's proclivity for blarney led him to considerably embellish the truth, a tendency which increased with the years.[29] In fact, Behncke announced the existence of ALPA shortly after the meeting of key men in Chicago, and the *New*

York Times carried a story on ALPA on November 1, 1931.[30]

The convention of key men had authorized a five-man Central Executive Council which would govern ALPA, but it had left the details and composition of the body to Behncke. Throughout 1932, Behncke operated with a Central Executive Council of sorts, which consisted of any group of pilots Behncke happened to designate as such for the evening. The creation of a more formal Central Executive Council had to await the 1932 convention, partly because ALPA was embroiled in the celebrated Century strike during early 1932, and partly because Behncke did not wish to have a governing body encumbering his freedom of action. In order to save money, the key men had already agreed that the Central Executive Council should consist only of pilots whose regular runs took them to Chicago, and that Behncke should appoint them subject to the approval of the general membership by ballot. The Central Executive Council was charged with the formulation of the by-laws, but given its loose construction and Behncke's domination of it, the by-laws were whatever Behncke said they were. A few members complained about having the Central Executive Council chosen only from the pilots who regularly flew into Chicago, but economics were more important than principle at this stage of the struggling organization's existence.[31] The first meeting of a Central Executive Council which was officially empowered to create by-laws did not convene until February 1933.[32]

The by-laws shortly became important in the dispute between Behncke and Frank Ormsbee. This controversy foreshadowed, in many ways, the one which resulted in Behncke's ouster from the leadership of ALPA in 1951. Ormsbee had been almost as active in the creation of ALPA as Behncke, and a great many pilots knew and respected him. He performed very effectively in organizing the Pan

American pilots, so effectively in fact that management instituted a yellow-dog clause in its employment agreements with all newly hired pilots. Largely because of his ALPA activities, Pan American fired Ormsbee in the fall of 1931, but the union was too new and weak then to do more than protest. Pan American answered Behncke's complaints on Ormsbee's behalf by saying that the dismissal was for reasons other than his union activities.[33]

The dismissal of Ray Brown left an opening on the ALPA headquarters staff, and Behncke hired Ormsbee for this job. Trouble broke out between the two men, at first over the direction of ALPA strategy and later over their personal approaches to leadership and administration. Ormsbee quite early decided that the main thrust of ALPA efforts should be in Washington. He argued that ALPA should concentrate on securing federal legislation which would force the operators to accept a standard set of working conditions and wages for all airline pilots. Behncke, on the other hand, was more inclined toward the traditional labor tactic of direct negotiations with the employers, using the threat of a strike as the principal weapon. In fact, Behncke's initial ideas about specific strategy and tactics were quite nebulous, and for a long time he seemed content to conduct a publicity war with the operators, hoping that somehow he could translate a favorable public opinion into a bargaining advantage. Since Behncke was still flying regularly, the daily operations of the ALPA headquarters fell increasingly under Ormsbee's control, and he persuaded Behncke that it was futile to continue circulating management-atrocity stories.[34]

The pressures and uncertainties incident to organizing ALPA had fostered a conspiratorial view of the world in Behncke, and he soon became convinced that Ormsbee was scheming to overthrow him. There is no doubt that ALPA was a one-man operation, despite Behncke's claims to the contrary, until Ormsbee's influence began to grow. It is also obvious that Behncke felt a deep proprietary interest in the association. In short, it seems likely that there would have been a conflict between the two men even if Behncke had been eminently fair-minded and an efficient administrator as well. Unfortunately, he was neither of these things. He never developed the knack of delegating authority and responsibility to his subordinates, and he knew nothing of efficient administrative procedures—a fact which led to increasing discontent among the membership over the years.[35] But the differences between Behncke and Ormsbee were not apparent until early 1932, and Ormsbee succeeded in convincing Behncke that ALPA should have a representative in Washington. Ormsbee spent much of his time in the nation's capital,[36] and he also paid frequent visits to the local councils around the country. Consequently, his reputation grew steadily among the pilots.[37]

Behncke grew increasingly apprehensive about the growing rapport between Ormsbee and several influential pilots. Adding to his apprehension, Behncke's "office manager," a man named Hugh Barker, frequently criticized ALPA's administrative procedures and Behncke's handling of *The Air Line Pilot*. Behncke proved to be a difficult man to work for over the years, and the harried Barker's complaints about his inefficiency were certainly justified. One of ALPA's charter members, Marion Sterling of United's National Air Transport division, began to echo Barker's criticisms, and he suggested that Ormsbee would make a better president since, unlike Behncke, he was no longer flying and would be able to devote full time to the job.[38]

While Ormsbee never took part in these criticisms, Behncke decided to dismiss him in order to preserve his own authority. Not content merely with removing him, however, Behncke wanted to prefer charges against him before the 1932 convention for "conduct unbecoming a member of ALPA." Behncke also dismissed Barker and accused him of conspiring with Ormsbee to "deliberately . . . overthrow the association and remove the present officers, which at this early stage of our development," he declared with typical modesty, "would have meant a complete collapse." Behncke nominally informed Cole and Huber of his plans, but he clearly intended to eliminate a potential rival for the leadership of ALPA, regardless of their feelings or advice in the matter.[39] To make an airtight case against Ormsbee and Barker, Behncke ordered Barker's replacement as office manger, Stuart Hayden, to reinvestigate Ormsbee's dismissal from Pan American. Hayden complied with Behncke's order by writing several letters to Pan American pilots and to the company itself. The pilots confirmed Ormsbee's story that Pan American had let him out because of his ALPA activities, but the company, naturally, declared that his dismissal resulted from his incompetence. The "reinvestigation" thus turned up no new evidence, but Hayden concluded, somewhat lamely, that Ormsbee "had been in disrepute for some time prior to his ALPA activities."[40] Behncke unhesitatingly took the word of Pan American's management over Ormsbee's, and decided ALPA could justifiably ignore all future attempts to gain reinstatement for him.

One must remember, at this point, that Behncke had been using the Central Executive Committee to give the trappings of authority to decisions which were his alone. Without much difficulty, he rounded up a group of stray pilots and persuaded them to support his condemnation of Ormsbee. Ormsbee seemed truly eager to return to flying, and he did not wish to create a major controversy within the organization. But he saw no way to avoid an internal fight unless Behncke retracted the charges that he was a "traitor" to ALPA. When Behncke refused to drop this charge, Ormsbee asked for an impartial investigation by a group of representative airline pilots. But he made it clear that all he really wanted was ALPA's help in getting him reinstated with Pan American, and he formally submitted such a request to the Central Executive Council, specifically denying any interest in continued administrative work with ALPA.[41]

But since Behncke controlled the Central Executive Council, Ormsbee got an unfriendly reception. None of the members of the council, including the officers, were in Chicago with any regularity, and they accepted Behncke's contentions almost by default. As a result, the Central Executive Council, with only Behncke, Cole, and Huber signing the letter, formally informed Ormsbee that he was fired, the "primary reason being disobediences, and primarily on incompetence" (a statement which bore the unmistakable stamp of Behncke's rambling grammar). The council rejected Ormsbee's request for a hearing and cited him for disloyalty, for complaining about his salary, and for being delinquent in his association dues, which was odd inasmuch as he was technically not liable for dues after his dismissal from Pan American. Nevertheless, Behncke declared that his failure to pay dues made him "subject to suspension by the by-laws," which of course did not exist at this time anywhere except in Behncke's mind. Capping the charge, the letter from the Central Executive Council informed Ormsbee that he had been forever barred from membership and his name stricken from the roster of charter members.[42] When Behncke set out to bury a potential rival, he did a thorough job!

Still acting under the auspices of the Central Executive Council, Behncke then circularized all local councils with a "Confidential Report" on the reasons for Ormsbee's dismissal. He might have gotten away with his hatchet job had he not required the "Confidential Report" to be read to all the members, and had Marion Sterling's name not appeared in it. The report was truly libelous, and it irritated a great many pilots.[43] It smacked of "railroading" and, for the first time, it caused many pilots to doubt Behncke's judgment. The local councils of Pan American were vociferous in their defense of Ormsbee, and Marion Sterling's local council in Cleveland was particularly outraged because Behncke did not furnish Sterling with a copy of the charges against him. Ralph A. Reed, Chairman of the Cleveland local council, requested that "an official investigation of . . . the charges against Ormsbee and Sterling be made by an impartial committee . . . as outlined in our association log."[44] Reed thus underscored the fact that there were no by-laws, and that the only written rules governing the organization up to that time were those approved by the convention of key men, which was merely a log stating the intention and general purposes of the association. Actually, Reed appeared to be rather friendly toward Behncke, and, in a handwritten aside included in the official letter requesting a formal investigation, he advised him that there was a good deal of support for both Sterling and Ormsbee among pilots all along the line. Reed further suggested that, in the interests of harmony, Behncke ought to retract his "Confidential Report."[45]

John Huber, who had signed the letter firing Ormsbee without really being aware of the details of the Ormsbee affair, also counseled Behncke to reverse himself. He pointed out that Fiorello La Guardia had also advised him not to make an issue of the matter because it seemed so transparently a case of petty jealousy and lent much credence to the rumors that the leadership of ALPA was wasting money on internal intrigues. Huber reproached Behncke: "You really . . . riled the boys up quite a bit," although he supported Behncke loyally throughout the controversy.[46]

Huber's reference to La Guardia underlined the growing friendship between the then Congressman, and later Mayor of New York City, Fiorello La Guardia. La Guardia had been an aviator in World War I, and he had capitalized on the glamour associated with aviation in his political career.[47] During 1931, Behncke and La Guardia had become acquainted and his friendship proved beneficial when ALPA took its case to Washington during the Century strike.

Ormsbee did his best to be accommodating and he obviously wanted to let the whole matter drop. But Behncke adamantly refused to help him regain employment with Pan American, and he refused to retract the charges against him, so Ormsbee had no alternative but to take the matter to the 1932 convention. The convention met in Chicago at the Morrison Hotel on October 17, 18, and 19, 1932, and it granted Ormsbee's request that he be given a hearing, overruling Behncke's notion that he did not merit a hearing since he was not a member of ALPA but merely an ex-employee. Even after the convention voted to create a special committee to hear the complaints of Ormsbee and Sterling, Behncke tried unsuccessfully to pack it with pilots whom he knew would be hostile to the complainants. The special investigation found Ormsbee blameless of the charges and ordered Behncke to help him find employment. Belatedly, after the affair began to arouse considerable complaint among the delegates about his "dictatorial" tactics, Behncke staged a temporary retreat. He insisted that he would do all he could to get any member of ALPA reinstated, Ormsbee included. As a witness before the committee, Behncke reluctantly admitted that the whole affair resulted from a clash of temperaments and that there was "no particular malfeasance on Ormsbee's part." [48]

While he had already hired another special assistant, Edward G. Hamilton, to replace Ormsbee, Behncke adopted

Ormsbee's original suggestion that the main duties of the assistant to the president should be in Washington. He tried to placate the pilots who felt that Ormsbee had been dealt with unfairly by occasionally dropping a note in *The Air Line Pilot* about his activities on behalf of Ormsbee. Also, by issuing cryptic warnings, he tried to frighten the pilots who continued to grumble into silence. In the December issue of *The Air Line Pilot*, he wrote: "Recently there appears to have been an epidemic of promiscuous talk. The worst offenders . . . have appointed themselves a committee of one [*sic*] to cure all our ills by criticizing us from every conceivable angle." [49]

But as soon as the furor died down, Behncke again tried to prefer charges aginst Ormsbee—this time because he had found employment, though not with Pan American and through no help from Behncke, and then had neither paid dues nor reapplied for membership. Operating with a new Central Executive Council created by the 1932 convention, Behncke sought to reopen the case, and he instructed the ALPA attorney to draw up a formal indictment on the old charges of conspiring to overthrow the organization. [50] This was too much for many of Ormsbee's friends, who had longer memories than Behncke expected, and they might well have led a revolt which would have removed Behncke from the presidency of ALPA. A renewal of the Ormsbee affair at the 1934 convention would surely have brought about a major rupture within ALPA. But fate intervened—Ormsbee died in a crash in early 1934, and the doubts about Behncke's competence and judgment which were beginning to spread among the pilots died with him. [51]

At the very beginning, many pilots doubted Behncke's competency and judgment owing to his obsession with destroying Ormsbee. But when Ormsbee died, the opposition which might have crystallized around him waned, and

Behncke's dominance went unchecked until he nearly destroyed the union he created. In retrospect, it is easy to see that the membership should have curbed Behncke's almost total control of ALPA long before they did. And yet, while Behncke never allowed a sentimental attachment to the abstract concepts of "democracy" to hinder him in union affairs, he generally made the correct decisions, so far as his pilots were concerned, until the mid 1940s. In addition, had Behncke not assumed a dominant and rather authoritarian control, ALPA might have foundered on the excessive individualism of the pilots.

While the might-have-beens of history are essentially futile, it seems that Frank Ormsbee would have made a better leader than Behncke. He was more flexible, better educated, and he had a grasp of the realities of power which Behncke lacked. Behncke had the capacity for growth, however, and he did an acceptable job of running ALPA as its full-time President after 1935. But certainly the membership should have insisted on more voice in ALPA affairs long before they did. That they waited so long to do so ultimately caused tragedy for both Behncke and the union.

6 | The Century Strike

Despite the temporary failures on T&WA and Eastern, ALPA membership grew steadily during the period between the organizational meeting of key men and the first national convention in October 1932. Most pilots were only dimly aware of the internal struggle for control of ALPA which was going on in 1932, and in any case it did not have a noticeable effect on recruiting. By the end of ALPA's first full year of formal existence, Behncke claimed support from 70 percent of all working airline pilots and at least a few members on every airline in the country.[1] When influential Congressmen and Senators in Washington began openly to applaud ALPA during the Century strike of 1932, most airlines quickly ceased opposing unionization among their pilots. Fear of losing government air-mail contracts forced even the managements of T&WA and Eastern to adopt a more conciliatory attitude, and Behncke won the support of most of the pilots of these two airlines without making a major effort. While Behncke expected that one of his chief tasks during the first year of operation would be explaining the affiliation with the American Federation of Labor, Brown's premature revelation forced him to make a straightforward announcement of it and most pilots simply accepted it. The affiliation was a *fait accompli,* and Behncke realized that he only needed to prevent a subsequent convention from repudiating it. He therefore decided to deemphasize the affiliation question at the 1932 convention.[2] He believed he could stifle criticism with articles in *The Air Line Pilot* describing the value of belonging to the AFofL. Frank Ormsbee wrote a series of articles which seemed to answer many of the questions for the time being,[3] but, more importantly, ALPA's first direct dispute with the management of an airline diverted the attention of most pilots from the affiliation issue.

While the depression continued to blight the prospects of most aviation entrepreneurs, it seemed to act as a tonic for the operations E. L. Cord. After the market crash of 1929, Cord achieved considerable notoriety as a wheeler-dealer in aviation, automotive, and related corporate operations. By early 1932, Cord's stable of industries included Auburn Auto, Yellow Cab, Checker Cab, and two airlines—Century Air Lines, operating in the midwest, and Century Pacific Air Lines, operating on the west coast.[4] Cord entered the air transport business too late to bid on a Post Office Department air-mail contract, but he soon expressed an interest in getting a share of the subsidy. Even relatively unsophisticated observers of commercial aviation recognized the connection between government subsidy and profits,[5] and Cord's lines, depending solely on passengers and freight for revenue, were managing to survive only by radically reducing operating costs. Pilot salaries were Cord's first target in reducing costs, and his pilots consequently received substantially less than pilots working for airlines with mail contracts. The lack of an air-mail contract as an excuse for low salaries was something of a subterfuge, however, for all of Cord's industries were notorious for their low pay.[6] The established operators were reluctant to reduce pilot pay drastically, because they liked to cite high pilot salaries as a justification for high air-mail subsidies. While Cord proved he could operate his airlines without a subsidy, he reasoned that his low operating costs would allow him to reap enormous profits if he were to secure an air-mail contract.[7]

At the end of 1931, the U.S. Bureau of Labor Statistics conducted a survey which covered 95 percent of the airline pilots in the country. The report showed that while the Department of Commerce set an upper limit of 110 hours of flying per month for pilots employed on regularly scheduled airlines, the average pilot flew only 80 hours per month. Taking into account "a certain latitude" which prevailed in methods of payment from line to line, whether hourly, monthly, or by miles flown, the survey arrived at $7.08 per hour as the average pay for a U.S. airline pilot in 1931, and it revealed that the top four pilots in the country received between $950 and $1,000 per month.[8]

Since the established operators with air-mail contracts could pass a large portion of this expense along to the Post Office Department, it was understandable that their principal organ, *Aviation* magazine, looked rather favorably upon high pilot salaries. *Aviation* declared that pilots received high salaries because they were "high-calibre" men, and it feared that widespread salary reductions would force many of them to seek other occupations. But to "deliberately take advantage of the economic necessities of a group of men who . . . cannot on the spur of the moment turn to any other well paid employment," *Aviation* believed, "would be an extraordinarily short-sighted policy."[9] *Aviation* had been tending toward a critical view of the pilots during the early months of the depression, and its remarkable turnabout indicated that the operators considered the pilots as potentially valuable allies should Cord, and the other nonair-mail operators, succeed in persuading Congress to cancel the old air-mail contracts and reopen them for competitive bidding. Many nonsubsidy operators, such as Paul R. Braniff, looked upon Cord as their champion in the effort to have Congress reopen the bidding, and Cord certainly had this object in mind. Late in 1931 he had approached influential lawmakers and senior Post Office Department officials with an offer to carry the air mail at exactly half the rate the current contractors were receiving. His offer was under serious consideration in Washington when his pilots went on strike over a reduction in their already low wages.[10]

In a way, the pilots were the catalytic agent in Cord's creation of Century Air Lines, and they also figured heavily in his decision to terminate operations. Cord became interested in aviation after adding the Lycoming Aircraft Engine Company to his collection of corporations. The acquisition of Lycoming led him to purchase the Stinson Aircraft Corporation in October 1929, and in so doing he became one of the largest individual entrepreneurs associated with aviation.[11] Cord learned to fly after he bought Stinson, and when he found that flying an airplane was relatively easy (presumably when the weather was perfect), he became an early dissenter from the mystique of the aviator as a superman. As a businessman, his purpose was to sell aircraft, and he sought to convince the general public that anyone could fly. Early in 1930, Cord remarked: "we feel that . . . 'aviators' have fostered an erroneous conception of the dangers of flying . . . There was a time when I was no different from any other person who looks upon flying as something only for especially gifted 'birdmen.'" But after earning a license, Cord indicated that the pilot mystique, which in part accounted for high pilot salaries, would receive short shrift in his enterprises. The pilots might have known they would eventually have trouble with Cord when he declared: "It is my conviction . . . that any normal person can easily and safely handle a ship."[12] Since he owned an airplane company and an airplane engine company, all Cord needed to open an airline was pilots. He decided to take advantage of the pool of able aviators who were out of work and who would be only too happy to work for substantially less than the annual average pilot salary of $7,000 which then prevailed.[13]

When Cord's Century Air Lines began operations in March 1931, the pilots operated on a pay scale which would eventually allow a pilot in command to receive $350 per month, plus $3.00 per hour for daytime flights and $5.00 per hour for night flights.[14] Partly because his pilot expenses were substantially lower than those of his competitors, Cord was able to offer frequent service between Chicago and St. Louis in ten-passenger Stinson trimotor aircraft.[15] His success in competing with American and United in the passenger trade in the midwest led him to open Century Pacific Air Lines on the west coast, where he engaged in a similar rate-cutting war with Varney, United, and T&WA between San Francisco and Los Angeles.[16] Intrigued by the potential profits of airline operations, Cord expanded into the southwest, directly competing with American on the Los Angeles to Phoenix run. He was on the verge of establishing Century Southwest Air Lines, which would offer through service from Los Angeles to Chicago via Phoenix, Dallas, and St. Louis, when American entered a suit against him before the Arizona Railroad Commission charging unfair competition.[17] By the time Cord halted his expansion because of the legal suit, however, he had created a major upheaval among the established operators and had succeeded in lowering the price of a transcontinental air ticket to below the price of a train ticket. Cord's competitors could not hope to match his operating costs, which, he boasted, were only 37.5 cents per mile.[18]

Since the Post Office Department paid a per-mile subsidy

of roughly double the amount Cord operated on without a subsidy, his activities in Washington sent cold chills down the spines of the established operators and whetted the interest of economy-minded Congressmen. Shortly after making his offer to carry the mail for one-half the prevailing rate, Cord returned to his Chicago headquarters and announced a pay cut for his Chicago pilots as of February 1, 1932. While lowering the monthly retainer from $350 to $150, he allowed the hourly rates to remain unchanged, and he pointed out that $150 per month was standard on Century Pacific Air Lines. Most of the Century pilots were members of ALPA, and they turned to Behncke for help. Without success, Behncke tried to get an appointment with Cord to discuss the pay cut, as he genuinely wanted to play the role of mediator in the first salary dispute to involve ALPA officially. Cord refused to see Behncke, but he did grant an interview to a committee of his unhappy pilots. The pilots were elated when Cord agreed to delay the pay cut for ten days, a period of time which seemed reasonable for discussion, but he had no intention of surrendering. At the end of the truce, the pilots still had not agreed to the new salary, so Cord hired armed guards to meet them as they reported to work at Chicago's municipal airport. The guards escorted the bewildered pilots into the presence of company officials who brusquely handed them sheets of paper which were dual resignations with applications for reemployment—at the lower rate of pay.[19] The pilots refused to sign them and trooped in a body to the ALPA office in the Troy Lane Hotel where they told Behncke: "Well here we are. We have been locked out . . . What is the Association going to do about it?"[20] Behncke, beset with other troubles, found himself and his union squarely in the midst of a dispute which would command national attention.

The Century strike, or "lockout" as Behncke always

At the time ALPA was organized, the Boeing 40, far more than the better known Ford and Fokker trimotors, was the standard plane in use on most of the country's airlines. It was designed primarily as a mail carrier, though there was also a small enclosed cabin that could hold two passengers.

The Douglas DC 2, precursor of the DC 3, carried fourteen passengers and cruised at 170 mph. It was a DC 2 that carried Senator Bronson Cutting to his death in 1935.

The workhorse of the domestic routes in the late 1930s was the famous DC 3, which carried twenty-one passengers and cruised at 180 mph.

By the late 1930s, when seaplanes such as this one began to fly the oceans with full replacement crews aboard, the connection between the professional sea officer and the professional air-sea officer was generally established in the public mind.

Behncke (right), negotiating with Jack Frye (left) president of TWA, during the 1946 strike, with the help of Chairman Frank P. Douglass of the National Mediation Board.

David L. Behncke (right) and Fiorello La Guardia at the head of the 1939 New York State Labor Day Parade. The union had already secured such affluence for its members that the "labor solidarity" theme evoked a weak response from most pilots. Although Behncke eventually persuaded a small number of ALPA members to join him in the march, at first not a single one volunteered, and many were infuriated by the request.

Clarence N. Sayen, a former Braniff pilot, who after a bitter fight succeeded Behncke as president of ALPA in 1951.

Charles Ruby, a former National Airlines pilot and the current president of ALPA.

called it, caught ALPA completely unprepared. William Green promptly wrote Behncke assuring him of the AFofL's "full backing," [21] and at Green's request Victor Olander offered the help of the Illinois State Federation of Labor. Olander advised Behncke to use the traditional practice of setting up a strike fund to support the locked-out pilots and to simultaneously use publicity to fight Cord. Since all the pilots discharged from Century were members of ALPA, Behncke immediately levied an assessment of $25 per month on all members and made this income available to the Century pilots.[22] Behncke considered the money ALPA paid the strikers to be a loan, rather than a gift, and he expected that the nearly $5,000 he distributed would eventually return to the union's coffers.[23] The Century strikers used part of their money to rent an airplane and paint "Century Is Unfair to Pilots" on its side. With this aircraft they flew alongside every Century plane arriving in Chicago in a unique attempt to persuade passengers to boycott the line through aerial picketing.[24]

Cord was a determined man, however, and his advertisements for new pilots brought an overwhelming response. He had to cancel his Chicago operations temporarily, but within a few days he was again offering daylight service between Chicago and St. Louis on a reduced schedule. Before he could resume night schedules, however, his pilots would have to "night-qualify," and the Department of Commerce obligingly sent a special team of flight examiners to Chicago to assist him. Cord insisted that he would resume full operations in a week as he had more applicants than he could use.[25]

When Behncke and the Century strikers saw that Cord was having no difficulty securing replacement pilots, they tried to shame the "scabs" into quitting by using the "brother-pilot" appeal for loyalty and unity. Cord became worried about this tactic, and he tried to insulate the new pilots from contact with the strikers, even going so far as to force them to live in a guarded dormitory, take their meals together, and journey to and from the flying field in a bus on which an armed guard was riding. Behncke later declared that "nearly every one of these scabs was brought to the Association office . . . I pointed out to them that they were jeopardizing their future as we meant business . . . and if they would stay off the job we would offer them all aid and cooperation." But only a few Century strike-breakers responded to Behncke's pleas, and he never forgave them for not helping in ALPA's "missionary work."[26]

When it became apparent that Cord would not reinstate his pilots, Behncke sought the help of the Chicago Air Commission, which operated and governed the municipal airport. He and a committee of Century strikers appeared before the commission to request that they order Cord either to negotiate or get off the public's airfield. The commission was not inclined to help ALPA, and some time afterward Behncke bitterly complained: "we found later that the Air Commission was usually about ninety per cent in sympathy with the operators." But the Illinois State Federation of Labor used its influence to have the Chicago City Council, which was very friendly to organized labor in the 1930s, order Cord to appear before it to explain why he had used armed guards to keep the pilots off city property. When Cord refused to appear, the pilots' situation began to improve, for city aldermen do not like to be ignored, and Cord's arrogance generated considerable sympathy among them for the strikers.[27] Cord would later prove that he could ignore even more august government bodies when, in 1934, he defeated the Securities Exchange Commission's efforts to investigate his stock manipulations by simply departing for Europe for a year, after which time the commission apparently lost interest in him.[28] At any rate, Cord's contemptuous disdain for governmental agencies did him no good in Washington, where his proposal to fly the mail cheaper than the regular contractors was then under serious consideration.

In addition, Behncke shrewdly exploited Cord's arrogance in a series of radio broadcasts over WCFL, a station controlled by the Chicago Federation of Labor. Olander advised Behncke to have the Century strikers describe an airplane trip to the radio audience, dramatically explaining the various hazards and problems. "When you have told that story," Olander counseled, "suddenly weave in a few words about Mr. Cord and Century Air Lines. You have everybody listening to you and they are sympathetic, and they are up in the air with you and are taking chances and are going to feel the same resentment you do toward the people opposing you." Olander later said the technical staff of WCFL felt that ALPA's broadcasts were very effective in swaying public opinion to the pilots' side.[29]

Shortly afterward, Cord's troubles began to multiply in Washington, where he could not afford enemies if he were to have any chance of securing an air-mail contract. Before the Century strike was a week old, Representative Melvin J. Maas of Minnesota denounced Cord and publicly urged the secretaries of the Army and Navy to "advise all Army and Navy pilots against taking leaves of absence [which were being encouraged just then owing to budget problems in the armed services] . . . for the purpose of flying for this line during this dispute." Maas added that if the secretaries allowed military pilots to fly for an unscrupulous operator like Cord, it would "bring disrepute upon the army and would work irreparable harm upon national defense."[30] Fiorello La Guardia also denounced Cord in bitter terms on the floor of the House of Representatives. "The profession of piloting . . . requires the highest degree of skill," said La Guardia, and he castigated Cord for allegedly stating that he was "going to 'take the romance out of aviation' and bring pilot salaries down to $125 a month. Imagine trying to get . . . trustworthy pilots . . . for less than a union truck driver gets in the City of New York." More ominously for Cord, La Guardia announced that he would lead the fight to keep Century Air Lines from receiving a government mail contract.[31]

La Guardia's speech seriously worried Cord, who had friends among the Congressmen from Indiana, where his biggest manufacturing enterprise, Auburn Auto, was located. Representative William R. Wood of Indiana inserted a letter from Cord in *The Congressional Record* which accused ALPA of "malicious attempts to . . . destroy a legitimate business." Wood also inserted an editorial from the notoriously anti-union *Los Angeles Times* which denounced ALPA as a labor racket. Wood announced on the floor of Congress that, in his opinion, ALPA was associated with "the racketeers and plug-uglies of Chicago," and he asked that Cord be given federal protection for his property.[32] Cord coerced nineteen of his twenty-four Century Pacific pilots, none of whom were directly involved in the Chicago dispute, into signing a telegram to the *Los Angeles Times* and Congressman Wood, which declared that they were "members of ALPA . . . in full sympathy with our courageous employer . . . in his attempts to obtain a right and just portion of the U.S. Air Mail contracts." [33] While Cord tried to show that some ALPA members supported him, he received unexpected help from Behncke's erstwhile business manager, Ray Brown, who denounced ALPA in general and Behncke in particular as labor racketeers. Brown later frequently repeated these charges in *The Aeronautical News,* an antagonistic little sheet which seemed to bear a special grudge against Behncke. He described the Century strike as a "bolshevistic stance," and he insisted that Cord had paid his pilots well "and treated them like gentlemen, but when it became necessary for the pilots to bear some of the load a few of them said 'we will show them, we will strike.'"[34]

But in Washington the clear balance of sympathy was with the pilots, and Congressman William W. Larson of Georgia expressed the feelings of a majority of lawmakers when he ringingly excoriated Cord as a "notorious exploiter of labor." Larsen added that Congress should prohibit Cord from operating because his aircraft were poorly maintained and unsafe, and because he did not "have satisfactory men to man the ships."[35]

On February 29, Cord replied to the criticism in a "patriotic interview" he sent to all members of Congress. He declared flatly that ALPA was infiltrated by "reds engaging in anarchistic activities," and he implied that most pilots did not support ALPA's affiliation with organized labor. Cord would have done better to remain silent, for his charges enraged La Guardia, who publicly replied to the "patriotic interview" by describing Cord as "low, dishonest, a liar, and a gangster." La Guardia declared that Cord had "deliberately attempted to deceive the Congress, in a desperate attempt to hide his own contemptible shame." In the course of this speech La Guardia introduced a committee of Century strikers who were present in the House gallery, and as the pilots rose the Congressmen also rose and applauded them. "Gentlemen," La Guardia intoned solemnly when the applause died down, "over fifty per cent of the pilots referred to as 'reds' by this miserable person are ex-servicemen who served as fliers in our army during the World War." La Guardia painted the pilots as true sons of the Republic who had altruistically gone on strike only because they were interested in safety, and because they objected to Cord's practice of working his mechanics seventeen hours a day at low wages. "There is not a meaner employer of scab labor than this man who disregards the truth and calls it a 'patriotic interview.' I hope to express the sense of this House when I say that we shall expect and insist that all operators of airplane companies having contracts with the government shall operate their planes safely and skillfully and shall treat their pilots and labor decently." La Guardia sat down to an ovation from his fellow Congressmen, and Cord's hopes for an air-mail contract were dead.[36]

Cord still had to go through the motions of presenting his case before the House Committee on the Post Office and Post Roads when it met early in March, but his position was hopeless and he refused to appear personally, instead sending one of his subordinates, L. B. Manning, to face the committee. Frank Ormsbee, acting for ALPA, was the principal anti-Cord spokesman, and he marshalled an impressive series of witnesses for the committee, including some Century strikers, several Congressmen, and Edward F. McGrady, the National Legislative Representative of the AFofL. Ormsbee made a good impression on Congressman Clyde Kelly, Chairman of the commission and the venerable "Father of the Air Mail," during his testimony, and the members of the committee seemed particularly impressed with McGrady's account of the abominable labor conditions prevailing in Cord's Auburn Auto plants.[37] As if to underscore the contention that Cord's operations with inexperienced pilots were unsafe, midway through the hearings a Century aircraft crashed in St. Louis while conducting training operations, killing two of the six pilot trainees aboard.[38] The hearings ended on a hopeless note for Cord, and several weeks later the Post Office Department formally rejected his offer to carry the mails and his request that the contracts be reopened for competitive bidding.[39]

ALPA proved it could effectively arouse public and Congressional opinion in its favor during the Century strike, but in some respects the outcome was not altogether satisfactory. The number of passengers boarding Century aircraft declined rapidly after the St. Louis crash seemed to verify ALPA's contention that Cord's equipment was unsafe, but for a while he succeeded in maintaining the semblance of normal passenger operations by hauling his clerical employees from city to city.[40] His revenues fell so drastically, however, that he suspended his Chicago operation altogether in April. Century Pacific also seemed to be foundering owing to the adverse publicity, but by a weird series of circumstances Cord managed to come out of the Century strike more deeply involved in air transportation than before. To begin with, the Arizona Railroad Commission ruled against him in the suit brought by American and forbade him to fly through Arizona airspace, which was within a state's power to do before federal legislation preempted this authority in 1934. Cord was enough of a gambler to see that luck was running away from him, as the series of reverses would seem to indicate, and he decided to get out of air transportation altogether. Aviation Corporation, the parent holding company of American, responded to his offer to sell out, and through a complicated series of stock deals, Cord gave up his aircraft, equipment, and personnel, in exchange for 140,000 shares of Aviation Corporation stock. Within a year, Cord had miraculously parlayed this block of stock into effective control of Aviation Corporation, and hence American Airways.[41] But because it might endanger American's government subsidy, Cord did not take personal control of the airline. Instead, he placed a friend, C. R. Smith, in charge of the airline, but he still remained the gray eminence behind the corporate structure which controlled it.[42] Cord was always careful in the future, however, to avoid direct conflicts with ALPA.

Neither the Chicago strikers nor strike-breakers were included in the merger with American. Century Air Lines had ceased to operate before the merger, so only Century Pacific's pilots automatically gained positions with American. Jobs were difficult to find in 1932, and as much as two years later many of ALPA's Century stalwarts were still without employment. Behncke did everything possible to help them, however, and by 1936 all of them were either employed or no longer seriously looking for a flying job.[43] But while the Century strikers paid a high price, the luckless scabs were ruined. For years ALPA conventions routinely rejected their pitiful applications for reinstatement or admission to the union. Behncke insisted on a very hard line toward them, and at the 1932 convention he secured a formal resolution which declared that the "strike breakers of . . . Century Air Lines did with full knowledge of their act and of their own free will violate the basic principles on which this, the ALPA, is founded and thereby forfeit the right now and forever more to membership in this association."[44] As ALPA's influence grew in the 1930s, good standing with it was almost a prerequisite to finding a flying job, and literally dozens of the Century scabs applied for membership during the 1934 and 1936 conventions. Behncke eventually allowed a few to become members, but only because he wanted to prove, as he put it, that "definitely ALPA has a heart."[45] In fact, Behncke pursued his vendetta against the unfortunate scabs by pressuring operations managers to discharge them when they found employment. He always claimed that he never tried directly to have scabs fired, but this was largely a semantic dodge, since his letters to various operations managers stressing their "undesirability" had precisely that effect.[46] Many

Century scabs who later got jobs were fired when management found out that they were on ALPA's blacklist. Most
loyal ALPA pilots refused to fly with them, and management
usually had no alternative but to dismiss them. A good example of how difficult ALPA made life for former Century
scabs was revealed in the case of Robert Cantwell, who secured an executive position with American after Century
Air Lines went out of business. When he lost his executive
job, American transferred him to a regular flying position,
but the pilots refused to work with him and threatened a
strike if the company did not dismiss him completely.
Management, fearful of the adverse publicity a pilot strike
would generate, acceded to these demands, and Cantwell
eventually had to go to the far reaches of South America
before he found employment with Panagra.[47]

One other aspect of the Century strike needs some explanation. The operators who did not have air-mail subsidies
originally looked upon Cord as their champion and spokesman in the effort to have Congress reopen the mail contracts
for competitive bidding. This effort finally succeeded
when Franklin D. Roosevelt's Postmaster General, James A.
Farley, canceled the air-mail contracts in 1934, charging
Hoover's Postmaster General, Walter F. Brown, and the
major airlines with fraud and collusion in the letting of the
original contracts. During the investigation into the circumstances surrounding the first competitive bidding, several
of the unsubsidized operators suggested that the Century
strike was a deliberate attempt by ALPA and the established
operators to discredit the nonmail airlines by creating an
erroneous public and Congressional opinion of their competence. Paul R. Braniff told the Black Committee investigating the air mail that it seemed "peculiar that a pilots'
strike should occur just before this body [the Mead Committee on the Post Office and Post Roads] met last March

and that Mr. Cord should take over control of the second heaviest subsidized air line and abandon the fight he was so instrumental in starting." [48] Certainly there were grounds for suspicion, and not the least of these was *Aviation's* sudden friendliness toward ALPA. The president of Cord's Century Pacific Air Lines made similar allegations at the time of the strike when he said it was "a fight by other interests to monopolize air mail contracts and has resulted in the union forces being used as a tool." [49] After investigating the strike, a *New York Times* reporter lent credence to this theory when he suggested that it was possible that the established operators had used the pilots as pawns in their struggle to preserve their air-mail contracts.[50]

But the "plot theory" of the Century strike seems untenable because it omits the fundamental fact that the individual strikers gained nothing from it and would hardly have knowingly allowed themselves to be used as pawns. The strikers had ample opportunity to return to work for Cord at the new rate of pay, and the fact that so many of them remained unemployed for a long time afterward indicates that at least a few of them, in bitterness, would surely have come forward later, during the Black Committee investigations, to tell their story. Certainly the nonmail operators would have offered them jobs as inducements to do so, but none ever did. Behncke certainly would not have supported a conspiracy which would have helped operators such as T&WA and Eastern, which at the time of the strike were trying their best to destroy ALPA. In addition, Behncke never blacklisted the Century Pacific pilots, although he was very hostile toward them for signing public letters and telegrams supporting Cord.[51]

It seems clear that the Century pilots walked out because, like any laborers, they did not like pay cuts, and because they were so imbued with the mystique of their own specialness as pilots that they believed Cord could not replace them and would have to come to terms. Certainly ALPA did not instigate the strike, and there is abundant proof that the strike caught Behncke completely by surprise.

Behncke and his ALPA emerged from the Century strike with a national reputation and several influential new friends in Washington. Postmaster General Brown voiced strong support for the pilots after Behncke flew him from Chicago to Washington during the strike. Behncke must have, characteristically, enjoyed himself hugely in impressing Brown with the intricacies of the cockpit of his Ford trimotor, for after the flight Brown declared that he was "a very good fellow . . . a splendid pilot. These pilots are the cream of the profession," he added, "highly educated and the fine type of men . . . I am personally willing to trust my neck with." [52] Needless to say, Brown was in no mood to argue when Representative James M. Mead of Pennsylvania introduced a resolution in the House of Representatives which resolved that "the Postmaster General be informed that it is the desire of the members of the Committee on the Post Office and Post Roads that in all future negotiations concerning air mail contracts . . . the privilege of collective representation be accorded to the pilots." [53]

This kind of support offered enormous opportunity for the pilots to pursue their goals in Washington, and from the Century strike until the passage of the Civil Aeronautics Act of 1938, gaining protection for airline pilots by lobbying in Washington for federal legislation was almost ALPA's only concern. But if the Century strike taught the pilots that they needed friends in Washington, it also dramatically demonstrated to them that they could not depend on their skills alone to preserve their jobs. After a determined fellow like E. L. Cord proved that he could replace them with other pilots, most of them accepted unionization as a necessity of life.

7 | The New Deal, The N.I.R.A., and Decision 83

The vagaries of Washington politics caused considerable turmoil in the air transportation industry during the early New Deal. The Century strike generated wide public awareness of the role subsidies played in airline operations, but the drama of the pilots' strike temporarily overshadowed the issue of government paternalism. Even though E. L. Cord temporarily got out of the air transportation business after losing his dispute with the pilots, he left a residual legacy of mistrust and suspicion hanging over the nonmail operators. However, the independent operators found many willing listeners among New Deal Democrats for their tales of fraud and malfeasance, and just prior to the end of the Hoover Administration the Senate created a special committee, chaired by Alabama's Hugo L. Black, to investigate Walter Folger Brown's air-mail policies. But even before the Black Committee began its work, the aviation trade journals were predicting severe cuts in the subsidy, since the "balanced-budget" campaign rhetoric of the early New Deal had forced Hoover to promise publicly new economies in government spending in the last days of his term. When the Post Office Department reduced the subsidies late in 1932, the temporary alliance between the major operators and ALPA, which was predicated only on their mutual fear of

E. L. Cord, collapsed.[1] Indicating the irritation of airline executives over high pilot salaries, *Aviation* magazine expressed dismay over the disparity between the high pay of pilots and the low pay of ground personnel. The implication was clearly, however, that pilot salaries should be lower, not that ground personnel salaries should be higher.[2]

Shortly after the lower subsidies became effective in December 1932, the operators announced their intention to decrease pilot salaries an amount compatible with the percentage of subsidy reduction. Eastern began with a 16 percent reduction, Northwest announced a flat 10 percent cut, and all the other airlines indicated that they too would reduce salaries in the near future. One of Behncke's most insistent rationales for the creation of ALPA was that a union would prevent pay reductions. Early in the depression it was the threat rather than the fact of pay cuts which alarmed pilots, and even on lines where the hourly system of pay prevailed, such as T&WA, pilot salaries remained fairly high. But late in 1932 reality stared the pilots in the face—the rhetoric and scares were over, the operators fully intended to cut pay, and ALPA would have to produce positive results in order to justify its existence.

At the same time, there were serious problems of technological unemployment facing the profession, since the airlines were rapidly introducing more modern aircraft, such as the Boeing 247, which, because they were larger and faster, vastly increased pilot productivity and resulted in some pilot layoffs. The Century strike proved there was no shortage of pilots, and Lyman D. Lauren, the aviation writer for the *New York Times* estimated that there were over 7,000 licensed transport pilots in 1933, but he placed the total number of jobs for them at only 1,500.[3] Faced with these dismal statistics, and the obvious financial difficulties of their respective airlines, a surprising number of pilots were willing to acquiesce in the pay reduction.

Behncke, however, had to deal with a credibility crisis among the remainder of his membership, and he desperately petitioned his new-found friends in Washington for help.[4] At his request, Congressman James M. Mead of Minnesota intervened directly on ALPA's behalf. He asked North-western's General Manager, Colonel L. H. Brittin, to with-hold action on the pay cuts until Congress and the Post Office Department had time to study the whole situation.[5] Mead also intervened with Captain Thomas Doe, the Presi-dent of Eastern Air Transport. Many Congressmen were becoming increasingly suspicious of the air-mail subsidies, and the situation at the time was very tense. As an indication of the antagonism the subsidy issue aroused in Congress, the Senate deleted the entire air-mail section in the Post Office appropriation, and a conference committee only barely succeeded in restoring it. The times were uncertain as the country awaited Roosevelt's inauguration, and nobody could be sure of the direction of aviation policy in the forthcoming New Deal. While expecting and preparing for the worst, most operators saw no advantage in prematurely alienating an important member of the House Post Office Committee. Brittin and Doe, therefore, reluctantly acceded to Mead's request.[6]

"Welfare Capitalism" and the anti-union activities of American businessmen during the prosperity decade of the 1920s had decreased the strength of the American labor movement, and the downward trend in union membership accelerated with the depression. But the confidence and enthusiasm which the early New Deal generated proved very helpful to union organizers, and the thrust of its policies seemed to offer organized labor a golden opportunity to write guarantees of maximum hours and minimum wages into federal law. The prestige of the entrepreneur in American society had sagged along with the index of industrial production, and many aggrieved and embittered people who formerly looked suspiciously upon unions were now willing to countenance them. While ALPA was already an organized union, it still had need of federal guarantees of the right to bargain collectively, and the new prestige of organized labor, particularly among influential legislators, gave Behncke cause for optimism.[7]

In the interim, however, before anybody could be sure of the shape of New Deal air transportation and labor policies, Behncke and the operators warily sparred over the pay issue. During the 1932 convention, Behncke told the delegates that the House Post Office Committee had promised to await ALPA's recommendations before passing any new air-mail legislation, and early in 1933 Congressman Mead asked the pilots for their views on a variety of aviation issues, including pay, hours, and air safety. Behncke undercut the stereotype of the individualistic aviator when he triumphantly informed the delegates that the pilots could "look forward to being adequately protected by some regulation or legislation during the coming 'session of Congress."[8] He wanted a firm commitment from his membership as to what they wanted, and, prior to the convention, he had polled all twenty-nine of ALPA's locals asking for their ideas on such things as salaries, hours, hazard pay, foreign-duty pay, vacations, and sick leave.[9] From the composite questionnaires he determined that the pilots preferred a base pay, plus mileage pay, with increased factors for the size, speed, and weight of the aircraft, and, of course, hazard pay for night, overwater, and mountainous terrain flying. At Behncke's insistence the convention established a National Basis of Pay Committee to aid him in the effort to have

Congress write federal guarantees which would apply to all airline pilots, but especially to pilots working for airlines which had air-mail contracts.[10]

The matter of a federal limitation of flying hours per month provoked some of the hottest exchanges of the 1932 convention. There was already a good deal of talk about limiting the hours of all workers to thirty hours per week, and William Green had endorsed the idea as early as 1930. The month following ALPA's convention, the AFofL formally endorsed the thirty-hour week on the theory that it would spread the available work.[11] Pilot interest in reduced hours of flying preceded such economic theorizing, deriving mainly from the fact that too many pilots spent three nights out of four away from their homes. While some pilots preferred the hefty paychecks they received for flying long hours, most pilots opted for a more relaxed routine even at the risk of lessened pay. The Department of Commerce set a maximum limit of 110 hours per month, but during busy seasons the airlines habitually exceeded this total on the theory, which the department never tested, that the maximum was meant to be an annual average rather than an arbitrary total for any one month. But to complicate matters for the pilots, many of the smaller airlines declared that they could not continue to operate if pilot hours per month were too low, and the pilots were genuinely worried about it. There was fundamental agreement, however, that the operators should not be allowed to exploit pilot labor, and John Huber spoke for the majority when he declared that "the idea behind all this is to set a regular scale . . . so there will not be any competition between the lines." The general discussion slowly yielded an understanding, for most of the delegates, that unless they stuck together and refused to fly more than other pilots, there would be anarchy within their ranks which would eventually destroy the union.

Many pilots evidenced a managerial mentality, and at times they seemed more concerned with their line's profit margin than with their own salaries. While there was some merit in this view, Behncke worried lest it dominate ALPA policy, and he insisted that ALPA must necessarily adopt a hard posture in favor of a uniform national scale. Despite this disagreement, it was apparent to almost all of the pilots that seniority should be the only factor in promotion. They openly derided the merit system, declaring that it was almost always used to favor management's cronies. They knew that they would eventually have to secure contractual agreements with the operators to use the seniority system exclusively, but Behncke persuaded them that it was better to seek federal protection before entering direct negotiations with the employers. The tricky problem of job security would necessarily involve a combination of federal guarantees and direct union-employer collective bargaining agreements. Still, until they got these agreements, federal rules governing their hours and wages would do them little good if, as one delegate put it, management could "fire an old man with a high base and start in a young fellow with a low base." [12] The times seemed propitious for a concerted effort in Washington, however, and Behncke persuaded a majority of the delegates that ALPA should delay action on direct collective bargaining.

At one point in the discussion the delegates seemed to be on the verge of adopting a variable scale on maximum hours and minimum pay which would allow for regional variations, the size of the airline, and the type of aircraft. Behncke adamantly opposed this idea, insisting on a single standard that would apply to all airline pilots everywhere. After a delegate offered a formal resolution that the hourly limit be subject to a "plus or minus fifteen hours" variation, Behncke blurted: "No! No! That is all wrong, that fifteen hour business. That leaves the sky for the limit." Since Behncke would not countenance a variable hourly limit, the convention seemed willing to adopt the Commerce Department's limit of 110 hours per month, until a delegate moaned that such a high hourly total would "just about drive us crazy on our line. With the run I'm on we would have to fly, well about damn near every day. And on account of the cancellations for weather we would just have a merry time." Behncke favored an 80-hour-per-month maximum, which was about what most pilots were then flying, and he stressed the fact that the Aeromedical Association, a private group of physicians interested in aviation medicine, endorsed his view. He had written to Frederick C. Warnshuis, the Chairman of the association, asking for a "scientific" determination of the maximum number of hours which would be compatible with safety. Warnshuis replied that, in his opinion, the Department of Commerce limit of 110 hours per month was too high, and he recommended 90 to 100 hours for day flying, 60 to 70 for night flying, with a standard figure of 80 hours per month for a combination of both types.[13] Behncke had a telling and effective point in the doctor's opinion, and the convention finally agreed to support him in his effort to make 80 hours per month the federal maximum.[14]

Behncke intended to make the Pay Committee his vehicle for Washington lobbying activities. The committee met for the first time on December 22, 1932, and promptly endorsed a pamphlet which Behncke had previously written entitled "The Truth About Pilot Pay." He subsequently circulated the pamphlet among all members of Congress and he sent dozens of copies to newspaper editors.[15] Behncke knew the operators would not delay their pay cuts much longer and he wanted to publicize the pilots' views as widely as possible. At this time he abandoned all idea of a strike, if and when the pay cuts became effective, partly because he felt that ALPA's structure was too weak to survive a major strike, but mainly because he wanted to pursue the issue in Washington.[16]

The uneasy truce which had existed between ALPA and the operators since Congressman Mead intervened to win a delay in the pay cuts ended abruptly on February 25, 1933, when a committee of executives from the nation's five largest airlines announced in New York that they were instituting a new, uniform system of hourly pay. All five lines declared that their decision to terminate mileage pay was irrevocable, and they set co-pilot pay at a flat $225 per month, regardless of the number of hours they flew. Three of the "Big Five" were already using the hourly system, but American and United, the two largest, were still paying their pilots on the old mileage basis. The new pay system raised pay very slightly on T&WA, Eastern, and Western Air Express, which were already paying on the hourly scale, but the impact of the new pay policy on United and American was to reduce salaries. United, which always treated its pilots gingerly, announced that there would be no lost pay the first year as a result of the new system of pay computation, because it would pay the pilots a "bonus" equal to the amount they would have made on the old mileage system. But United's management adamantly insisted that the new hourly method of computing pay was in effect and permanent.[17]

Behncke promptly objected to the new pay method, and he condemned the operators for deceptively calling it a "pay raise" when in fact it was a pay cut. He took a few days off to go to Washington in the hope of enlisting the aid of his friends on the House Post Office Committee, and William Green issued a statement from AFofL headquarters condemning the operators. Green insisted that it was folly for the government to cut the pay of its own employees, thus reflecting Behncke's notion that the airline pilots were "quasi-governmental" employees.[18] The operators had lent credence to this idea by citing cuts in the mail subsidy as their reason for reducing pilot pay. The President of the AFofL seemed genuinely to like Behncke, and the two were on very friendly terms. Green went out of his way to be helpful to ALPA from the very beginning of its connection with the Federation, perhaps because ALPA was one of the few unions to affiliate with it in the bleak years between 1929 and 1933. Green and Behncke shared a common Horatio Alger story background, since both had risen in the world from rural, working-class backgrounds, despite their lack of formal education.[19] But there was little the House Post Office Committee, William Green, or anybody else could do to prevent the operators from changing the basis of pay in the uncertain period before Roosevelt's inauguration. Green promised Behncke that he would use whatever influence he had with the new President,[20] and owing to his efforts Behncke received an invitation to attend a presidential "Industrial and Labor Conference" in Washington on March 31.[21] In the frantic atmosphere of Washington, however, where ardent New Dealers were already busily planning their assault on the depression, there was no place for the leader of a small union to present his case. Other far larger issues were on the minds of officialdom, and Behncke realized that he would have to swim with the tide of events for the time being.

The labor provisions of the National Industrial Recovery Act (N.I.R.A.), which the President signed on June 16, 1933, were enormously important for organized labor, but for ALPA the vital aspect of the measure lay in its basic assumption that cooperation between labor, capital, and the government offered the best solution to the problem of economic collapse. The heart of the Blue Eagle crusade was its insistence that agreements between the various participants in an industry, as stated in an industry-wide "code," could restore prosperity.[22] The Air Transportation Code, which became effective on November 27, 1933,[23] had no effect on pilot laborers because they were not in it—they wanted no part of it and they fought furiously to avoid any definition of their maximum hours and minimum wages under the code. Ordinarily it might seem that the code offered an ideal vehicle for ALPA to achieve its goals. But Behncke distrusted airline management more, perhaps, than any other pilot in America. He never evidenced any sign of the managerial mentality which characterized so many pilots, and he stubbornly insisted that ALPA adhere to its original objective of specific federal laws covering the wages and working conditions of airline pilots. He refused to depend on the good will of airline managers for the simple reason that he did not expect to have their good will very long.[24]

Initially, however, Behncke had to go through the motions of cooperating in the effort of the National Recovery Administration (N.R.A.) to draft a code for the air transportation industry. While many people in the N.R.A. regarded it as a straightforward method for introducing government planning into the economy, another faction worried that the charge of "czarism" might discredit their work. General Hugh Johnson, the head of the N.R.A., was in a difficult position when it came to the harsh realities of actually hammering out workable codes for each industry. He had grave doubts about the constitutionality of the N.I.R.A., and quite early he decided that, in order to avoid court tests, labor and capital would have to voluntarily assent to a code before the N.R.A. could approve it. The N.R.A., then, simply provided a forum at which the bargaining between labor and management could take place.[25]

Prior to coming to Washington for the final approval of a code, both labor and management were supposed to engage in preliminary discussions with the assistance of an N.R.A. functionary. General Johnson began the codification process almost as soon as the basic framework of the N.R.A. was operable in June 1933.[26] The June 15, 1933, meeting of ALPA's Central Executive Council was devoted exclusively to discussing the kind of labor provisions the pilots wanted in the Air Transportation Code. Many of the members believed the code could guarantee the kind of wages and working conditions they wanted. Behncke, while not overly critical of the idea, was skeptical and he tried to tone down the enthusiasm of the council members. He warned that ALPA must exercise extreme caution before committing itself to support of the code.[27] In order to present a united front of all airline labor, Behncke suggested to the July 6 meeting of the Central Executive Council that ALPA take the lead in forming a "Directorate" of all airline labor groups. Only a few airline workers were fully organized at the time, but Section 7(a) of the N.I.R.A. was stimulating the growth of unionization among several groups of unorganized air workers, and Behncke wanted ALPA, as the senior air transport union, to occupy a dominant position. After an exceedingly lengthy meeting, however, the Central Executive Council for once failed to act as a rubber stamp for Behncke, and ordered him to concentrate strictly on the part of the code affecting pilots. The council decided that if the results of the code discussions with the various operating companies were satisfactory, Behncke could then pursue his rather visionary idea of creating an Air Line Labor Executives Association similar to the organization of executives of railroad labor groups.[28]

The code conference which United held with its pilots on July 25 at the Edgewater Beach Hotel in Chicago produced an unexpectedly satisfactory result. United's management was always inclined to be lenient in its dealings with

ALPA. The President of United, William A. Patterson, personally represented his company, while J. L. Brandon headed the United pilots' committee, although Behncke was a member. United's various division managers had previously held a series of meetings with their pilots in which they pointed out that changes in working conditions would be necessary with the introduction of the new Boeing 247. While there would be pilot layoffs in the future owing to the greater speed and consequent decrease in the need for pilot crews to fly the new aircraft, Patterson agreed to reemploy his old pilots as soon as possible and to abide by the rule of seniority in doing so. The old basic conflict between pilots and management over who should gain the benefits from improved technology underlay these meetings, however, and Patterson could not agree with the pilots' notion that only by retention of the mileage pay factor could they be fairly recompensed for their increased labor productivity. Patterson necessarily insisted that since the companies took the risk by investing in new aircraft, they, and not labor, should reap the rewards. The conference was tense and at times strained, but Patterson's genuine desire to retain good relations with his pilots eased the situation. To prove his good will, Patterson overrode his lower-echelon managers and partially gave in to the pilots on the mileage pay question by agreeing to support some kind of mileage pay increment in the final code.[29]

Although ALPA's victory on United was significant, it was isolated. The Eastern pilots got no satisfaction from their employer, and the Chairman of the Eastern pilots' committee, Wallace S. Dawson, informed Behncke that the company had openly irritated ALPA members by hiring two Century scabs the week before the conference.[30] A few Eastern pilots favored a wildcat strike of short duration to protest the hiring of the two scabs, but Behncke counseled against it because he thought it would make ALPA appear irresponsible just when N.R.A. officials were studying the industry as a whole.[31] The Eastern pilots accomplished very little in the way of influencing the labor provisions of the code during the conference, which was held from July 28 to August 2, despite the presence of an N.R.A. official to smooth the proceedings. All the other "Big Five," with the exception of United, copied Eastern in refusing to retreat on the hourly pay issue.[32]

Shortly after the code conferences with United and Eastern were completed, Behncke formally requested similar conferences with the remaining airlines. Most of the operators proved reluctant to meet with ALPA, and they suggested that Behncke take his request to their agent, the Aeronautical Chamber of Commerce. The N.R.A.'s policy of dealing mainly with the employers and slighting labor in the initial codification process alarmed Behncke, and he grew increasingly uneasy about the kind of labor provisions the code would eventually contain. Furthermore, he realized that management would undoubtedly dominate the Code Authority which would administer the code. Fearing disaster, Behncke dropped all idea of further negotiations with the individual airlines and instead resorted to the approach he originally favored of taking his case directly to Washington.[33]

In the intervening period, Behncke concentrated on lining up a battery of supporters to testify at the code hearings. He wanted William Green to appear in ALPA's behalf, but the AFofL President was too busy, and as a substitute he arranged for Victor Olander of the Illinois State Federation of Labor to be present.[34] Olander was a lawyer, and Behncke hoped that by having him there ALPA's depleted treasury could be spared the expense of hiring legal help.[35] At Behncke's request, the August 15 meeting of the Central

Executive Council named a committee of prominent airline pilots to attend the hearings, among them E. Hamilton Lee, the veteran United pilot who had been one of the principals in the air-mail pilots' strike of 1919, and Mal B. Freeburg of Northwest, who had won the first "Air Mail Pilot Medal of Honor" by saving his aircraft and passengers after a spectacular in-flight explosion and fire.[36] In addition, Dr. Ralph Green, former Chief Medical Examiner for the Department of Commerce and current head of the Aeromedical Association, agreed to testify on behalf of the 80-hour-per-month maximum.[37] A covey of congressmen would speak for ALPA, but Behncke's star witness was to be the nimble and vibrant Fiorello La Guardia, who, despite his liberalism, had been defeated in the Republican debacle of 1932 and was then running for Mayor of New York on a fusion ticket. The hearings promised La Guardia some badly needed public exposure, and he eagerly honored Behncke's plea for help. Behncke secured yet another leave of absence from United, and he was on hand at Washington's National Airport, along with a committee of pilots, to meet La Guardia when he took time out from the mayoralty campaign to fly down. They went into an immediate conference with William Green at AFofL headquarters to plan their strategy during the hearings, which would begin the following day.[38]

When the code hearings convened in the ballroom of the Hotel Mayflower under the supervision of Deputy N.R.A. Administrator Malcolm Muir, Behncke's urgency in assembling his all-star cast of witnesses received immediate justification. The rumors which had been circulating in the aviation trade journals that the operators intended to impose ridiculously high hour and low minimum-wage provisions proved to be true, thus confirming Behncke's worst fears.[39] La Guardia responded with his usual pugnacity when he discovered that Title III of the operators' proposed code established 140 hours per month as the maximum, and $250 per month as the minimum pay. The industry's spokesman was Frederick W. Coburn, a former President of American Airways, but there were four current airline chiefs in attendance as well. Lester D. Seymour of American denied that management intended to decrease the status or wages of pilots, and he cited Title V of the code, which guaranteed the right of collective bargaining, as proof. The hour and wage provisions, he insisted, were simply minimums and maximums, and he ridiculed the idea that the major operators would ever pay their pilots so little or work them so hard. The particular figures, Seymour maintained, were "fixed with consideration for the smaller operators, at least one of whom now pays his pilots as low as $100 per month." La Guardia displayed his usual histrionics when he attacked Seymour's contentions, and he had a telling argument when he pointed out that, in the codes so far adopted, the working conditions and wages specified usually corresponded very closely to actual conditions.[40] La Guardia's argument struck a responsive chord with most air travelers. There was a rather general uneasiness among airline patrons that the operators might unduly reduce pilot salaries, and the *New York Times* expressed this fear when it pointed out that in the first six months of 1933 the airlines had flown over 25,000,000 passenger miles with only two fatalities. The newspaper attributed this safety record to pilot skill, and it believed that the industry's profit level was secondary in importance to preserving "the highest type of pilot morale."[41] Indicative of the public's support for high pilot salaries, even during the depression, the following day the *New York Times* printed a letter which declared: "If the captain of an ocean greyhound can be called a 'glorified ferryboat skipper,' . . . if an eagle can be called a 'glorified sparrow,' then a scheduled air transport pilot can be called a 'glorified chauffeur.'"[42]

Deputy Administrator Muir, harried and tired and with more important industry codes demanding his immediate attention, was inclined to approve the code despite the various objections to it. As this fact became increasingly clear to Behncke and La Guardia, they decided to press for total exemption of the pilots from the code, rather than take a chance on the hour and wage provisions becoming industry-wide standards. The thrust of their argument was that the pilots were professional workers whose wages and hours were subject to the regulation of the Department of Commerce, and hence they did not belong in the code. In his testimony, Behncke suggested that rather than writing arbitrary standards, the code should instead provide for a "planning, coordinating, and conciliating" committee to study the question of pilot labor. He believed that the committee should have one member each from the N.R.A., the Aeronautical Chamber of Commerce, and the AFofL. He preferred that the committee's recommendations be the subject of direct negotiations between the operators and the pilots. Clearly, Behncke's motive in suggesting this cumbersome arrangement was to obfuscate the issue, to use some last desperate ploy to delay approval of the Code's provisions for pilot labor.[43]

N.R.A. head Johnson, in the meantime, was in a quandary over the Air Transportation Code. It presented curious problems to begin with, because of the close association of business and government, and the pilot labor sections were even more obtuse since the Department of Commerce actually had the statutory power to regulate such things, regardless of what the code said. Malcolm Muir recommended that he accept the code despite the pilots' objections, but Johnson, with his deep fear of court challenges of the N.I.R.A.'s constitutionality, insisted that both sides agree to the code before it received final N.R.A. approval. Since the pilots adamantly refused to accept the code as it was, Muir had no alternative but to accede to their demands and exempt them from the code altogether.[44] Behncke had demonstrated once again that his appeals to government agencies and officials could be very effective, and the decision to omit the pilots from the code was one of the stepping stones which led to complete victory for the pilots later on.

One of the factors which aided the pilots in this victory was the editorial support of the Hearst newspapers. Hearst was generally antilabor, but aviation fascinated him and for some reason he liked the pilots.[45] Before the code hearings in Washington began, Behncke wrote to the sage of San Simeon to ask for his help. Although Hearst never answered the letter, the Hearst newspapers responded with a series of editorials favorable to the idea of exempting the pilots from the code, notably in the *Washington Daily News.* Behncke always believed that Hearst had personally intervened with Hugh Johnson to help ALPA, and he later told the 1942 convention: "I got in touch with Mr. Hearst, and I don't know to this day what happened, but the next day the air carriers' code . . . was withdrawn and General Johnson announced that the airline pilots were taken out of the Code because theirs was a profession and not just a job."[46]

With ALPA out of the code and the situation highly nebulous, there was no reason for the operators to delay the institution of a national, uniform basis of computing pilot pay on the hourly system. Early in September they formally announced that the new system was in effect and permanent. Behncke had about exhausted his sources of appeal among government officialdom, he had been in Washington continuously for almost two weeks, and he knew his job with United was in jeopardy owing to his absenteeism. The last thing he wanted was another strike, since he knew that it would in all probability fail and totally discredit ALPA in the process. Behncke reassessed his position, frantically telephoned local chairmen around the country, and concluded that while some locals could endure a strike, the majority would collapse. He told the 1934 convention: "I believe that American Airways was the best balanced of all operating companies . . . They were pretty much together and I believe that [they] . . . would have walked out to a man. T&WA would have collapsed completely and I know that on United everything south and east of Chicago would have gone out, and west of Chicago it would have been just a little bit better than half."[47] Still, he could see no alternative to an old-fashioned strike confrontation with the operators over the new pay scale. While hoping that the operators would not call his bluff, he decided to threaten a strike. Behncke set October 1 as the deadline for the operators to restore the mileage system, and in order to dramatize his contention that the strike would be nationwide, he prepared a set of color charts and graphs for use in his news conference showing the geographic extent of the national airline network.[48]

At this point, the kid gloves were off and the bare-knuckles battle between ALPA and the operators was in earnest. A national strike of airline pilots was heady stuff to the press, and it faithfully reported the charges and countercharges which Behncke and the operators traded. Each side declared that the other was trying to force a national strike, and the operators even went so far as to take out full-page advertisements in several newspapers accusing ALPA of trying to wring the neck of the Blue Eagle. Behncke was rapidly developing into a major-league polemicist, and he gave as good as he got in the exchanges with airline public relations men. But in one area Behncke was highly vulnerable— he was still only an employee of United, and there were limits to the patience of W. A. Patterson. Disquieting rumors began to reach Behncke that his future with United was in deep jeopardy, and at this time he began to think seriously about devoting full time to ALPA.[49]

Behncke's threat of a national strike moved Secretary of Labor Frances Perkins to arrange a thirty-day truce, which was a godsend for ALPA since it allowed time for maneuver. In the meantime, Behncke tried desperately to get ALPA's case before the National Labor Board (N.L.B.) of the N.R.A. He believed the board would take the case because a clause in the N.I.R.A. stipulated that no industry operating under a code could reduce pay levels below the pre-code level, and he argued that the operators had done precisely this. In formally requesting that the N.L.B. take jurisdiction, Behncke told the board's Secretary, W. M. Leiserson, that the operators were "gradually cutting down on salaries. Now they want us to accept starvation pay."[50]

The function of the N.L.B., composed of three members each from labor and industry, was to iron out disputes which arose over the interpretation of the codes. But as Arthur M. Schlesinger, Jr., said of the N.L.B.: "Its mandate was vague, its procedures were undefined, and its direct power of enforcement, beyond appeal to public opinion, was nonexistent."[51] On this curious body, however, Behncke staked the entire future of his organization. Fortunately, only he knew that the threat of a strike was a hollow bluff. During the 1934 convention Behncke told the delegates: "The only way you can keep a striking element in line is to keep them informed . . . I figured it would cost $1,000 a day to conduct the strike . . . and our treasury had $5,000 and we would have lasted about five days. After that our communications would have been cut, we would have been completely broke." Furthermore, he admitted that the strike would have caused "a perfect split in our organization that would probably have never been able to mend back together."[52]

In fact, the mere threat of a strike was enough to unravel some of ALPA's locals on T&WA. ALPA's strength on T&WA was always weak, and management had considerable success when it embarked on yet another of its efforts to wreck the union. This time, the company persuaded the Master Executive Council to declare itself independent of the National on the strike issue, and former Master Executive Council Chairman W. A. Golien led the move. While a few ALPA members held out against the company union idea, most of them went along, and ALPA's strength on the line collapsed. There was also considerable restiveness among Eastern pilots because of the proposed strike, and although a company union drive there failed, Behncke had to resist pressure to withdraw the strike decree.[53] But nothing could sway Behncke at this point—the whole ALPA idea was a desperate long shot, he was determined to play the game out, and he exhibited the fanaticism of the confirmed gambler who had nothing to lose. One favorable omen for him was that the major airlines were again making profits by late 1933, general revenues were up an average 20 percent despite the mail pay cuts, and the operators were, consequently, very reluctant to engage in a ruinous shutdown.[54] Still, they were in a better position to weather the strike than ALPA. Behncke's only real hope, then, was to get the shaky N.L.B. to accept jurisdiction so he could call off the strike before the October 1 deadline revealed ALPA's weakness.

But persuading the N.L.B. to take ALPA's case proved a difficult task, for it was inundated with code disputes and strikes in industries which were far more important than air transportation. During late September, the N.L.B. held all its meetings behind closed doors in order to keep the swarm of persistent leaders of small unions from interfering with its deliberations. William Green was on the N.L.B., but he was ill at the time, and the remaining labor members were either too busy or too tired to bother with ALPA. As the strike deadline neared, and Behncke still had not established contact with the board through conventional methods, he decided to adopt a direct approach and personally seek out one of the members he vaguely knew. Professor Leo Wolman of Columbia University was a member of the N.L.B. whom La Guardia had once introduced to Behncke, and he seemed the likely candidate for a personal contact.[55] Because of the pressure on board members, most of whom had other New Deal jobs (Wolman, for instance, was on the N.R.A. Labor Advisory Board), their home addresses were secret. By following the professor home after he emerged from a twenty-four-hour N.L.B. session, however, Behncke learned his address. Wolman as well as other pro-labor N.L.B. members had been dodging Behncke for two weeks, and needless to say he was unhappy to see the dogged aviator burst into his living room at ten o'clock at night with a wide-eyed tale of a national pilot strike. But he sat down on the front porch with Behncke and, after listening to his side of the dispute, agreed to use his influence to get the case before the board. In exchange, Behncke promised to cancel the strike. The exhausted academic then retired, but Behncke spent most of the remainder of the night calling ALPA's local chairmen on his living room telephone.[56] Professor Wolman subsequently persuaded Senator Wagner to contact the "Big Five" with a request that they voluntarily withhold the pay cuts until the N.L.B. could study the situation.[57] Once again, under what had seemed impossible odds, Behncke had staved off defeat.

The N.L.B. began its hearings on the airline pay dispute on October 4, 1933. Behncke, Hamilton, and American's Master Executive Council Chairman Clyde Holbrook represented ALPA, with Victor Olander present to give them legal advice. The presidents of all the "Big Five" plus several executives from smaller lines attended the hearing, bringing with them complete batteries of corporation lawyers. The disparity between the overblown management group and the spare ALPA delegation gave the pilots an underdog's psychological advantage which outweighed the merits of the miles versus hours argument. Hamilton gave most of the oral presentation for ALPA, trying to build a case that the pilots were quasi-governmental employees and, hence, deserving of government protection. With a bow to the ghosts of Grover Cleveland and Richard Olney, Hamilton declared that even should the pilots strike they would "not be a party to retarding the U.S. Mail" but would only refuse to carry passengers and freight. He also used the rhetoric of class warfare in a tub-thumping anticapitalist harangue against the "powerful financial interests that are behind these . . . big operating companies" who were trying to crush "this spendid corps of airline pilots who are . . . going through all kinds of dangers losing one of their number . . . every twenty-nine days, and who incidentally are the first line of defense material in time of war." While he conceded that pilots frequently made more money than airline executives, he maintained that they were nevertheless a group of "mass wage earners" and that they needed special protection in order to retain the high state of morale which was essential to air safety.[58]

Things went poorly for the operators from the beginning, when Senator Wagner and Victor Olander, who were old friends, exchanged just enough banter to make them feel like they were sitting before a hanging judge. In fact, Wagner's predisposition to favor the underdog pilots and his sharp criticism of the airline executives for bringing lawyers to the hearing meant that the pilots were almost certain to receive a favorable verdict from the N.L.B. To make matters worse, the operators allowed their lawyers to begin with the legalistic argument that since the pilots were not in the Air Transport Code, the N.L.B. had no jurisdiction. Wagner replied that the labor policy of the New Deal was to play fair with unions and he rather pointedly hinted: "You are doing government work and I thought you would be first in line." Sensing Wagner's rising irritation at the operators' lawyers, Olander interjected: "If we find ourselves in a position . . . where the opposition presents its case through some distinguished lawyers who are trained in the technique of merely defending their clients, we will not get very far." The Senator agreed and promptly condemned any further "legalistic quibbling." "I am a member of the law profession myself," he said, "but we are always looking for technicalities and we can do better when these technical gentlemen are not around at all." A lawyer representing American quickly succeeded in antagonizing Wagner even more by beginning his presentation with the courtroom pleasantry that he regretted "bothering gentlemen like you and asking for your intervention in a matter like this when there are so many other affairs . . . which should be taken care of." Wagner virtually exploded: "Nobody's rights are too small to be taken care of. I do not know whether you understand that!" "Nothing is greater than the individual's rights and the smaller he is . . . the more he needs our help."[59]

The nervous airline executives squirmed as their lawyers, who were supposed to keep them out of trouble, only succeeded in getting them in deeper. In an effort to discredit ALPA, T&WA's lawyers declared that most of their pilots had resigned from the union and that it could not, therefore, speak for them. Behncke was prepared for this argument, and he called attention to a petition which a majority of T&WA pilots had previously signed designating ALPA as their bargaining agent. He denounced T&WA's labor policies and declared that the line's executives were intimidating pilots and pressuring them to resign from ALPA. He asked Senator Wagner to consider the case of T&WA pilot Wayne Williams, who was present in the room, who had been fired when he refused to cease his organizational work on behalf of ALPA. Senator Wagner was immediately interested in Williams's case because it personalized the issue, and he asked the T&WA lawyer, whose name was Henry M. Hogan, to explain his position in the light of Behncke's signed petition. Hogan declared that many T&WA pilots had resigned from ALPA since signing the petition, and the subsequent exchange between the Senator and the lawyer ruined the operators:

WAGNER: How did you happen to see them?
HOGAN: Because I have seen copies of some letters of resignation.
WAGNER: How did you happen to see them?
HOGAN: Because I represent the company . . . and the letters were sent to us . . .
WAGNER: You are not an officer of the Association. Why should they send letters to you? How did they know the company was interested in them . . . ?
HOGAN: I imagine if you were a pilot you could answer that.
WAGNER: What? No. It might indicate that the company was evidencing a little interest in their resigning.
THOMAS B. DOE [President of North American Aviation]: We are interested in everything they do, Senator.
WAGNER: That is something you ought not to be interested in because it is none of your business. When a man

working for a concern is a member of a union and he
resigns from that union and then hurries to tell his
employer—well now, I am not a child . . . Wayne
Williams was discharged for no other reason than his
activity in organizing the pilots . . . That sort of thing
must stop . . . If certain rights are given to them
under the law, to organize, the government should not
permit employers to discriminate against them . . .
You must understand that this is a new era. There is
an equality of rights that we must take into consideration. We are not living in an old century.[60]

The operators were beaten at this point, and all they could
do was to try to minimize their losses. Almost in chorus the
airline representatives began to sing praises to their pilots.
Ernest R. Breech, a lawyer for Eastern, declared: "I for one
will never subscribe to paying these fellows chauffeurs's
wages because they are the greatest salesmen we have."
J. Bruce Kremer, a managerial spokesman for United, added:
"Candidly, knowing their fearless spirit, I think a man shows
a great deal of temerity who tries to intimidate any one of
them." Unimpressed, Wagner replied that it did not take
much courage to fire a man, and he insisted that the pilots
must receive fair treatment or he would see to it that the
airlines received no more "liberal mail subsidies." He
ordered T&WA to reinstate Wayne Williams immediately,
and he appointed a special fact-finding board, to be composed of Behncke, Lester D. Seymour of American, and
Judge Bernard L. Shientag of the New York Supreme Court,
to study the pay question. He required that the committee
report its findings to the N.L.B. within three weeks, and he
asked the airlines to voluntarily retain the mileage pay system until then. Considering the Senator's irate mood, the
airline executives would probably have agreed to anything
just to get out of the disastrous hearing.[61]

The fact-finding committee was essentially a device whereby Behncke and Seymour could present their views to a neutral, Judge Shientag, who would then make a decision. Each side could call witnesses, and the operators scored an initial victory when Eugene Vidal, Director of the Bureau of Air Commerce, agreed to testify in behalf of the hourly pay system.[62] There were a number of complex factors in the hearing, which was held on October 27 and 28 in New York City, but the essential conflict came over ALPA's contention that increased speed meant increased hazard, and that accidents were a function of the number of miles flown, rather than the number of hours flown. From this notion, Behncke could argue that the pilots should be paid on the mileage basis because of the risks involved.[63] Vidal demolished this argument in his testimony, correctly pointing out that most accidents occurred on takeoff or landing and that the new aircraft, while they flew faster when cruising at altitude, actually had lower landing and takeoff speeds than the old trimotored aircraft. Before Judge Shientag, the operators at last were able to make good use of their expensive legal talent. They presented an exhaustive series of charts and legal briefs showing that airline stockholders were sacrificing current profits in order to invest in the new aircraft, and that the stockholders, rather than the pilots, deserved the productivity gains which accrued from investing the risk capital. The presidents of all five major airlines assured Judge Shientag that they "considered their pilots in a class at least semi-professional and out of self interest wished to maintain their morale at a high level." They argued that pilot pay would average $6,000 per year under the hourly pay system and might go as high as $9,000 per year in some cases. To bolster their contention that this amount was satisfactory, they produced the startling information that the master of the largest ocean liner in America's merchant marine fleet, the 2,600 passenger Leviathan, earned only $6,000 per year. To refute ALPA's contention that the new aircraft were more difficult to fly, the operators submitted letters from famous aviators Wiley Post and Captain Frank M. Hawks declaring that the new aircraft were easier to fly. Post said that he accomplished a ten-hour flight in a Boeing 247 "without noticeable mental or physical fatigue."[64] The pilots looked bad in the exchange, and Behncke later ruefully admitted: "they really ganged up on us that time."[65]

Fearing that Seymour was winning the argument, Behncke asked that a "scientific study" be made of the safety factor by the Department of Labor. He had a naive faith in "statistics," and he believed that the Department of Labor would render a "good report because they would only deal with the facts, there would be no politics . . . it would be submitted to their statisticians . . . and they would make a report."[66] Judge Shientag leaned to the operators' side, but he decided he could not make a final decision on the available facts, so he returned the controversy to the N.L.B. suggesting that "the rates proposed by the operators should continue without prejudice to the contentions of the respective parties, pending a prompt, thorough, and scientific investigation . . . to be made by a government agency to be designated by the N.L.B."[67]

The Shientag decision was a blow to Behncke, but Senator Wagner reprieved him by rejecting the report. The Senator wanted a clear-cut decision, once and for all. He was tired of studies and investigations and inconclusive disputation. He allowed the operators to begin paying on the "new standardized scale," retroactive to October 1, but he warned them that the final decision, regardless of the fact-finding committee's views, would rest with the N.L.B. itself.[68]

Thinking they had won, the operators did not mount a second major offensive to influence Judge Shientag. Only

Lester D. Seymour of American came to the second meeting, held in mid-November, and he left the floor largely to Behncke. Behncke later remarked that he felt ALPA had scored well in the second hearing because "I could argue and Eddie [Hamilton] could figure." But Behncke's forensic talents were a dubious advantage, and Judge Shientag was less impressed with the substance of the debate than with the obvious fact that he would have to arrive at some kind of compromise in order to satisfy the N.L.B. He was in poor health, suffering from heart disease, and he wished to rid himself of the troublesome case. In order to resolve the question he simply combined the basic hourly pay (which would increase with the speed of the aircraft), with a very small mileage increment, and called it a compromise. In similar fashion, the Judge resolved the hours per month question by splitting the difference between the operators' preference for a ninety-hour limit and ALPA's preference for an eighty-hour limit. Needless to say, Seymour, representing all the operators, was horrified at this turn of events. What had originally shaped up as a sparkling triumph for the operators had inexplicably turned into something quite different. Shientag's report represented a clear retreat from his first position in favor of straight hourly pay, and Seymour refused to sign it. Although the report established an hourly component, Behncke was willing to accept it because it was geared to the speed of the aircraft and therefore gave pilots a share of the increased productivity. Principles aside, Behncke later admitted that he liked the report because "the amount [of money] was not so bad and that is the controlling factor in a thing like that." [69]

The N.L.B. subsequently spent about two weeks converting Judge Shientag's report into a definite wage formula, and when Senator Wagner summoned all interested parties to Washington for a conference on December 14, the reluctant operators had no alternative but to attend. Wagner, however, still operating under the Johnsonian policy that labor and management must, if at all possible, voluntarily assent to all N.R.A. decisions, insisted that the pilots and the operators meet one last time in an effort to iron out their difficulties. The meeting which took place on December 15 in the May-flower Hotel produced no general agreement, except that both sides acknowledged that there had to be *some* limit on the number of miles a pilot could fly each month, regardless of whether an hourly or mileage system of pay prevailed. The operators were well aware of the problems involved in Judge Shientag's complicated system of pay computation, but there was very little they could do about it. After the meeting broke down, Behncke formally requested binding arbitration by the N.L.B. because he believed that it would favor ALPA.[70]

Behncke had been in either New York or Washington al-most continuously since August, and he had not flown enough for United to remain "current," according to De-partment of Commerce regulations. When he returned to Chicago for the Christmas holidays, United fired him, claim-ing that his repeated absences had made it necessary to fill his position. Whatever good will once existed between Behncke and Patterson had long since disappeared in the heat of repeated confrontations. While Patterson probably expected to face Behncke across a bargaining table for years to come, he was not particularly anxious to continue paying his salary while doing so. Behncke did not intend to lose his job without a fight, and he lined up support from Green, Olander, and several Congressmen in an effort to have the N.L.B. reinstate him. Mayor Edward J. Kelly of Chicago, who owed the Chicago Federation of Labor a great deal, also offered to come to Washington to testify in his behalf. Simultaneously with United's dismissal of Behncke, T&WA

raised the absurd claim that ALPA was connected with the Chicago underworld. As proof, T&WA complained to the N.L.B. that pro-ALPA "elements" had assaulted one of its anti-ALPA pilots in the parking lot of the Newark Airport. Despite this climate of recrimination, however, Behncke successfully presented his case to the N.L.B., and, on January 18, Senator Wagner ordered his reinstatement.[71]

Judge Shientag's compromise report eventually emerged as Decision 83 of the N.L.B. and it was, as a leading expert on airline labor relations has said, "without doubt . . . the most far-reaching ruling ever issued in the air line labor field."[72] Because it embodied both mileage pay and an hourly pay rate which increased as the speed of the aircraft increased, it guaranteed the pilots a huge share of the productivity gains associated with improved aircraft technology. The essentials of this pay formula still apply to airline pilots today.[73] But perhaps even more importantly, for the first time the airline pilots had persuaded an agency of the federal government to grant them special protection. In a sense, Behncke won his argument that the pilots were "quasi-governmental employees." Although Behncke would later score a stunning victory in keeping Decision 83 in the Air Mail Act of 1934, the fight over the pay scale would always remain the classic example of his effectiveness in obtaining his goals through appeals to Washington.

8 | Victory in Washington

Despite the crises and heated encounters, the nation's airlines as well as their pilots did very well for themselves in 1933. Largely through consolidations and mergers, the number of operating companies fell from twenty-eight to fifteen, but the number of cities with scheduled air transportation service rose from 143 to 156. The Bureau of Labor Statistics noted that the industry had continued to grow "even in the presence of unfavorable economic conditions," and that the airline pilots had succeeded in maintaining their share of that growth. There were more pilots working in 1933 than in 1931, and, after a survey covering over 90 percent of all airline pilots, the bureau reported that the average monthly salary for a captain was $628.23, while co-pilots earned $231.13 per month. These 1933 salaries were up an average of 10 percent over the salary levels of 1931 (there was no survey in 1932). The bureau found no real pay reduction even on the airlines which had begun to pay on the hourly rather than the mileage basis, for the average captain earned $7.36 per hour, an increase of 28 cents per hour over 1931. Even more startling, of the 452 pilots tabulated, thirty-three averaged making over $1,000 per month in 1933, whereas only two had reached this level in 1931.[1]

The profession's well-being owed nothing to Decision 83,

however. Even the initial impact of the N.L.B. ruling was limited because of the Roosevelt Administration's spectacular cancellation of all the air-mail contracts in February 1934. The cancellations followed many months of investigation by the Black Committee into the circumstances surrounding a series of conferences between the major airline operators and Hoover's Postmaster General, Walter F. Brown. During late May and early June of 1930, Brown had asked the operators to discuss, under Post Office Department auspices, the creation of a coherent and unified national air transportation network. He was in many ways Hoover's ablest cabinet member, and he faithfully reflected the ideas of the "great engineer" on efficiency and order. As Secretary of Commerce under Coolidge, Hoover feared that the airlines would develop in the same helter-skelter fashion as the railroads in the nineteenth century. His policy was to force the mail carriers to expand their operations so that they might attract enough paying passengers to become independent of the government subsidy. The corporations entering aviation during and after the Lindbergh boom had the financial capacity to purchase the large aircraft which such a passenger service required, but in a system which required periodic open competitive bidding for the mail routes, they could be consistently underbid by the small operators who flew open-cockpit planes designed solely for carrying mail. The first contracts let under the Watres Act of 1926 were to run for four years, at which time they were to be up for open bidding again.

In line with Hoover's basic ideas, Postmaster General Brown had consistently rigged the ground rules for entering bids to favor the large corporations, as only they could afford the large multi-engined aircraft which made a passenger service feasible. After virtually forcing the operating companies to invest a considerable sum of money in the new aircraft, he could not in good conscience allow them to lose it when the contracts were reopened. Accordingly, he extended the original contracts for six months past the expiration date, which the law allowed, and in the interim he arranged a series of conferences with the major operators to insure that they would be the successful bidders, which opponents claimed the law did not allow. These meetings, which later became known as the "Spoils Conferences," established a national route structure and a set of ground rules for bidding on the contracts. In order to qualify, a potential bidder had to show that he already had the multi-engined aircraft and the experience, stated in terms of route length and night-flying capability. When the bidding belatedly took place, Brown awarded ten-year contracts to the major operators, much to the disgruntlement of the small operators. They complained that the contracts were awarded through fraud and collusion, and Democratic politicians began to listen to them, almost in direct proportion to the amount of money they contributed to the party's campaign coffers.[2]

In fact, Brown was acting in a completely legal, although somewhat devious manner. There was less collusion involved than there was coercion, since the exasperated Postmaster General had to repeatedly bludgeon the reluctant and suspicious major operators into cooperating with each other in the kind of national airline system he wanted. In the Black Hearings, however, a different picture emerged. An obscure Hearst reporter named Fulton Lewis, Jr., (later to become famous as a conservative radio commentator) had discovered that Luddington Airlines, a nonmail carrier flying between New York and Washington, D.C., had bid low on the New York to Washington run but had lost the contract because of the route length limitation. The contract, instead, went to Eastern, which Brown preferred because as a subsidiary of North American Aviation it had powerful financial backing. Luddington subsequently merged with Eastern, but Black regarded this case as the most blatant example of the conspiracy to favor Wall Street at the expense of the "little man" who only knew how to fly.

Actually, Luddington could not have fit well into Brown's overall picture because the relative shortness of its runs made it only marginally better than the railroads for transporting either mail or passengers. Luddington's bid was very low in comparison with Eastern's, but had it been forced to operate over an extended low-population density route, such as Eastern, it could not have entered such a low bid. In all truth, however, there seems little doubt that Brown imposed certain conditions specifically to disqualify Luddington because he was suspicious of its financial resources. While this incident showed that Brown could be ruthless and imperious in forging the kind of national air transportation system he wanted, there was nothing technically illegal about it.

Black thought otherwise, however, and he gradually won the President to his view. After a brief investigation, Solicitor General Karl Crowley concurred in Black's opinion that the original contracts were let fraudulently, and he told the President that sufficient grounds existed to cancel the contracts. The President secured the assurance of General Benjamin D. Foulois that the Army Air Corps could carry the mail after its pilots had ten days to familiarize themselves with the routes, and on February 9, 1934, he canceled the air-mail contracts effective February 19.[3]

The cancellation of the air-mail contracts was as much a blow to the pilots as it was to the operators. While the N.L.B. had not yet officially promulgated Decision 83, it was an accomplished fact, and the airline operators had conceded defeat on the pay issue. But their basic willingness to comply with the N.L.B. educt stemmed from their desire to court favor with the government, since without the government subsidy they could not operate profitably, regardless of pilot salaries. The cancellations removed the mantle of government protection from both the pilots and the operators, and since management no longer had anything to fear from the government, it could do pretty much what it pleased with respect to pilot salaries, Decision 83 notwithstanding.

In a way, Behncke had been partially responsible for the rising discontent with the air-mail situation which had built up in Congress. While the Black Committee's investigation ground relentlessly on, he had repeatedly insinuated that the air-mail contractors were, in effect, government-sponsored monopolists, and that the government therefore owed the flying workers employed in these monopolies special protection. Engaged as he was in a bitter battle over the particular issue of pilot compensation, Behncke lost sight of the fact that his general interests were the same as the operators'. He short-sightedly gloated when the Black Committee first began to disclose publicly what seemed to be a pattern of underhanded behavior on the part of the operators, and he used these disclosures to win sympathy for ALPA in Congress. Behncke told the January 10, 1934, meeting of the Central Executive Council that Senator Black had contacted ALPA's Washington representative with a request that he "suggest lines of questioning which might reveal interesting facts." At Behncke's insistence, the council agreed that Hamilton should cooperate fully with the Senator.[4]

The cancellations came as a distinct shock to Behncke, and the tone of his public pronouncements became remarkably subdued. Shortly after obtaining the order from the N.L.B. which required that United reinstate him, he returned to Chicago and resumed flying. He was in Omaha, the western extension of his regular route, when he learned of the cancellations. He promptly telephoned the *New York Times* to protest that the airline pilots were "entirely innocent of any fraud that may have entered into the air mail business," and he pointed out that the cancellations would have a disastrous effect on all airline workers. He insisted that most airline operators were honest, and, while not directly criticizing either Senator Black or the President, he argued that the "graft of a few government officials and air operators" ought not to discredit the entire industry.[5] Once again, as in the fight against E. L. Cord, ALPA and the operators found themselves engaged in a common cause.

But at first Behncke was uncertain as to the position ALPA should adopt. The cancellations created a storm of controversy and provided the growing ranks of New Deal critics with a perfect focal point for their discontent. Charles A. Lindbergh promptly castigated the President for canceling the contracts without due process of law. His opposition was a matter of serious concern to the Administration, for he was perhaps the only man in America whose popularity rivaled Roosevelt's.[6] Will Rogers added his voice to the rising ride of protest. Writing in his nationally syndicated column, Rogers, who was an aviation buff, declared: "You are going to lose some fine boys, these Army fliers, who are . . . [not trained] in night cross country flying in rain and snow."[7]

The Administration declined to reply to Rogers, since he was more a professional entertainer than a political commentator, despite his pretensions. Lindbergh, however, bore no such immunity, and Administration spokesmen counterattacked by insinuating that he was a mere hireling of T&WA, which billed itself as the "Lindbergh Line." They pointed out that T&WA and Pan American had paid Lindbergh handsomely for "consulting" work, and that T&WA had once given him $250,000 in stock. Administration stalwarts scathingly announced that with his criticisms of the cancellation, Lindbergh was at last earning it. The breech thus opened between Lindbergh and Roosevelt endured through the bitter "America First" movement and even beyond, with the famed aviator gradually becoming the most popular figure in the conservative coalition against the New Deal.[8]

The Administration would not have blundered so badly in the air-mail controversy had General Foulois not misrepresented the readiness of his aviators. After a very short period of route familiarization, the poorly prepared Army pilots tried to match the veteran airline pilots. The typical Army pilot of the day was like Colonel Robert L. Scott, who later described the difficulties the Army encountered in flying the mail. After graduating from West Point, Scott went through flight training in Texas, where he received the latest instrument instruction. But upon joining his squadron, Scott found that the Curtiss Falcon, known as the 0–39, was totally without modern instrumentation. In fact, because of the austerity program of the late 1920s and early 1930s, Army pilots were generally limited to about four hours a month of *total flying,* and even that had to be in good weather inasmuch as the Army feared that bad-weather flying might result in the loss of scarce aircraft. A few pilots managed to stay "current" by flying weather research flights for the Department of Commerce, but these billets were scarce and the competition for them was fierce. As a result, only a few Army pilots had flown any instruments at all since leaving training. To complicate matters even more for the Army pilots, the winter of 1934 was exceptionally severe. In order to avoid the harsh northern climate, most Army squadrons wintered in Florida, hardly an ideal training ground for the kind of flying they were about to undertake. "Here we were," Scott wrote, "about to start flying the mail in tactical planes with open cockpits in the blizzards of the Great Lakes. It must have looked peculiar to air mail pilots to see

Army pilots taxiing out to take off over a course they had never flown before. Not only that, but flying the mail in P-12's and P-26's holding some fifty pounds."[9]

The results were predictable; within a week five pilots were dead, six were critically injured, eight aircraft were destroyed, and worse was to come. On March 10, Secretary of War Dern ordered the Army to stop carrying the mail "except under such conditions as would insure against constant recurrence of fatal accidents." The following day General Foulois halted all Army mail flights pending further training. What the General had originally welcomed as an "ideal peacetime test" had become something very close to war as the toll of dead pilots mounted. On March 17, the General, by now the object of the President's ire, ordered the resumption of mail flights, but covering only 40 percent of what the private operators had formerly covered, and then only in good weather.

While the Army fliers were not incompetent, they were ill prepared owing to lack of training and inadequate equipment. The cancellations had at least one beneficial side effect in that they revealed the inadequacies of the Army Air Corps. Secretary of War Dern ordered a special investigation of the Air Corps, and he asked Lindbergh, Orville Wright, the transatlantic flier Clarence Chamberlain, Foulois, and five other generals to participate in it. Wright declined on grounds of ill health, and Lindbergh too refused. When Dern publicly asked him to reconsider in the interest of national security, Lindbergh curtly replied that he would not "directly or indirectly lend his support to the operation by military forces of American business and commerce."[10]

The Administration reeled as such prominent men in the industry as Eddie Rickenbacker of Eastern Air Transport denounced it for committing "legalized murder." It seemed that every prominent aviator in America was joining the chorus of condemnation of what Arthur M. Schlesinger, Jr., called the New Deal's first "fiasco." Only Behncke's airline pilots, curiously, for they were gravely injured by the cancellations, voiced open support for the President.[11] At the time of the cancellations, Roosevelt had been toying with the idea of reestablishing the old Post Office Department Air Mail Service, and he told Harold L. Ickes that he thought it might be "possible to have the Army Air Corps train the Post Office pilots and perhaps supervise the service."[12] The Army's collapse quickly ended that plan. Behncke, like most pilots, was decidedly cool to the idea of becoming a Post Office employee, and he urged the President to abandon the notion.[13] Behncke was rapidly establishing himself as an Administration loyalist. Since Lindbergh had emerged as the bitterest critic of the Administration, and since he was associated with T&WA, ALPA's blood enemy, it was fairly logical for Behncke to enter the lists on the Administration side. He very cleverly managed to seem to be agreeing with the President, at least in public, while in private he was urging that the operators be given another chance. He had returned to Washington within a week of the cancellations (this time with the full cooperation, needless to say, of W. A. Patterson), where he applied steady private pressure in behalf of the operators.[14]

Roosevelt really had no alternative but to allow Postmaster General Farley to advertise for new air-mail bids, and on March 28 he announced that he would let temporary ninety-day contracts to the low bidders, pending permanent air-mail legislation.[15] Lindbergh maintained his opposition, contending that Farley's decision that executives tainted by the "Spoils Conferences" might not participate in the bidding was a violation of due process. Behncke, however, declared that Farley's decision was "regarded by the air mail pilots, who are perhaps closer to the industry than any other single group, as being the soundest and most constructive move yet taken in the entire history of air commerce."[16] Admittedly, neither Behncke nor his fellow airline pilots, even in the aggregate, could rival Lindbergh in prestige or counterbalance his attacks on the Administration. But at least they tried, and the President did not forget their loyalty. Underneath this public show of support for the Administration, however, Behncke was alarmed at the prospect of the small operators, who paid notoriously low wages, gaining a foothold in the aviation business. With masterly equivocation, he announced that he favored competitive bidding for the new air-mail contracts, but only so long as there were minimum specifications to keep "shoestring operators" from entering the field—a position which was not too different from that of the much abused Walter F. Brown.[17]

Growing pilot unemployment following in the wake of the cancellations was an important factor forcing Behncke toward an accommodation with the major operators. While the Army took some airline pilots on active duty during the crisis, most found themselves on either reduced work schedules or not flying at all. Western Air Express temporarily canceled all its operations and laid off its entire pilot force. While other lines did not react to the cancellations quite so drastically, by early March nearly one-third of ALPA's members were out of work.[18] Behncke tried to alleviate the problem by having the Army temporarily employ all the airline pilots as a special "reserve force" for flying the mail. Very few of his pilots were interested in a permanent relationship with the Army, however. Most of them had been in the Army at one time or another, and they much preferred their civilian employers.[19] By March 8, unemployment had become so worrisome that a mass meeting of unemployed Chicago-area pilots preceded the regular Central Executive Council meeting, but there was little

ALPA could do for them.[20] In fact, the treasury was so low that ALPA could no longer even investigate cases of members being fired.[21]

Without doubt, however, the air-mail tragedy enhanced the prestige of the professional airline pilot. Even before the death toll among Army aviators began to mount, Will Rogers worried about the fate of "all the hundreds of airplane pilots . . . who make an honest living in the airplane business." "I trust an air line," he added, "for I know that pilot has flown that course hundreds of times."[22] Lindbergh added his voice to those praising the professional transport pilots,[23] and *Aviation* also extolled the virtues of "professionalism" while trying at the same time to defend the Army Air Corps from an "utterly undeserved loss of public confidence." "Foremost among the Army's afflictions," *Aviation* editorialized, "was the failure to realize the extent to which successful . . . operation in bad weather depends upon the pilot's specialized knowledge of the route he flies." Apparently unaware that unionization among pilots had made such thinking obsolete, the editorial further insisted that the airline pilot, "even though in some cases he will ultimately become an executive of the line, functions for the time being purely as a professional pilot."[24] The prestige of the pilots was so high, in fact, that at the 1934 convention Behncke could gloat: "They are never going to try to replace you because they had their lesson. Some smart alec walked up to some high officials in Washington and put over the idea that anybody could fly the air mail. Well it was a bitter lesson."[25]

By May of 1934, the private operators were once again flying the mail, and ALPA's unemployment problem had eased. Because the Congress was in the process of writing new air-mail legislation, Farley limited the contracts to only ninety days, and he made it very clear to the operators that their contracts were temporary. Although the operators were unhappy with the limited contracts, they were desperate for the government subsidy and had no alternative but to accept Farley's conditions. They also agreed to his demand that the officials involved in the "Spoils Conferences" be excluded from any further bidding on mail contracts and that the offending airline companies reorganize themselves. American Airways became American Airlines, Eastern Air Transport became Eastern Airlines, T&WA simply added "Inc." to its name, and United, since its subsidiaries had bid on the original contracts, simply unified its bid and did not bother to change its name at all.[26]

In essence, the old companies remained the same, but they were technically and legally new companies. This fact put the pilots in a delicate position, for Decision 83 had been issued with specific regard to the old companies, and hence, legally, the new companies were not affected by it. There was a stipulation in Decision 83 that it was to apply to all government carriers, but as time passed and the legality of the N.L.B. came more and more into question, employers found that they could safely ignore its dicta altogether, since it had no direct powers of enforcement.[27] The N.L.B. had been on the verge of promulgating Decision 83 when the cancellations became effective, but the staff workers decided to await the outcome of the air-mail controversy before doing so. Behncke continually pestered the N.L.B. staff to publicize the decision right away, but his pleas were unavailing. "There we were," Behncke later declared, "waiting around Washington, and it is a cold-hearted town, between the devil and the deep blue sea and with no place to hook onto." [28]

Congressional skirmishing over a new air-mail law started almost as soon as the President announced the cancellations. There was a pressing need for new legislation to govern aviation, since the existing federal statutes divided basic authority between the Post Office Department and the Department of Commerce. While the Kelly and Watres acts granted the Post Office Department control of the all-important subsidy, the Air Commerce Act of 1926 conferred the power to regulate the industry on the Bureau of Air Commerce of the Department of Commerce. Congressional dissatisfaction with the Post Office Department mail subsidies spread quickly to the Department of Commerce. The internal division of authority within the Bureau of Air Commerce hamstrung Director Eugene L. Vidal's efforts to exert tighter control over aviation, but he irritated many Congressmen because he devoted an inordinate amount of time to supporting the hopelessly visionary scheme of a "flivver" airplane costing under $700 for every family. Congressional irritation manifested itself in the more than forty bills which were submitted in the first month after the cancellations. The Administration supported a bill written by Senator Black of Alabama and Senator Kenneth McKellar of Tennessee, Chairman of the Senate Post Office Committee. The Black-McKellar Bill was essentially just another air-mail law on the order of the Kelly and Watres acts, and it would leave basic authority to govern aviation divided. A competing bill, written by Senator Patrick A. McCarran of Nevada, complicated matters for the Black-McKellar law because it contained the germ of the idea for an independent regulatory agency for aviation. McCarran had been a member of the Black Committee, and he came to the conclusion that aviation should have one central controlling authority, either the Interstate Commerce Commission (I.C.C.) or a special agency for aviation similar to it. While Congress eventually passed the Black-McKellar Bill as the Air Mail Act of 1934, the pressure for an independent regulatory agency would grow until it finally succeeded in the Civil Aeronautics Act of 1938.[29]

The Black-McKellar Bill was the subject of heavy debate, much of it politically inspired. Behncke stayed in Washington almost continuously from February to June, and he, Hamilton, and frequently a "committee" of miscellaneous pilots attended every hearing or other event at which air-mail legislation was likely to come up.[30] He kept "boring in" and gradually became a familiar figure on Capitol Hill. Whenever an opportunity presented itself, he would, as he put it, "start talking and swing my arms."[31] When the House Post Office Committee began hearings on the Black-McKellar Bill, Behncke tried desperately to persuade the Congressmen to write a pilot minimum-wage guarantee into the law. Many famous aviators, such as Amelia Earhart, opposed the minimum-wage idea, sometimes very strenuously. Celebrity fliers irritated Behncke because they usually reflected management's views. Like most of the celebrity-flier breed, Miss Earhart was formally connected with an airline—she was a Vice-President of National Airways, a subsidiary of the Boston and Maine Railroad. Eddie Rickenbacker also opposed the minimum-wage law for pilots. Rickenbacker was one of Behncke's special pet hates, and he never lost an opportunity to criticize the World War I glamour boy. On the last government air-mail flight before the cancellations became effective, Rickenbacker and Jack Frye, a T&WA executive, had flown one of the Douglas DC–2's, the prototype of the famous DC–3, from California to New York in record time in an effort to dramatize the progress and efficiency of commercial aviation. Behncke protested Rickenbacker's being called a pilot. He told the 1934 convention, "Rickenbacker is a World War ace, all credit to him for that . . . but he doesn't hold a license, he has drifted completely away from it. He flew this plane . . . and tried to set himself out in the press as the pilot . . . Then it came out that he was just riding. The other guy was the one who was following the beam." [32] In fact, among the high officials and famous aviators who frequented Washington, Only W. A. Patterson of United was willing to have Congress specify a minimum wage for pilots in the new air-mail law. [33]

Since there was every chance that the pilots might not win any protection in the law, Behncke decided to mount a major campaign. He had to have something definite to center his campaign on, and he selected the N.L.B.'s as yet unpublished Decision 83. "We began to see," he said, "that we could not get anything definite unless we had something definite for these people to put in it." Decision 83 was definite enough, but the problem was that the N.L.B. had never officially promulgated it. The N.L.B. staff had seemingly forgotten all about it, and only Behncke's constant pleading finally induced them to publish it officially. "We went back to the labor board," Behncke later related, "and we said, 'now we have got to have that decision . . . we played along . . . when we could have blown this thing wide open and been as radical as the devil.'" Since the legitimacy of the N.L.B. itself was increasingly suspect, the staffers decided to humor Behncke, and with an almost visible shrug they formally promulgated Decision 83 on May 10, 1934. This action was a great relief to Behncke, for he had been talking to Congressmen for months as if the decision were already in effect. [34]

Behncke's verbal loyalty to the President paid dividends shortly after Congress began considering new air-mail legislation. Behncke became friendly with the President's personal secretary, Marvin McIntyre, and largely owing to the latter's influence the Chief Executive issued a statement praising the airline pilots and urging Congress to include some kind of protection for them in the new law. "Public safety calls for pilots of high character and great skill," the President told Congress in a special message. "The occupation is a hazardous one. Therefore the law should provide for a method to fix maximum hours, minimum pay, and a system of retirement annuity benefits." Behncke could scarcely contain his elation over this statement, and at the least provocation he would repeat it to anybody who would listen.[35]

On March 7, Senator McKellar introduced new air-mail legislation. The President supported the McKellar Bill, and the lawmakers regarded it as an Administration measure, but the section dealing with pilots was rather vague, and it did not specifically mention Decision 83. Alarmed, Behncke repeatedly wrote McKellar and other members of Congress, suggesting that the bill include something specific about the mileage pay system or Decision 83.[36] The original draft of the bill would have authorized the Department of Commerce to set maximum hours and minimum pay for pilots on "air mail lines," but by the time the Senate began to debate the bill Senator McKellar had added Section 13 which specifically declared: "It shall be a condition upon the awarding and holding of any air mail contract that the rate of compensation for all pilots . . . shall not be less than the rate . . . paid by air mail operators during 1933, *as modified by the decisions of the National Labor Board*" (emphasis supplied). Equally important for ALPA, the new law required air-mail contractors to bargain collectively with their employees. The revised draft of the law removed the power to regulate pay from the Department of Commerce, a vital necessity for ALPA, since Eugene Vidal had earlier made his support for the hourly system of pay a matter of record. The Department of Commerce still had the power to set maximum flying hours per month for pilots, however.[37]

When the Senate began to debate the new air-mail law on April 17, there was intense partisan wrangling over almost every part of it except the pilot's section. Republican critics concentrated their fire on the original cancellation issue because they believed the Administration was vulnerable on it, and by creating an atmosphere of scandal they hoped to undermine popular support for other New Deal measures. Senator Simeon D. Fess of Ohio declared that the cancellation of the air-mail contracts was "the most important single issue since . . . the Civil War," and Senator Austin of Vermont, a clever and successful critic of the Black Committee, presented the Republican viewpoint in a nationwide radio broadcast. Even the Republicans favored protecting the pilots, however, for in his address Senator Austin argued that the old operators had played fair with labor, and had therefore attracted a corps of exceptionally skilled pilots. During the debate on the Senate floor, Senator Black counterattacked, using the pilots as his shield too. "The time has come," he said, "when we ought to raise the wages of the men who do the work." He praised the airline pilots, insisted that his committee's investigation had the best interests of the pilots at heart, and he criticized the operators for "strangling the life out of the men who actually do the work in the planes." [38]

The lawmakers seemed to universally favor protecting the pilots, and the pilot sections of the Black-McKellar Bill included everything Behncke wanted. He was inveterately suspicious, however, and to the very end he feared that victory might somehow be euchered away, despite the specific language of the law. He asked William Green to obtain verbal assurance from Postmaster General Farley that he would uphold the law, and Green reassured him: "I called Postmaster General Farley by telephone. In response . . . he assured me that it was his purpose and determination to protect the wage standards of air pilots in awarding contracts for air mail service." [39] Behncke worried needlessly, for Congress clearly intended to protect the pilots and it would insist that Administration officials adhere to that intent.

Behncke had so successfully associated the concept of air safety with pilot skill that most Congressmen considered the relationship self-evident. Since Congressmen were frequent air travelers, air safety elicited enormous interest among them. In fact, Washington lawmakers appear to have been among the nation's first habitual air travelers, the first steady clientele of the airlines. The time they saved by flying enabled many of them from western districts to function more effectively both at home and in Washington. Needless to say, the airline pilots always gave them special attention, and a visit to the flight deck or some other explanation of the mysteries of a Ford or Fokker or Douglas could be very effective. Even the relatively primitive aircraft of the late 1920s had a bewildering collection of dials, switches, and levers, and most Congressmen were terrifically impressed with the technical mastery the pilots displayed. Senator Wagner once remarked: "When you go up in the air you know that those fellows have got your life in their hands. I know that my life is in that man's hands and a sort of affection grows up between the customer and the pilot. It is sort of indefinable." [40] In short, most traveling lawmakers felt about pilots like patients feel about doctors after a successful operation—a feeling of respect tinged with awe. They wanted to rule out the possibility that underfinanced companies might try to increase their profits by using poorly paid, inferior pilots. Congressmen Mead and Dobbins, in a joint "Congressional Opinion" radio broadcast over CBS in March 1935, stressed the "human element" in air safety. "We took particular care to include in the 1934 Air Mail Act a provision that pilots' wages be maintained," Mead said, "to guard against a natural tendency to lower costs through reduction in pilots wages." [41] Pilot salaries, then, were to be nationally uniform, high, and under federal protection. Behncke had won a total victory—he had made the professional airline pilot a ward of the state.

In retrospect, the Air Mail Act of 1934 was the crucial victory the pilots needed. Behncke's adroit use of a variety of approaches and appeals to secure federal protection for his airline pilots was his greatest achievement as President of ALPA. While everybody realized that the new air-mail law was temporary, Behncke's hardest fight was over, for he had established the precedent.[42] For the time being Behncke had everything he could conceivably want, but he realized that he would have to monitor Washington developments with steady vigilance if he were to maintain the pilots' favored position in subsequent legislation. In the final analysis, both the operators and the pilots emerged from the ordeal of cancellation with new prestige. The operators had proved that they could fly the mails better and more cheaply than the Army, and the pilots, under Behncke's leadership, had proved that they were a formidable pressure group.

9 | Ceiling and Visibility Unlimited

The problems confronting ALPA after the passage of the Air Mail Act of 1934 were relatively minor. The union had what it wanted—now it merely needed to protect its gains. The job of protecting the existing laws governing pilots promised to be far easier than the job of getting them written in the first place. Behncke was always on hand, ready with advice or comment, whenever Congress considered any kind of legislation affecting aviation. It was a foregone conclusion that federal law would protect the airline pilots after 1934, and even the operators realized it.

The successes of 1934 turned ALPA's convention, which met in the Shoreland Hotel in Chicago on October 29 and 30, into a jovial celebration. The new prestige and status of the union were reflected in Movietone News film coverage and in the stream of congratulatory telegrams from friends and foes alike. Honorary memberships for William Randolph Hearst and Will Rogers guaranteed wide newspaper coverage of the event, and CBS Radio recorded a fifteen-minute interview with Behncke. Behncke's right-hand man in the Washington battles of 1934, American's Master Executive Council Chairman Clyde Holbrook, had died in a flaming crush shortly before the convention, thus lending it a certain maudlin and dramatic immediacy which appealed to the

161

mass media. Behncke, needless to say, adeptly exploited it when he read the roster of departed pilots and intoned: "To fly west, my friends, is a flight we all must take for a final check." [1]

Prospects for the union's future were bright. ALPA now officially represented the vast majority of airline pilots, claiming over 600 dues-paying members. The pilots of American, United, and several lesser airlines approached 100 percent allegiance, a clear majority of Eastern and Western Air Express pilots were members, and Pan American's far-flung pilots were an astounding 90 percent in the fold. Braniff, the former independent which had become a major carrier as a result of the cancellations, was very weak with only 12 percent of its pilots paying dues, but a nucleus of senior pilots had joined and organizational success seemed assured. T&WA pilots were making covert inquiries about rejoining ALPA, and it was apparent that the company union there was rapidly falling apart. The leader of the T&WA company union, former ALPA official W. A. Golien, let it be known that he was willing to lead the T&WA pilots back into ALPA, and shortly before the convention he formally petitioned for readmittance. Most of the delegates to the 1934 convention felt he had prostituted himself by leading the separatist movement, however, and they turned him down. But because of his early services for ALPA, the convention declared that he might rejoin the union without penalty in ten years, if he did no further harm. All other T&WA pilots, even those who had testified in opposition to ALPA during the N.L.B. hearings, could rejoin the union without penalty, since the delegates understood that management pressure had forced their resignations in the first place. The separatist movement on T&WA underscored the problem of local union autonomy. While this problem occurs in virtually every union,[2] ALPA's neophytes found it particularly distressing, and the best method of controlling locals without establishing a central dictatorship was the subject of a long debate during the convention. The final solution, to the extent that there was one, the delegates decided, was to have each local forward its minutes to national headquarters for review. Such a review, they hoped, would nip incipient challenges to the national's authority in the bud.[3]

The co-pilot problem had a bearing on ALPA's difficulties with T&WA. In the early days of airline flying, even after multi-engined aircraft began to come equipped with dual controls, there was frequently only one pilot aboard, and a mechanic might occupy the right seat. In the interests of air safety, Walter F. Brown had forced the companies to have two qualified pilots aboard as a condition for receiving a mail subsidy. For a long time, co-pilots were neither fish nor fowl to ALPA, although they were grudgingly admitted to membership in an inferior status. Because of their vulnerability, T&WA's management easily intimidated or cajoled their co-pilots into deserting ALPA for the company union, and many senior pilots believed that if they had not joined the company union, T&WA would have replaced them with co-pilots. Behncke was particularly incensed because he believed that had it not been for the co-pilots' wholesale defection to the company union, the senior pilots would have remained loyal. Because of their alleged disloyalty on T&WA, Behncke for a long time regarded all co-pilots as dangerous threats to ALPA's security, and he therefore insisted that they occupy a clearly inferior position within the union. Until 1938 co-pilots could not vote, and even afterward their votes were worth only half a captain's vote in ALPA affairs. Furthermore, no co-pilot could serve as chairman of either local or master executive councils, and there could not be more than one co-pilot on any ALPA committee or council. This policy of treating the co-pilot as an "enemy within" always worked poorly, for there was the troubling question of equality of working conditions under the N.L.B. ruling to consider. Gradually Behncke came to realize ALPA could not allow co-pilots to work longer hours than captains, or else their longer hours might become a rationale for changing the N.L.B. decision. Accordingly, insofar as the hourly limitation applied, ALPA demanded full equality for co-pilots, and this step toward equality in union affairs was the first in a long line which would eventually, by the late 1950s, lead to the erasure of all distinctions between the first and second man in the cockpit.[4]

ALPA had spent nearly $25,000 in 1934, and its financial condition was shaky. Dues collection was a perennial problem, and at the time of the convention there were over $18,000 in dues outstanding. The pilot delegates authorized an annual budget of $40,000 for 1935 based on the projected income from dues. There was no special assessment on the membership to cover the cost of the 1934 convention, and the twenty-two delegates expected to bear the expense for attending it out of their own pockets. (After ALPA's financial condition began to improve, however, the Central Executive Council levied a special assessment of over $2,000 on the membership to reimburse the delegates for both "lost time" and expenses.)[5] The convention opted for a "get-tough" policy on delinquent dues, insisting that when a member resigned, either through "misinformation or cussedness," as one delegate put it, he still had to pay back dues in order to regain good standing. In addition, several delegates pointed out that the dues of $60 per year could be higher without hurting anybody.[6]

The 1934 convention made one momentous change in ALPA's affairs by electing Behncke to the full-time presidency. His difficulties with United had subsided, but he had begun to think seriously about resigning and devoting full time to ALPA even before he was fired. Early in ALPA's history there had been a good deal of sentiment among the membership in favor of an annual rotating president. Although Behncke was not thinking of giving up flying at the time, he argued for long-term continuity in the higher offices. "A one-year term of office . . . ," he said, "is really a short time. It amounts to this; you are elected and by the time you get into your work and know what it is all about you are already on a downhill grade on your term of office."[7] In addition, he frequently cited the common practice of union leaders giving up their regular work while serving as chief executive of a national as an argument in favor of a full-time president for ALPA. Behncke queried the Central Executive Council and the general membership on his becoming the full-time president after his troubles with United, and the response was overwhelmingly favorable.[8] It was obvious to almost every pilot that Behncke was working himself to death trying to fly and oversee ALPA's affairs simultaneously. Furthermore, everybody knew that the tricky business of negotiating direct collective bargaining agreements with the operators would be a full-time job, and it never seems to have occurred to the pilots that anybody other than Behncke would do it.

Behncke openly solicited the job at the 1934 convention, asking only that the union pay him a salary equal to the average captain's pay on United, which he reckoned at $7,000. The convention's finance committee studied the feasibility of paying Behncke this amount and decided that it was reasonable, but favored meeting it through special assessment rather than out of general dues revenue. With only one dissenting vote, the convention approved the idea of a full-time president, and then promptly elected Behncke to a two-year term.[9] In addition, the convention created a series of regional vice-presidents and combined the offices of secretary and treasurer, electing Homer Cole to the office. John Huber had been transferred away from Chicago and he gave up his ALPA office.[10] After his election, Behncke agreed to resign from United effective January 1, but he did so with great reluctance. It seems that he genuinely wanted to remain a pilot, but he realized that he simply could not do justice to both jobs. He explained his willingness to forsake flying in the following manner: "I have been a pilot for eighteen years. I started out in the game and worked my way up. I have now got a job which . . . I believe is with as fine a company as there is on the transcontinental mail route. It takes a long time to get that far. I like to fly. I think a lot of my job. But there are circumstances here where fate seems to have dealt the cards and I believe there are responsibilities which must be met fairly and squarely." [11]

Before Behncke could resign, however, fate dealt the cards in a way he never expected. On December 20, 1934, he took off on what was to have been his last flight, piloting a Boeing 247 westbound from Chicago to Omaha. He reached altitude, retarded the throttles to cruising position, and sat back for what promised to be an uneventful flight. It was a gray day, with a high overcast and a good deal of visible moisture in the air, but at his altitude Behncke was not in the cloud layer. Below him the forests rimming the western suburbs of Chicago lay under a blanket of ice and snow. Unknown to either Behncke or his co-pilot, the visible moisture in conjunction with an air temperature inversion had created atmospheric conditions which were conducive to that silent killer of unwary aviators—a rapid and uncontrollable build-up of internal ice in the carburetors. The ice accumulated so quickly that Behncke had none of the usual advance warnings of carburetor ice, such as gradual loss of engine manifold pressure or decreased airspeed. Instead, he was greeted with the loudest of all silences, which occurs only when an aircraft's engines abruptly quit.

Behncke applied full carburetor heat and desperately tried to restart his engines. After deliberately opening his throttles in an effort to backfire the ice out of the intake manifolds, he finally regained partial power on one engine; this was not enough to maintain flight, but sufficient to allow him some leeway in seeking an emergency landing area. With his frightened passengers strapped to their seats, and his co-pilot urgently radioing the aircraft's position, Behncke scanned what appeared to be an endless expanse of ice-coated forest below, searching for a break. There was no break, no meadow, not even a road. He was faced with that early barnstormer's nightmare—an emergency landing into trees. He had two choices; he could either drive the aircraft into the trees and hope the fuselage would miss the trunks of the trees, or he could stall the big ship into the tops of the trees and hope that it would come to rest in the trees and not break up. The forest was so thick that he opted for the latter. Shortly before impact, he closed the throttles, cut all electric switches to avert fire, and eased the yoke back, tentatively feeling for the tops of the trees with the tail of his ship. With incredible gentleness, the aircraft skipped from one tree to another and came to rest in the fork of a huge oak tree. None of the passengers was injured.

It was an amazingly successful emergency landing. After lowering his passengers to the ground, Behncke, curious as to the cause of the engine failure, climbed back to the airplane and crawled out onto the wing. A light freezing rain had begun to fall, coating the wing's surface and making the footing treacherous. After removing part of the cowling, Behncke stepped back to look at the engine, inadvertently slipped off the wing, and fell some sixty feet to the ground, breaking his knee, several ribs, and his leg in two places. He was hospitalized in traction for several weeks into early

1935, and he could not resign because there were insurance, pension, and accident-investigation problems to be worked out. It took nearly a year before Behncke was exonerated from any blame in the accident, and he did not finally resign from United until January 1, 1936, a full year after he intended to do so. He was on reduced salary from United during the period of his convalescence, and while he borrowed a little money from ALPA, he did not begin drawing a regular salary from it during 1935. He devoted full time to ALPA affairs, of course, and the unhappy President of United, W. A. Patterson, had no alternative but to continue paying his disability salary during that period.[12]

As full-time President, Behncke continued to focus his attention on the Washington scene. It was apparent to almost everybody that the Air Mail Act of 1934 was a temporary measure. Indeed, one section of the act called for the creation of a special commission to study the whole aviation industry. President Roosevelt appointed Clark Howell, editor and publisher of the *Atlanta Constitution,* Chairman of the commission, which included such aviation experts as Edward P. Warner, editor of *Aviation* and Professor of Aeronautics at M.I.T. After months of careful study, the Howell Commission recommended an independent regulatory agency for aviation, similar to the I.C.C. and much along the same lines which Senator McCarran had suggested in the previous session of Congress. Behncke and Hamilton appeared before the commission arguing that Decision 83, along with the pilot provisions in the Air Mail Act of 1934, be made a permanent part of federal aviation legislation. The final report of the Howell Commission, which emerged in February 1935, called for the new regulatory agency to subscribe to "the principles contained in Section 7 (a) of the N.I.R.A. and to function in adherence thereto . . . and to use its influence to bring together employers and duly chosen representatives of labor . . . on all questions involving hours, wages, and conditions of employment."[13] While this statement was vague and lacking in specifics, Behncke was not unduly worried about it because he knew the real test would come later when Congress actually wrote legislation. Furthermore, he knew that influential members of the Howell Commission and Congress favored full retention of Decision 83 in subsequent legislation.[14]

The inadequacies of the Air Mail Act of 1934 affected the pilots as well as the operators. The provision calling for annual bidding on air-mail contracts discouraged the operators from investing in new aircraft, and the airlines entered a period of stagnation.[15] While the law made adherence to Decision 83 mandatory for any carrier holding a mail contract, there was a difficult problem of enforcement involved. What could ALPA do if an operator simply refused to abide by Decision 83? There were disputes between ALPA and most of the operators over this issue at one time or another, but the most persistent trouble came from Long and Harmon Airlines, a small company holding a mail contract for the route from Tulsa to Amarillo to Brownsville, Texas. Long and Harmon employed only three pilots, and it disappeared in a merger with Braniff after a year, but in that year it caused ALPA major headaches. After a desultory and unsatisfactory exchange with E. L. Harmon and William Long, the operators of the line, on the pay issue, Behncke appealed to Washington.[16] Hamilton corresponded with Representative D. C. Dobbins, a member of the Post Office Committee, asking if ALPA could seek redress on behalf of the Long and Harmon pilots only through the extreme measure of petitioning for cancellation of the company's contract.[17] Not only would such a course of action deprive the Long and Harmon pilots of their jobs, but Dobbins warned Hamilton that it would also give Long and Harmon an opportunity to challenge the legality of Decision 83 in the courts. Dobbins feared that the only method of enforcement open under the law was outright cancellation, which would be unsatisfactory for everyone concerned. He promised to discuss the situation with Representative Mead, the Chairman of the House Post Office Committee,[18] and a few days later Mead wrote Behncke that he too saw no legal method of forcing compliance other than by asking the Post Office Department to cancel Long and Harmon's contract. But he promised to take the matter up with postal officials and he hoped that unofficial pressure from them through Solicitor General Karl Crowley might yet yield satisfactory results. Mead reaffirmed that in fixing pilot hours and wages in the Air Mail Act of 1934, it was the clear intention of Congress that the "operating companies be on an equal footing, and when bidding each would take this fixed cost into consideration. If this were not done," he said, "it is obvious that unfair operators would be given an advantage over their more conscientious competitors which would result in the employment of cheap help . . . which would have ultimate evil effects." [19]

In an effort to frighten Long and Harmon into compliance, Behncke flooded ALPA's friends in Washington with complaints about the line's safety policies and operating procedures. Senator Black promised to interest himself in Long and Harmon's affairs, and Lionell Thorsness, ALPA's attorney, filed a formal petition with the Post Office Department asking it to force the line to comply with the N.L.B.'s ruling, but not specifically asking for contract cancellation.[20] Long and Harmon were tough-minded, independent pioneer fliers, however, and they refused to budge. Instead, they launched a counterattack of their own and fired all three of their pilots, even though only two of them were ALPA members. Needless to say, their comments on Behncke,

the pilots' union, and Washington politicians were un-
printable. Behncke took the cases of the three fired pilots
before the N.L.B. and secured an order for their reinstatement which Long and Harmon refused to honor. The
N.L.B. was at that time increasingly under fire and ineffective and nothing came of the order. Since he now did not
care what happened to the scab pilots working for Long
and Harmon, Behncke formally asked for cancellation of
the line's air-mail contract under Section 17 of the Air
Mail Act of 1934. The Post Office Department ordered Long
and Harmon to appear in Washington to show cause why its
contract should not be terminated, but since the line was already in process of merging with Braniff, Long and Harmon
could safely ignore Washington. Braniff, which took over
the Long and Harmon route, was abiding by the pay rules
specified in the law.[21] The three dismissed pilots, however,
were left out in the cold, and two years later one of them
added a final note of tragedy when he committed suicide,
apparently because he despaired of ever finding employment.[22] While ALPA had once again demonstrated the
strength of its influence in Washington, it was impossible
for its pressure group activities to be completely effective
because of the deficiencies in the enforcement procedures
of the Air Mail Act of 1934.

In order to correct these deficiencies, Congress amended
the Air Mail Act in early 1935, allowing the operating companies which then held the temporary contracts to extend
their bids for three-year periods. Although the amendment
did nothing for ALPA, its enforcement problems tended
to disappear after postal officials, acting under Congressional
pressure, decided that they could force compliance through
a system of fines and by refusing to pay the full subsidy to
companies which it deemed to be in violation of the law.
This method proved effective, and from mid-1935 on there

was no challenge to the labor provisions of the air-mail acts from the operators themselves. Rather, ALPA's main problem came from Department of Commerce rulings which injected an element of considerable ambiguity into the interpretation of the law. Certain lower-echelon officials of the Department of Commerce decided that the eighty-five-hour monthly maximum specified in the law was meant to be an annual average per month rather than an arbitrary limit for any one month. Eugene Vidal supported this decision, although with considerable misgiving, and Behncke's savage criticism added to his doubts. In an effort to placate the pilot union leader and to turn away Congressional wrath, Vidal declared that while he supported the monthly average idea, he felt that there should be an upper limit of 100 hours per month, regardless. This decision was clearly illogical and it did nothing to assuage Behncke, who loudly complained that the operators were trying to sabotage the clear-cut labor provisions of the law through administrative action. Because the basic Air Mail Act of 1934 and the 1935 amendment to it, known as the Mead Amendment, left ultimate authority divided, Behncke decided that it was necessary to have a single governing agency. The Howell Commission had recommended an independent regulatory agency, but the President opposed it, arguing that the I.C.C. had sufficient personnel to handle aviation regulation. Behncke, always loyal to the President, publicly supported the idea of I.C.C. regulation, but privately he expressed interest in a new agency devoted solely to aviation.[23]

Owing to the President's control of Congress, there was little chance that aviation legislation he opposed would pass. But overwhelming sentiment for an independent regulatory agency began to develop in Congress after the death of Senator Bronson Cutting of New Mexico in the crash of a T&WA DC-2 near Kirksville, Missouri, in May 1935. Senator

Cutting had boarded the specially chartered plane, piloted by Hugh F. Bolton, whom T&WA considered one of its best pilots, at Albuquerque on May 5 for a flight to Washington via Kansas City. It was a night flight, the weather was reported good en route, and Kansas City itself was forecast to remain clear. The forecast was inaccurate, however, and the weather began to deteriorate while the T&WA airliner was still more than an hour away from its destination. The pilot would have to make a "blind" instrument approach using the low-frequency radio range at Kansas City. While a pilot could, by carefully flying on the specifically directed radio beam, fly his ship down to an altitude of about 500 feet above the ground, he still needed to be able to see the ground from that point on in order to complete the landing. If at the end of this "instrument approach," which ended at 500 feet above the ground, the pilot could not actually see the runway, he had to execute a "missed approach" or "go around," which simply meant that he must fly on the radio beam back to a specific altitude above the station, and then either try the approach again or go to another airport where the weather was better. Department of Commerce regulations required a forty-five-minute fuel reserve in such cases, as a safety margin.

Bolton began his first approach at Kansas City shortly after midnight. The weather, while poor, was still good enough for a successful instrument approach to a landing, but it was changing rapidly owing to a frontal passage. The low-frequency directional radio ranges in use during the 1930s could broadcast either the directional electronic beam or voice message, but not both at the same time. Whenever the voice weather reports interrupted the beam, the pilot could not continue his approach and had to execute the missed-approach procedure. The Department of Commerce radio operator normally interrupted the beam to broadcast the current weather at thirty-minute intervals, fifteen minutes before and after each hour. Pilots knew that the beam would be interrupted for two or three minutes at those times and accordingly they could plan to either expedite or delay their instrument approaches. But Department of Commerce regulations also required the radio operator to broadcast "significant" weather reports immediately upon their receipt. Since weather conditions were changing rapidly in the Kansas City area, the radio operator repeatedly interrupted the directional beam to broadcast weather reports. Each time he did, Bolton, by now trying to make an instrument approach, had to discontinue it and start all over again as soon as the station began transmitting the steady "A's" and "N's" by which he could orient himself. When Bolton first began his approach, he undoubtedly could have completed it to a landing. But after several minutes had been lost owing to the beam interruptions, the weather had deteriorated until a landing was out of the question. In addition, Bolton's fuel was now running low.

After consulting with his company dispatcher, and checking the weather reports from other airports within his range, Bolton decided to go to Kirksville, Missouri. He would have just enough fuel, and there was another airport with an instrument approach en route at Macon, Missouri. The weather at Macon was, curiously, much worse than the weather the Department of Commerce "airport keeper" at Kirksville was reporting. The discrepancy in the weather reports between two stations which were so close to each other puzzled Bolton but he had no alternative to believing that the report from Kirksville was accurate.

As Bolton and his sleeping passengers proceeded on toward Macon and Kirksville, fate and Department of Commerce inefficiency began to play the dominant roles.

The northeast leg of the Kansas City radio range was off course, and had been for several days. Instead of flying toward Kirksville, Bolton was being lured in a more south- easterly direction. But even worse, Bolton began to suspect that the weather report from Kirksville was seriously in error. Actually, the weather in Kirksville was, if anything, worse than the weather in Kansas City. The Department of Com- merce "airport keeper," charged with maintaining a constant vigil of the weather at the Kirksville airport, was in fact at home in bed. Periodically he would telephone an imaginary weather report on through the weather network, then turn over and go back to sleep. Since ordinarily no planes landed at Kirksville at night, he never expected to be found out in his dereliction.

Worried because he had not yet picked up the Kirksville radio beam, Bolton reoriented himself and found that he was south of his intended flight path, owing to the erroneous signal he had been flying from Kansas City. He was by now seriously low on fuel, and he elected to descend in an effort to contact the ground visually, which he should have been able to do if the weather report from Kirksville was accurate. When upon reaching the lowest possible safe altitude Bolton could still see nothing but fog and gloom, he knew he would have to make an emergency landing. After searching as best he could for a suitable landing site in the murky darkness, he eased the big ship into what appeared to be a farmer's field. Unfortunately, there was a railroad track embankment at the end of the field. In the grinding crash which followed, Hugh Bolton, Senator Cutting, and three other passengers were killed.

The Senate created a special committee, chaired by Senator Royal S. Copeland of New York, to investigate the crash. The investigation lasted more than a year and it revealed severe deficiencies in the Department of Commerce's aviation bureaus. Even worse, the committee discovered that certain Department of Commerce officials had attempted to "cover up" for the derelict "airport keeper" at Kirksville. This revelation turned the investigation into a searching review of aviation safety policy and the department's role in it. Bolton had been at the controls of the aircraft for more than eight hours, and many Senators were shocked to learn the Department of Commerce regulations permitted flying that long. Since federal law limited railroad engineers to eight hours, it seemed to them that pilots should be subject to similar restriction, and that department officials had not insisted on such a restriction indicated to many Senators that the department's attitude toward air safety was generally lax and complacent.

The committee's formal report eventually cited Department of Commerce safety regulations, T&WA dispatching procedures, and general bureaucratic incompetence as the principal causes of the accident. The report had nothing but praise, however, for the pilot, and its verdict on him is worth repeating in full: "Bolton himself, mortally wounded and bleeding profusely, displayed such nerve and coolness in the few minutes that followed, that no one could possibly allege carelessness, lack of loyalty to duty, selfishness, or a character that would shirk, or under any circumstances disobey the law of tradition. Uncomplainingly, he told everyone who asked him what had happened that he was 'out of gas,' an expression that the schools teach the pilot to say when he is forced down. Bolton was low on gas—too low to venture up again into the overcast, which would have meant another time-consuming orientation, but he did not whimper even though he knew he had been 'let down' . . . He was the victim of fallible ground aids to navigation in which he trusted implicitly." Bolton's martyrdom, and Behncke's own near-fatal crash, provided Behncke with an excellent stage from which to express his ideas about air safety. During and after the Copeland Committee's investigation, he became, for many legislators, "the authority" on matters relating to aviation. Ostentatiously stumping the halls of Congress with his cane and injured leg, Behncke became in the years to come a welcome guest and expert witness at literally dozens of sessions and hearings, and his message was nearly always the same—that only the pilot could truly speak for aviation safety, since he had, ultimately, the most to gain from it.[24]

The Copeland Committee's exoneration of Hugh Bolton was deeply gratifying to all airline pilots. The Department of Commerce frequently cited "pilot error" when it could not otherwise explain a crash, and Behncke insisted that it did so in order to cover up its own failings.[25] After the Copeland Committee verified Behncke's contentions, most legislators realized that accident investigations should be conducted by an independent agency which would have nothing to gain by hiding unpleasant facts from the public. Indeed, as early as 1929 there was criticism of the government's accident-investigation apparatus, and many responsible observers pointed out that the use of "pilot error" to explain crashes was, in effect, a way to exonerate the living by placing blame on a dead pilot. After a fatal crash in 1929, *Aviation* wondered editorially if the Department of Commerce and the operators were not fastening blame on the pilot in order to protect themselves against lawsuits brought by relatives of deceased passengers.[26]

After a rash of fatal crashes in the winter of 1932–33, Behncke began preaching the doctrine that ALPA was necessarily more interested in safety than either management or the government. He made "Schedule with Safety" the official motto of ALPA,[27] and beginning with the Howell Commission's investigation he tried to plant the idea in the mind of the nation's lawmakers that the airline pilots were the only truthful source of information about air safety. He derided fliers like Rickenbacker who presumed to speak for men who were still flying regularly. "The Commission will be surprised," he declared, ". . . to find that the pilots who usually do the talking . . . are not even licensed." Driving home his point in a later appearance before the Howell Commission, Behncke maintained: "the pilots are not motivated by any selfish interest, as is attested to by the fact that they are accepting less pay . . . The pilots are doing this in the interest of public safety." Needless to say, most Congressmen were receptive to Behncke's ideas. Many of them were inveterate air travelers, and like Senator Wagner they respected and liked the airline pilots. Behncke's argument before the Howell Commission that "a tired pilot is an unsafe pilot" seemed self-evident to most of them.[28]

Behncke took advantage of his favorable position to press for a pilots' amendment to the Railway Labor Act of 1926. Strikes on the railroads were a great inconvenience to everyone, and Congress began trying to avoid them as early as 1888 when it passed the Arbitration Act. Repeated Congressional forays into the thicket of railroad labor legislation during the late nineteenth and early twentieth centuries produced the Erdman Act of 1898, the Newlands Act of 1913, the famous Adamson Act of 1916, which guaranteed the eight-hour day for all railroad workers, and the Transportation Act of 1920. The 1920 law established the Railway Labor Board, designed to avert strikes through mediation and arbitration, but after the board failed to prevent the disruptive national strike of 1922, Congress began to consider yet another law. It finally passed the Railway Labor Act in 1926, which carefully laid out a complicated system of adjustment boards, arbitration, and other machinery, which, if it were effective, would satisfy the railroad brotherhoods, the public, and the employers. The law proved to be less than satisfactory, however, for its vague language was susceptible to such a variety of interpretations that company unionism seemed to have a stronger legal basis than before and thus continued to flourish, at least among the nonoperating employees. In addition, the law's system of mediation and arbitration never really worked very well. Still, there were no major strikes in the late 1920s, and even though the Railway Labor Act of 1926 was only indirectly responsible for this happy state of affairs, it gained a certain measure of prestige as a "model labor law." [29]

The law had obvious application to the airline pilots, and as early as 1932 Frank Ormsbee persuaded Fiorello La Guardia to sponsor an amendment to it which would include pilots.[30] Behncke was rather cool to the idea because at the time he was trying to stress his identification with the AFofL, and he feared that overt association with the railroad brotherhoods might irritate William Green. But more importantly, the law's toleration in practice of company unionism left Behncke with an uneasy feeling, since he knew from bitter experience how easily a determined employer could crush a legitimate union by sponsoring a competing captive union. He liked certain provisions of the law, but because of his native suspicion he preferred to press for a completely separate law covering all air transport workers. Behncke could never bring himself to believe that anything which management favored could help his pilots, and the 1926 law was therefore highly suspect in his view. Together, Ormsbee and La Guardia convinced Behncke that the law's potential benefits outweighed its liabilities, and that a completely new law would be extremely difficult to pass. La Guardia particularly stressed the relative ease with which he could get an amendment to the old act passed in 1932, and Behncke reluctantly assented, probably because the

idea of short-circuiting "the system" and stealing a tactical
march on the operators appealed to him.[31] In the final
analysis, it really did not matter, since the opposition of
the Aeronautical Chamber of Commerce was sufficient to
kill the bill in the House Committee on Interstate and
Foreign Commerce, even though the chairman of the
Federal Mediation Board testified in favor of it. But Behncke
knew that he had lost little of real value.[32]

An amendment to the Railway Labor Act in 1934 eliminated the troubling company union problem, and Behncke
threw his full support behind the pilot's amendment idea.
ALPA's influence and prestige had grown steadily through
1934 and 1935, and Behncke sensed correctly that he
would have little trouble getting the pilots' amendment
through Congress. Senator Black agreed to sponsor it in the
upper house, while its sponsor across the way was the
Chairman of the House Post Office Committee, James M.
Mead. The two legislators introduced their bills simultaneously and they were identically worded by Edward
Hamilton.[33] The measure encountered no opposition in
either chamber, other than inconsequential changes in
the wording of a few sections. In appearances before the
Senate Interstate Commerce Committee and the House
Committee on the Post Office and Post Roads, Behncke
stressed the safety theme, although it had no real bearing
on the legislation in question. He had found that it was a
popular subject among Congressmen, however, and he was
reluctant to let it go.[34] After perfunctory hearings, both committees reported the bill favorably, and the Senate version
received final action, passing the Senate as Title II of the
Railway Labor Act of 1926 as Amended in June 1935 during
the first session, and the House in April 1936 during the
second session of the Seventy-Fourth Congress.[35] The ease
with which Behncke secured this special-interest legislation
provided a ready indication of the esteem and authority

which most Congressmen accorded ALPA. In addition, it was a practical demonstration of Behncke's growing mastery and knowledge of the intricacies and byways of Washington political channels.

Title II of the Railway Labor Act was rather anomalous in that its structure of adjustment boards and mediation services was designed originally to settle disputes which arose over the interpretation of existing employment contracts. ALPA had no contracts, but Behncke hoped he could use the machinery of the National Mediation Board (N.M.B.) to settle the myriad cases of employee grievances which members continually referred to him. Local adjustment boards could be established by the N.M.B. to settle employee grievances. The act also provided for a National Air Transportation Adjustment Board (N.A.T.A.B.) to settle any disputes which local adjustment boards could not settle.[36] (The N.A.T.A.B. never became operable because both ALPA and the carriers preferred to settle their disputes through System Boards of Adjustment composed of one management representative, one ALPA representative, and a neutral to break tie votes.)[37] One other aspect of Title II which deserves some mention was the provision guaranteeing the right of collective bargaining. This right was redundant, since the Air Mail Act of 1934 and the Wagner Act also guaranteed it, and few other workers were interested in piling one law on another. But Behncke wanted it because he believed the adjustment board apparatus would allow him a working tool other than a strike through which he could confront the employers, since in the absence of direct agreements with the operators, the adjustment board was ALPA's only formal contact with management. This scheme failed to work, however, since no System Boards of Adjustment were established until after ALPA negotiated employment contracts.

Despite constant and heavy pressure from his members,

Behncke refused to initiate direct contract talks with the employers until he had herded the provisions protecting pilots through Congress and into the new aviation law which was coming. He always did things one at a time, and he would not even consider direct negotiations until the convention of 1936 created a permanent committee to study the problem and advise him. Before direct talks with the operators could begin, Behncke insisted on a careful series of conferences between the headquarters staff and the Master Executive Council of each line to agree on the terms they would seek. While the negotiating team would include representatives from the Master Executive Councils, Behncke was to be the chief bargainer and, in line with traditional union practice, the final agreement would have to receive the approval of the Central Executive Council.[38]

ALPA's position was so strong by the time of the 1936 convention, which again met in the Shoreland Hotel in Chicago in October, that it no longer had to worry about attracting members. Accordingly, it adopted a very stringent policy toward "fence sitters." If a pilot would not join the union within a year of the time he became eligible, he was formally declared "undesirable" and in order to join subsequently he would have to directly petition the general convention. Newly hired co-pilots, rather than the few remaining adamant veteran holdouts, were the primary target of this policy. Older ALPA members wanted to indoctrinate them and make them understand that they owed their primary loyalty to the union, rather than to management. After 1934, allegiance to ALPA among new co-pilots was nearly unanimous, and there was a very cogent reason for it. "If a fellow is not going to join the Association," one delegate admitted to the 1936 convention, "he is not going to get a lot of instruction from the first pilots. If he joins . . . we will help him along and do everything we can for him."[39]

As membership increased, Behncke began to expand office facilities and hire new employees. ALPA now rented the entire second floor of the Troy Lane Hotel and had acquired a vacant store-front building next door, and Behncke repeatedly suggested that a union-owned building would soon be necessary. He believed that having its own building would give ALPA stability and prestige, but for the present he preferred to use available money to hire "imminent legal counsel" in Washington. He hoped to hire Donald Richberg, whose price would be high, but nothing ever came of it.[40]

The character of ALPA was changing rapidly between 1934 and 1936. Many old faces were now gone from its gatherings, and the increasing professionalization of the staff had diminished the easy informality and volunteer atmosphere which had previously been its chief characteristics. Homer Cole and John Huber had both left the profession by 1936 and were no longer active in the union.[41] Walter Bullock, another charter member, had resigned after an inconsequential spat with Behncke, and one by one, through death and other attrition, most of the old names were fading away. While the pilots with whom Behncke had plotted and schemed to create ALPA were less in evidence at the 1936 convention, his personal position was never stronger. He was unanimously reelected to another two-year term, and he attempted to persuade the delegates that ALPA should adopt a more openly political posture. Specifically, he wanted the convention to endorse Roosevelt for reelection. "I'm a strong Roosevelt man myself," he told the delegates. "You can just take the simple facts and put them on the table. Had it not been for him the picture would be pretty black today." But the growing affluence of the pilots had fostered a more conservative viewpoint, and they turned down Behncke's request for a direct endorsement. Behncke desperately argued that it was not only politic but necessary for ALPA to endorse its friends, in both parties, for reelection. "I do not believe we should become involved in partisan politics," he tried to explain, "but this convention should go on record as endorsing Congressmen and Senators . . . on the basis of what they did for you. If we do not . . . we are going to be back in Washington in a couple of months with our hands out again . . . and they are going to say 'Where were you? Why didn't you send me a wire or something?'" Behncke's reasoning proved persuasive, and the convention formally approved "non-partisan" letters of endorsement for several politicians.[42]

Behncke could get almost anything he wanted from his pilots because he had indisputably proven that he could fatten their paychecks. During 1936 he had challenged several airlines on the pay issue, contending that they were not paying the scale prescribed in the law. Not only did the operators give the pilots the pay Behncke thought they should have, but on several occasions, using governmental pressure, he forced the lines to give pilots back pay. Braniff, for instance, owing to the Post Office Department's threats to cancel its contract, paid its pilots $30,000 in back pay in 1935 alone. Needless to say, such a demonstration of muscle was very impressive, not only to Braniff pilots, most of whom had joined ALPA by the end of 1935, but to all airline pilots.[43]

Partly because of ALPA's effectiveness, in 1936 the operators organized a federation of their own, the Air Transport Association (ATA). The ATA was an outgrowth of the old transport department of the Aeronautical Chamber of Commerce, and many of the same personnel served in both. The Aeronautical Chamber of Commerce had proved ineffective, and in an effort to copy ALPA's centralized organization, which allowed one man to speak for everyone, the operators named Colonel Edgar S. Gorrell to head the ATA. Acting as the operators' spokesman after 1936, Gorrell ended the era when ALPA, with its streamlined apparatus, could easily outmaneuver the operators in Washington. As time passed, Behncke, with his penchant for personalizing issues, began to identify Gorrell as the source of ultimate evil.[44]

Despite the operators' new organization, there was little they could do to prevent the transfer of the provisions protecting the airline pilots from the Air Mail Act of 1934 into the Civil Aeronautics Act of 1938. Gorrell ineffectually argued that it was unnecessary to write specific guarantees of salary and hours into the new law because Title II of the Railway Labor Act would enable the pilots to bargain for adequate working conditions. Behncke paid little attention to Gorrell's half-hearted efforts, for he knew that there was almost no chance that Congress would leave the pilots unprotected.[45] Instead, he was shooting for something far more important, he thought, for the future. Because he had achieved success playing upon Congressional anxiety about air safety, Behncke decided to press for an amendment to the new law which would create an independent board, composed of three members, to investigate accidents. One of the three Aviation Safety Board (A.S.B.) members would have to be, by law, an active airline pilot. Although Behncke did not specifically advocate such a provision in the law, he obtained private assurances from several Congressional leaders that ALPA would be able to nominate the pilot who would serve on the A.S.B. The Hearst newspaper organization editorially supported the A.S.B. idea, and it publicized the activities of the committee of pilots Behncke had recruited to support him in Washington, dubbing them the "Lobby to Save Lives."[46]

A series of terrible crashes in the winter of 1937–38 lent special urgency to Behncke's constant admonitions about air safety. The Department of Commerce accident-investigating teams still designated the probable cause of too many accidents as "pilot error," and Congress was becoming openly skeptical. Behncke hammered away, insisting that investigatory and regulatory functions could not be entrusted to a single agency or there would inevitably be a tendency to "cover up" unpleasant facts. The independent A.S.B. would separate the functions, and it could be funded out of the appropriations for the new Civil Aeronautics Authority (C.A.A.). One of Behncke's most important converts to this idea was Montana's crusty Senator Burton K. Wheeler, who, after listening to Behncke, publicly declared that it was "time the United States government stopped playing politics with human lives . . . The airline pilots, who fly the industry's planes and who are personally responsible for the safety of their passengers," he said in an interview with the Hearst organization, "have appeared several times and publicly pleaded for the speedy removal of air safety from politics." [47]

Wheeler's support for the A.S.B. idea as an independent arm of the proposed C.A.A. was crucial. As Chairman of the Senate Interstate Commerce Committee, he was the man whose opposition could ruin not only the A.S.B. but the whole concept of an independent regulatory agency for aviation as well. Earlier, Wheeler had been less than enthusiastic about the idea of creating a new federal bureaucracy. Although the Howell Commission had recommended the new agency, Roosevelt at first opposed it and favored confining such regulation to the I.C.C.[48] Despite howls of protest from aviation enthusiasts, Senator Wheeler concurred in the President's decision. Behncke, proverbially loyal to the President, was the only major spokesman in the industry to support the I.C.C. as the chief regulator of aviation. But his loyalty was largely semantic, for the kind of "bureau" within the I.C.C. he wanted to see regulating commercial aviation bore a striking resemblance to the kind of independent regulatory agency everybody else was talking about.[49] Eventually, the President changed his mind, but Wheeler still had to be convinced, and it appears that Behncke's air safety argument was the deciding factor.

The Civil Aeronautics Act of 1938, the cornerstone of modern commercial aviation, was really an outgrowth of the competing bill Senator McCarran of Nevada introduced in opposition to the Black-McKellar Bill which eventually became the Air Mail Act of 1934. McCarran had continued to talk about his idea for an independent regulatory agency after 1934, but he did nothing concrete about it until the President began to favor it. McCarran then polished up his old bill and resubmitted it, with Congressman Clarence F. Lea of California sponsoring a similar bill in the House. The Air Mail Act of 1934 had given the I.C.C. the power to set rates the airlines might charge, and advocates of a new centralized agency only slowly overcame the reluctance of many legislators to see a single agency both setting rates and totally regulating the industry in every other respect. Behncke's advocacy of an impartial and semi-independent accident-investigation and safety agency within the new bureaucracy eased the fears of many Congressmen. The operators were eager to have the C.A.A. both regulate the industry and set rates, but Gorrell had no particular interest in the A.S.B. idea. Without Behncke's active support, however, the whole law might have run into serious trouble. In order to forestall such an impasse, Gorrell and Behncke arranged a deal. The ATA agreed to support the A.S.B. in return for Behncke's support for the C.A.A. as the sole rate-making agency. Despite some minor irritations, Behncke and Gorrell worked harmoniously during the C.A.A.'s passage into the statute books, and as a result the A.S.B., with an active airline pilot as a member, became a part of the law.[50]

Basically, the new law superseded and repealed the Air Commerce Act of 1926 and all subsequent air-mail legislation. It established the Civil Aeronautics Authority, consisting of an administrator and a five-man board to make basic policy decisions. The C.A.A. was to administer the law as well as the policy decisions. The administrator was appointed directly by the President, thus allowing the executive branch some control, but the other five members of the authority were supposed to be nonpolitical and beyond presidential recall. The C.A.A.'s decisions were the law of civil aviation, and in its basic area of responsibility it was beyond the control of the courts. The C.A.A., in addition, was charged with carrying out all functions which were previously under the control of the Department of Commerce, the Post Office Department, and the I.C.C. Everybody was satisfied with this arrangement, including, for once, Behncke, since the President promptly appointed ALPA's First Vice-President, Thomas O. Hardin, as the airline pilot member of the A.S.B.[51]

The pilots' sections of the new law contained everything Behncke wanted, and although Congressman Lea gave him a scare by omitting specific reference to Decision 83 in the first draft of the House version, the friends of the pilots were so numerous and vociferous that there was never really any cause for alarm. The impassioned description of the airline pilots given by Representative John Martin of Colorado is worth repeating in full, because it provides an illustration of literally dozens of similar and, in some cases, even more flowery encomiums which the legislators were wont to render:

In my opinion, the piloting of these great airplanes, which hurtle through the air at 200 miles per hour, loaded with human lives, is the most responsible, the most skillful, and the most dangerous occupation that mankind ever engaged in. Nothing in the past history of the world, nor anything today is equivalent to the position of a pilot at the controls of one of these gigantic airplanes . . .

They are the picked men of the country. These men must not only be perfect mentally and physically, but the art of flying a plane must be born in them. It is a profession in which many are called but few chosen. These men ought to be as free from worry or concern about their economic condition or future as it is humanly or legislatively possible to accomplish. If there is anything we can put in the legislation that will keep worry from the air pilots, it ought to be done.[52]

By 1938, the period of ALPA's greatest success was over. Behncke had accomplished everything he originally set out to do, and the future of the union, as well as the economic position of its members, was assured because of an astounding array of federal protective legislation. While ALPA would, beginning in 1939, negotiate direct collective bargaining agreements with the operators, federal law created a set of conditions which were so favorable that the union literally had nothing to fear. Through a combination of luck, special circumstance, and decisive leadership, Behncke had succeeded in institutionalizing an image—Congress regarded the dashing aviator as the indispensable man and it made his occupational well-being a matter of national policy.

Epilogue

By the end of World War II, ALPA had secured direct employment agreements with all the major air carriers in the country, and foreign airline pilots marveled at the resulting affluence of American pilots. British and Canadian pilots soon followed the American example, and after the war Behncke spearheaded the creation of the International Federation of Air Line Pilots (IFALPA), which he headed until 1951.

At the outset of World War II, Behncke expected to receive a high appointment in the Air Transport Command (ATC), which the government established to mobilize the nation's air transport industry. He still retained his reserve rank of captain, but when the Army ordered him to active duty it offered him neither a promotion nor a significant position. Since several airline executives had received direct commissions at high ranks in the new ATC, Behncke thought he deserved at least equal treatment. Neither his previous loyalty to the New Deal nor his urgent appeals had any effect, however, and his outrage was such that he fought successfully to avoid serving on active duty. He was bitter about what he regarded as Roosevelt's lack of gratitude, and consequently he was particularly diligent in looking after the interests of airline pilots serving with the ATC. His stubbornness in insisting that the ATC adhere to federal regulations, despite the wartime situation, elicited several monumental outbursts of patriotic indignation from Rickenbacker during the course of the war. But Behncke stuck to his guns, treated the ATC as if it were must another employer, grudgingly permitting *temporary* wartime increases in flying time but insisting on reciprocal concessions. As a result, he won substantial pay benefits for civilian pilots employed in the ATC, thus setting a precedent for even higher postwar salary scales on the domestic airlines.

The great postwar expansion of domestic airline operations brought a rapid influx of new members into ALPA, and Behncke's position began to weaken because most of them were ex-military pilots. Military aviators generally had a low opinion of Behncke and his union, since it was widely rumored that ALPA members flying with the ATC earned fabulous salaries for their relatively unhazardous work. Ernest Gann's splendid little memoir *Fate Is the Hunter* points out that the rumors were not true, but they were standard fare among service fliers nonetheless. In addition, nearly every service flier was aware of Rickenbacker's denunciation of Behncke, and many of them had heard of his attempt to physically assault Behncke during a 1942 conference because of his "unpatriotic" attitude. (Rickenbacker's fellow airline executives restrained him after a fist-shaking interlude, but perhaps many service fliers secretly wished the famed ace had succeeded in socking the union leader.)[1]

In fact, Behncke's apparent lack of regard for the conventional "can-do" patriotic fervor of World War II irritated many ALPA members. At one point during the long struggle between ALPA and the operators over pay scales for airline pilots working overseas, Behncke ordered a group of American Airlines pilots not to go to Natal to fly the dangerous "Hump" route over the Himalayas to China until management signed a contract. The pilots went anyway, and Behncke would have disciplined them for violating ALPA orders had not an irate reaction from the membership developed.[2]

This background of discontent was at least partially responsible for ALPA's first true nationwide strike, which came against TWA in 1946. Behncke needed to impress his members with his toughness and devotion to their well-being, and the strike seemed an ideal vehicle. ALPA's principal concern in the immediate postwar years lay in writing new employment contracts to cover operation of the new four-engined aircraft, which had been perfected during the war, and which were entering domestic service by early 1945. The airlines were vigorously advertising travel by four-engined aircraft, and Behncke, with an eye to publicity, believed that a strike over higher wages for flying the new aircraft would not only win public approval but also shore up his shaky relations with the rank and file.

Partly because he harbored ancient resentments against TWA from ALPA's early organizational days, but mainly because TWA was operating more four-engined aircraft than any other airline, Behncke singled it out for a strike. Unfortunately for Behncke, the strike came amidst the great postwar epidemic of strikes, and an exasperated public opinion was in no mood to support what *Time* magazine called the "golden boys." It seemed outrageous to many people that the pilots should strike when they already earned average salaries of over $10,000 a year, and Behncke's image in the popular press, as a "suave, self-assured, retired pilot who looks about as radical as a Philadelphia main liner" did not inspire much affection either. When the CIO's Phillip Murray at a press conference snorted, "Labor dispute hell! That's a row between capitalists," the nadir had been reached.[3]

Although ALPA failed to win its specific demands, the strike did demonstrate its power to totally shut down an airline for an extended period of time. Unruffled by the strains which the strike had placed on the union, Behncke methodically continued to negotiate with the operators one at a time, and, perhaps because of the new credibility of the strike threat, he began to win generally favorable settlements. But the slow pace of contract negotiations irritated many pilots, who frequently worked for several months without a current contract. Furthermore, Behncke's peculiar flamboyance and use of obsolete terminology led many young pilots to regard him as a relic of a bygone era. He had not flown an airliner in well over a decade, and he seemed increasingly out of touch. As a result, for the first time in ALPA's history, there was a serious challenge to his leadership in 1947, when Captain Willis Proctor of American Airlines unsuccessfully sought the presidency.

Behncke won reelection to a new two-year term without opposition the following year, and he also persuaded the delegates to appropriate money for a building. The idea of a union-owned building had obsessed him for years, and he believed that it would be a permanent monument to his leadership. Ironically, the building turned out to be more of a tomb than a monument. He insisted on "aircraft specifications" for the building, with the inevitable result that costs soared. When he had exhausted the original $250,000 appropriation, Behncke simply spent more union funds, without consulting anybody. In addition, he spent almost every waking hour supervising the construction of the new building, located on the edge of Chicago's Midway Airport, and he neglected ALPA's administrative work.

In an effort to improve administration of union affairs, the membership insisted on structural changes after 1948. They provided Behncke with a bright young assistant, a former

Braniff pilot named Clarence N. Sayen, to oversee administrative details, but Behncke, afflicted with an almost constitutional inability to delegate authority, made little use of him. Discontent with his leadership finally reached such proportions that in 1951 a specially constituted Executive Board removed him from office and named Sayen to replace him. In 1952, after a bitter and costly struggle, a federal court confirmed Behncke's ouster, but in the interim ALPA operated with two presidents and a court-appointed "receiver." The "receiver" seemed intent on looting the union's treasury, authorizing enormous fees for legal services, among other things, and before the pilots regained control of the union it was practically bankrupt. It took Sayen and his successor, Charles Ruby, a National Airlines pilot, years of patient effort to restore the union to health.

While the airline pilots found it necessary to remove Behncke from office, they still admired and respected him, despite his incompetence to deal with a world of aviation which no longer depended on fabric-covered wings, trimotored Fords, and open cockpits. They thought he would accept a "President Emeritus" position at full salary for life, but they underestimated his tenacity. By the early 1950s most pilots had never heard of Frank Ormsbee or his celebrated 1932 dispute with Behncke. Had they known of it, and had they been aware that Behncke demonstrated an essential inability to compromise during it, they might have realized that he would never retreat. The aging giant simply did not know how.

David L. Behncke was a man of tremendous energy and drive, and these very traits, which were so important in creating an organization such as ALPA, contributed to a certain rigidity of mind which became more pronounced as the years passed. From the creation of ALPA to the end of World War II, his contributions to the pilots and the success of commercial aviation in America were enormous. But when great technological changes began to occur in the industry after World War II, Behncke's tenacity in sticking to the old ways generated a revolution among the rank and file of his union, and the strain of the battle to retain his control so undermined his health that he died of a heart attack shortly after it was over. At his own request, he was cremated and his ashes were scattered along the old air-mail route between Chicago and Omaha which he had flown in the 1920s. This final sentimental gesture perhaps symbolizes the estrangement between Behncke's generation of scarf and goggle barnstormers and a more modern generation of flying technocrats. It seems unthinkable that a modern jet captain would make such a request.[4]

Bibliographical Note
Notes
Index

Bibliographical Note

Of the archival sources for ALPA's history, the transcripts of the semi-annual conventions are by far the most valuable and voluminous. Running to thousands of pages for each session, the bound typescripts provide information on almost every aspect of the union's activities through the late 1940s. Unfortunately, as challenges mounted to Behncke's leadership after 1948, the conventions tended to go "off the record" when sensitive issues were discussed. Karl M. Ruppenthal's dissertation, "Revolution in the Air Line Pilots Association," which he wrote at Stanford University in 1959, is actually a primary source for these events. Ruppenthal was a participant in the revolution, and he kept careful notes at the conventions. It is, however, impossible to reconstruct the events in the conventions leading up to the ouster from the transcripts alone.

The minutes of the meetings of the Central Executive Council are useful for the 1930s, but since that body met irregularly there is little continuity in the subjects it covered. Behncke's penchant for preserving historical records led him to have a stenographer present at the meetings, however, and on certain subjects the council's minutes are more specific and helpful than the transcripts of the conventions. The internal and external correspondence of ALPA is incomplete for the early period, but, again, Behncke's habit of preserving records apparently accounts for the scattered items which have survived.

The material is stored in a long row of metal file cabinets in a basement hallway of what was formerly the union's Chicago

headquarters.* There are also several cardboard boxes of correspondence stored in what was formerly a shower room for pilots
wishing to freshen up during their Chicago layovers. The library,
on the main floor, contains a complete file of Behncke's speeches,
copies of mimeographed letters to all members, and a complete
run of *The Air Line Pilot*. In addition, several boxes of memorabilia
are scattered throughout the building.

In 1966, the Executive Board of ALPA agreed to deposit archival
material which it deemed to be of purely historical interest in the
Labor History Archives of Wayne State University. The union has
for some years been microfilming its records in order to make room
for current files, and as the microfilming progresses batches of the
material will be turned over to Wayne State. As of the summer of
1967, however, all the primary manuscript sources were still in
ALPA's possession.

Perhaps the most valuable source for the history of ALPA among
public documents is the hearings conducted by the House Committee on the Post Office and Post Roads. The Senate Interstate
Commerce Committee also held hearings at which ALPA presented
its views during the 1930s. In addition, the hearings conducted
by the National Labor Board of the N.R.A. provided valuable information. The *Report of the Federal Aviation Commission* (Senate
Document 15, 74th Cong., 1st Sess., 1935) contains a wealth of
background information on aviation during the 1920s, and the report of the special investigative committee chaired by Senator
Royal S. Copeland (Senate Report 2455, 74th Cong., 2nd Sess.,
1936), covering the death of Senator Bronson Cutting, is also
valuable.

Among periodical sources, *Aviation* magazine, and its successors
of various names, is the most important. As the industry's primary
organ, *Aviation* provides an almost day-to-day record of the development of civil aviation. The aviation section of the *New York
Times* offers substantial background information in this area.

---

* In 1968, after years of hesitation, ALPA finally moved its national headquarters to Washington. There was never any real reason for its headquarters
to be in Chicago, except that it was Behncke's home. That the union waited
until sixteen years after his death before moving, even though the bulk of
its activities have always been in Washington, is in a way a final tribute to
Behncke's pervasive influence.

Aerial Age Weekly is an important source of information on aviation prior to 1920. The union's newspaper, *The Air Line Pilot,* can be rather unreliable owing to Behncke's eclectic editorship. However, as a chronicle of names and attitudes, it is invaluable.

Henry Ladd Smith's *Airways: The History of Commercial Aviation in the U.S.* (1944) is still the best single volume on the subject. Frederick C. Thayer's *Air Transport Policy and National Security* (1965) tries to pick the story up where Smith left it. Elsbeth E. Freudenthal's *The Aviation Business* (1940) is marred by a strong bias against the operators during the cancellations controversy. R. E. G. Davies, *A History of the World's Airlines* (1964), contains brief synopses of the development of almost every airline in the world. The author, a retired BOAC executive, has an encyclopedic knowledge of the internecine mergers which have characterized the industry. The principal book on government intervention in commercial aviation is Richard E. Caves' *Air Transport and Its Regulators* (1962). Malcolm A. MacIntyre's *Competitive Private Enterprise Under Government Regulation* (1964) adds little to Caves' book, although its focus is somewhat different. David C. Corbett, *Politics and the Airlines* (1965), is a strange little book with some interesting conclusions, but it is lightly footnoted and therefore difficult to evaluate. Arthur M. Schlesinger, Jr., *The Coming of the New Deal* (1958), contains by far the best analysis of the air-mail controversies of the 1930s.

Most of the major airlines have at one time or another subsidized the publication of a history of their operations. With a few exceptions, they are uniformly inadequate. The sensitive nature of the connection between government subsidy and their operations has made airline executives extremely skeptical of independent scholars, and they have therefore, in direct contrast to ALPA, generally refused to open their records. Significantly, the only first-rate academic study of an airline is Robin D. Higham's study of BOAC's predecessor, Imperial Airways, *Britain's Imperial Air Routes, 1918 to 1939* (1961). Frank J. Taylor's *High Horizons* (1951), covering United Airlines, is the best of the subsidized remainder. Airline pilot memoirs are fairly plentiful with Basil L. Rowe, *Under My Wings* (1956), Byron Moore, *The First Five Million Miles* (1955), William Grooch, *Winged Highway* (1938), and Lew Reichers, *The Flying Years* (1956), among the most significant.

In evaluating the relationship between ALPA and the organized labor movement, Joseph G. Rayback, *A History of American Labor* (1959), provides general background information in one concise volume. The literature of labor history is massive, but David Brody's *The Butcher Workmen* (1964) stands out as the model of what a monograph in this area should be. John M. Baitsell, *Airline Industrial Relations* (1966), and Mark L. Kahn, *Pay Practices for Flight Employees on U.S. Airlines* (1961), deal specifically with ALPA's labor relations practices. Reed C. Richardson's *The Locomotive Engineers* (1963) is helpful in drawing analogies between the pilots and a group of workers they closely resemble, while Adolf Sturmthal, ed., *White Collar Trade Unions* (1966), contains a number of provocative articles which deal with elite unionism.

Notes

1. The Pilot Mystique

1. R. E. G. Davies, *A History of the World's Airlines* (London: Oxford University Press, 1964), pp. 1–55; Henry Ladd Smith, *Airways: The History of Commercial Aviation in the United States* (New York: Alfred A. Knopf, 1944), pp. 86–87; Elsbeth E. Freudenthal, *The Aviation Business: From Kitty Hawk to Wall Street* (New York: Vanguard Press, 1940), pp. 62–64.

2. *Ibid.;* "Our Winged Postmen," *Scientific American,* 118 (May 25, 1918), 476–477.

3. Smith, *Airways,* pp. 94–102; Lester D. Gardner, "German Air Transport," *Aviation,* 23 (Aug. 1, 1927), 253–254.

4. U.S., Federal Aviation Commission, *Report of the Federal Aviation Commission* (Washington: U.S. Government Printing Office, 1935), Senate Document 15, 74th Cong., 1st Sess., 1935, pp. 1–5; "The Connecting Link," *Aviation,* 24 (May 21, 1928), 1449. See also Roger Eugene Bilstein, "Prelude to the Air Age: Civil Aviation in the United States, 1919–1925," Ph.D. diss., Ohio State University, 1966.

5. Dixon Wecter, *The Hero in America: A Chronicle of Hero-Worship* (New York: Charles Scribner's Sons, 1941), pp. 415–444.

6. Edward L. Fox, "Fatalism of the Fliers," *Century,* 83 (April 1912), 841–849; Smith, *Airways,* pp. 19–34; Don Dwiggins, *The Air Devils: The Story of Balloonists, Barnstormers, and Stunt Pilots* (New York: Lippincott, 1966), *passim;* Lester J. Maitland, "Knights of the Air," *The World's Work,* 57 (November, 1928), 88–103.

7. Anonymous, *The Essays of an Aviator* (London: Aeronautics, 1914), p. 38.

8. Andrew J. Cooper, III, "The Wages of Airline Pilots: The System of Wage Computation, the Wage Level, and the Wage Structure of Pilots Employed by United States Scheduled Airlines," Ph.D. diss., Princeton University, 1961, p. 3.

9. Smith, *Airways*, pp. 47–49; F. T. Courtney, "Stunt Flying and the Commercial Pilot," *Scientific American Supplement*, 88 (Nov. 8, 1919), 259; interview with Walter Bullock, former barnstormer, retired airline pilot, and charter member of ALPA, July 6, 1967 (hereinafter cited as Bullock interview).

10. *New York Times*, Sept. 18, 1933, p. 16.

11. "Flying Supermen and Superwomen," *Literary Digest*, 122 (Nov. 14, 1936), 22.

12. Beirne Lay, Jr., "Airman," *Fortune*, 23 (March 1941), 122–123.

13. Earl D. Osborne, "Ten Years of Civil Aviation," *Aviation*, 21 (Aug. 2, 1926), 214–216; Arthur Ruhl, "It's a Temperamental Job," *New Republic*, 28 (Sept. 28, 1921), 126–128; "Three Years of the Aerial Mail," *Aerial Age Weekly*, 13 (May 23, 1921), 249; "Transcontinental Mail in Twenty-six Hours," *The World's Work*, 46 (October 1923), 567; Donald Wilhelm, "Flying the Mail," *The World's Work*, 42 (May 1921), 49–59, and 42 (June 1921), 199–204.

14. Burt M. McConnell, "The Air Mail Pilot," *American Review of Reviews*, 76 (August 1927), 167–173.

15. *New York Times*, Feb. 25, 1929, p. 15.

16. "Dearth of Transport Pilots Lanphier Says," *Aviation*, 26 (Mar. 2, 1929), 644.

17. "Air Transport Growth Announced," *Aviation*, 26 (Mar. 16, 1929), 817.

18. H. T. Lewis and George I. Meyers, "Selecting and Training Transport Pilots," *Aviation*, 30 (November 1931), 648–649; Charles H. Wooley, "Training Pilots for Airline Operations," *Aviation*, 27 (Nov. 16, 1929), 967–969.

19. *Aviation*, 25 (Aug. 4, 1928), 448.

20. "The Cost of Training," *Aviation*, 26 (Jan. 5, 1929), 23.

21. Swanee Taylor, "Daring Young Men Needed," *Aviation*, 21 (Aug. 16, 1926), 294.

22. Myron M. Stearns, "The Men Who Fly the Planes," *The World's Work*, 59 (July 1930), 62–65; Kenneth S. Davis, *The Hero: Charles A. Lindbergh and the American Dream* (Garden City, N.Y.: Doubleday, 1959), pp. 76–78; Edward V. Rickenbacker, *Ricken-*

backer (Englewood Cliffs, N.J.: Prentice-Hall, 1967), pp. 21, 58–67, 85–86.

23. Cooper, "Wages of Air Line Pilots," pp. 5–23.

24. Beirne Lay, Jr., "Airman," *Fortune*, 23 (March 1941), 138.

25. *Chicago Sun-Times*, Apr. 27, 1969, p. 3.

26. "NAT Begins Passenger Service Between Chicago and Kansas City," *Aviation*, 24 (Feb. 20, 1928), 439.

27. Velva G. Darling, "Across the Continent in Forty-eight Hours," *The World's Work*, 59 (September 1929), 53–56; Myron M. Stearns, "All Aboard by Air," *The World's Work*, 58 (May 1928), 34–41, 144–150.

28. "How Much Can a Pilot Make?" *Literary Digest*, 99 (Nov. 24, 1928), 60–61.

29. "On Good Pilots," *Aviation*, 20 (Apr. 19, 1926), 583.

30. James P. Wines, "Operation of the Pan American Airways System," *Aviation*, 26 (Apr. 27, 1929), 1422–1429.

31. Ralph Deggers, "Give Service Plus to the Air Travelers," *Aviation*, 26 (Feb. 9, 1929), 396–397.

32. "Passenger Pilots," *Aviation*, 26 (Mar. 16, 1929), 797.

33. "Passenger Impressions," *Aviation*, 25 (Dec. 15, 1928), 1981.

34. "Sailors of the Sky," *Popular Mechanics*, 74 (December 1940), 866–869; "Pacific Overture," *Aviation*, 34 (December 1935), 38.

35. ALPA, *Proceedings of the 1934 Convention*, pp. 112–113.

36. U.S., Bureau of the Census, *Statistical Abstract of the United States*, 88th ed. (Washington: U.S. Government Printing Office, 1967), p. 588; *ibid.*, 90th ed. (1969), p. 572.

2. Early Pilot Organizations

1. ALPA, *Proceedings of the 1932 Convention*, p. 50.

2. *Ibid.*, pp. 39–40. Gladys Behncke did all the secretarial work for ALPA in the beginning, handling all the paperwork and correspondence, and it seems that her husband's efforts to organize a union wrought considerable personal hardship on her. In early 1931 Behncke rented office space for ALPA in the Troy Lane Hotel in Chicago, but prior to then a converted bedroom in his house was ALPA's office. Behncke complained of this period: "There was practically no home life in my house, the telephone people and the telegraph boy never stopped calling . . . When we

finally moved out my wife was broken in health due to the terrible strain."

3. Smith, *Airways*, p. 59.

4. Manufacturers' Aircraft Association, *Aircraft Year Book* (1919), p. 318. Emphasis supplied.

5. "The Aerial Mail Service—One Year Old," *Aerial Age Weekly*, 9 (Apr. 26, 1920), 218.

6. *New York Times*, July 25, 1919, p. 5.

7. "Aerial Mail Strike Settled," *Aerial Age Weekly*, 9 (Aug. 4, 1919), 968.

8. "Leon D. Smith, Aerial Mail Pilot," *Aerial Age Weekly*, 9 (May 5, 1919), 383; "Air Mail Pilot E. H. Lee Trained Navy Stunt Fliers for the Service," *Aerial Age Weekly*, 9 (June 2, 1919), 589–591. One of Lee's aviation records was for consecutive loops. On June 18, 1918, he performed 105 of them and landed on the last one—out of gas.

9. *New York Times*, July 26, 1919, p. 1.

10. *Ibid.*

11. *Ibid.*

12. "Aerial Mail Strike Settled," *Aerial Age Weekly*, 9 (Aug. 4, 1919), 968.

13. *New York Times*, July 26, 1919, p. 1.

14. U.S., *Congressional Record*, 66th Cong., 1st Sess., 1919, LVIII, Part 3, p. 3171.

15. *Ibid.*, pp. 9046–9047.

16. *Ibid.*

17. *New York Times*, July 26, 1919, p. 1.

18. *Ibid.*, p. 8.

19. *Ibid.*, p. 1.

20. *Ibid.*, p. 6.

21. *Ibid.*, July 27, 1919, p. 4; July 28, 1919, p. 8.

22. "Aged Squaw Makes Flight," *Aerial Age Weekly*, 10 (Nov. 22, 1920), 293. Smith at this time made one of the trade journals by taking a 106-year-old Indian woman for a flight during a county fair he was working in Batavia, New York.

23. "Aero Mail Pilots Receive Increase," *Aerial Age Weekly*, 9 (Aug. 11, 1919), 1008.

24. Burt M. McConnell, "The Air Mail Pilot," *American Review of Reviews*, 76 (August 1927), 167–173.

25. Manufacturers' Aircraft Association, *Aircraft Year Book* (1920), p. 297.

26. "To Rate Aerial Mail Divisions," *Aerial Age Weekly,* 11 (Apr. 26, 1920), 218.

27. "The Air Mail Pilots of America," *Aviation,* 21 (Nov. 22, 1926), 884. In 1926, as the government air-mail service was being phased out, the association had forty-five members, scattered from coast to coast across the transcontinental air route. The majority of the members had been with the air-mail service for more than five years, and together they had flown 200 years of actual flying time.

28. "Transport Pilots Get a Rating," *Aviation,* 31 (June 1932), 276. As late as the early 1930s, PPA was still being consulted by the government as to its opinion of certain airmen's ratings. Needless to say, the organization was moribund by that time and that it presumed to speak for "pilots" was a source of extreme irritation for ALPA.

29. Waldo D. Waterman, "The Professional Pilots Association: An Organization for the Protection of Pilots and the Encouragement of Reliable Air Transport," *Aviation,* 20 (Mar. 15, 1926), 369.

30. "Waldo D. Waterman Tours Industry," Aviation, 21 (Nov. 29, 1926), 916.

31. "Transport Pilots Get Rating," *Aviation,* 31 (June 1932), 276.

32. "Who's Who in American Aeronautics," *Aviation,* 28 (June 29, 1925), 722.

33. "New Air Mail Head," *Aerial Age Weekly,* 13 (July 4, 1921), 388.

34. *New York Times,* Oct. 25, 1925, p. 13.

35. *Ibid.,* July 22, 1927, p. 6. One may infer that Egge was well regarded by the air-mail pilots he had formerly supervised since Lloyd W. Bertaud and James DeWitt Hill, both air-mail pilots, kept him well informed as to the progress of their proposed New York to Rome flight. Neither was an air-mail pilot at the time and they owed Egge no due as their superior, but they apparently just liked him.

36. *New York Times,* Mar. 30, 1927, p. 44.

37. "Air Mail Pilots of America Now the National Pilots Association," *Aviation,* 24 (Jan. 2, 1928), 34.

38. *Ibid.*

39. *Ibid.;* interview with Homer F. Cole, first Secretary of ALPA, first Director of the Cleveland Air Traffic Control Center, Aug. 11, 1967 (hereinafter cited as Cole interview).

40. Cole interview; ALPA, *Proceedings of the 1932 Convention,* p. 51. Cole described NAPA as "sadly negligent" in 1932.

41. ALPA, *Proceedings of the 1932 Convention,* p. 7.

42. ALPA, *Proceedings of the 1934 Convention,* pp. 525–565.

43. *The Air Line Pilot* (Apr. 20, 1932), p. 4.

44. Bullock interview; letter from R. J. Little, "key man" for Salt Lake City-based pilots, to D. W. Behncke, May 12, 1931. Little heard rumors that Egge was trying to play some part in ALPA's affairs and expressed himself on Egge: "Word has reached us that Mr. Egge is to act for the pilots . . . I do not know if that is so . . . but I wish to state what most of the pilots out here feel about Egge. They do not want Egge to have anything to do with this matter and they also do not want him to know that they have signed any letters of resignation. There is strong feeling against him in this section. In fact, some of the pilots feel that he might be drawing a salary from the operators."

3. The Impact of the Depression

1. U.S., Federal Aviation Commission, *Report of the Federal Aviation Commission,* pp. 2–3.

2. Smith, *Airways,* pp. 86–88; "Aeronautical Stocks," *Aviation,* 25 (Feb. 16, 1929), 467.

3. "Investment Trusts," *Aviation,* 26 (Apr. 13, 1929), 1249.

4. "Wall Street's Crash," *Aviation,* 27 (Nov. 2, 1929), 875.

5. "Guggenheim Aviation Fund to Disband at End of Year," *Aviation,* 26 (Nov. 2, 1929), 898.

6. Smith, *Airways,* pp. 156–166.

7. "Air Transport Progress," *Aviation,* 30 (January 1930), 18–21.

8. Rudolph Modley, ed., *Aviation Facts and Figures* (New York: McGraw-Hill, 1945), pp. 66–67.

9. "What's Next in Air Transport," *Aviation,* 29 (October 1930), 193.

10. Bullock interview.

11. U.S., Department of Commerce, *Statistical Handbook of Civil Aviation* (Washington: U.S. Government Printing Office, 1944), p. 33.

12. "A Separate Corner for the Student," *Aviation,* 27 (Oct. 19, 1929), 777.

13. Cooper, "The Wages of Airline Pilots," p. 3.

14. Bullock interview.

15. "Pilot Responsibility—The Question of the Hour," *Aviation*, 28 (Mar. 29, 1930), 629–630.

16. "Air Transport Progress," *Aviation*, 30 (January 1931), 20.

17. "Air Transport," *Aviation*, 31 (March 1932), 102–105.

18. *Airway Age*, 12 (May 9, 1931), 16.

19. ALPA, *Proceedings of the 1932 Convention*, p. 167.

20. *Ibid.*, pp. 7–8.

21. Interview with W. W. Anderson, Director of Personnel Services of ALPA, July 3, 1967 (hereinafter cited as Anderson interview).

22. "Behncke Wins Chicago Air Derby," *Aerial Age Weekly*, 14 (Sept. 19, 1921), 28.

23. The biographical information on Behncke comes from a variety of sources: interviews with Homer F. Cole, Walter Bullock, and W. W. Anderson, a magazine article by Wesley Price, "Labor's Biggest Wind," *Saturday Evening Post*, 220 (Aug. 2, 1947), 118, and Oscar Leiding, "Pilot Union President," a thirty-page pamphlet prepared under ALPA auspices in 1944.

24. Minutes of a meeting of the Representative Council of United Air Lines Pilots, June 19, 1931.

25. *Ibid.*

26. *Ibid.*

27. ALPA, *Proceedings of the 1932 Convention*, pp. 7–8.

28. Bullock interview.

29. *Ibid.*

30. "Mutual Protection for Pilots," *Aviation*, 28 (Jan. 25, 1930), 143.

31. ALPA, *Proceedings of the 1932 Convention*, p. 8.

32. Air Line Pilots Association, *The ALPA Story* (Chicago, 1966), p. 12. This pamphlet is of the standard promotional type, designed to encourage young pilots to join ALPA. It stresses, almost urgently, that "Pilot pay *was* cut. Pilots' monthly flying hours *were* increased," although, of course, such appears not to have been the case on all airlines.

33. Anderson interview.

34. Price, "Labor's Biggest Wind," *Saturday Evening Post*, 220 (Aug. 2, 1947), 117.

35. Interview with R. L. Oakman, Aug. 1, 1967. Mr. Oakman, who headed the Statistical Research Department of ALPA from

1946 until 1953, kept a notebook or daily log of his activities with ALPA, which he graciously allowed me to copy. In his notebook he included anecdotal material on Behncke, or "Behncke-isms" (sample: Behncke on preciseness, "The wording in this paragraph is too broad. It is like shoveling rice out the window."). Hereinafter cited as Oakman diary.

4. Creating a National Union

1. ALPA, "Information Sheet for Air Mail and Transport Pilots," Apr. 22, 1931.

2. *Ibid.* Behncke suggested the following divisional alignment: Division 1—National Parks Line; Division 2—Varney; Division 3—Boeing Air Transport; Division 4—Boeing Air Transport; Division 5—Boeing Air Transport; Division 6—Boeing Air Transport; Division 7—National Air Transport; Division 8—Pacific Air Transport; Division 9—Western Air Express.

3. ALPA, *Proceedings of the 1932 Convention,* p. 11. Behncke arranged for Victor Olander, who was Secretary of the Illinois State Federation of Labor, to address the convention. It is difficult to say just when Behncke and Olander came to know each other. Behncke always maintained that he did not meet Olander until he began trying to organize ALPA, but it is obvious that he had found out a great deal about the labor movement somehow before meeting Olander, despite his protestations to the contrary.

4. *Webster's New Collegiate Dictionary.*

5. Joseph G. Rayback, *A History of American Labor* (New York: Macmillan, 1959), p. 55, points out that the Philadelphia cordwainers used this technique as early as 1799.

6. ALPA, "Evidence of Authentication of the Formation of an Organization for Air Line Pilots Only . . ." This is a folder containing several hundred pilot escrow agreements. The escrow the pilots used on United was typical of the common wording. It was a mimeographed form letter which stated: "Enclosed you will find my letter of resignation . . . The time of the resignation is left blank. I hereby empower you to deliver my resignation to said employer anytime you see fit. Particularly in the event that any United Aircraft Corporation pilots should be discharged because of their activity in the movement now underway to protect the interests, working conditions, wages, and hours of pilots. I

hereby authorize you to negotiate for and on my behalf with my employer in all matters concerning my working conditions, wages, and hours, and to enter into an agreement with my employer binding myself to service . . . when agreed to by majority vote . . .

"In the event that you should see fit to deliver the enclosed resignation I hereby agree to cease working at the time designated by you in the enclosed resignation and not to return to work until your committee has so desired. The above authority is granted to you for a period of one year from date."

Page two of the escrow was an agreement to pay $50, "to be used as a majority of said committee may direct."

7. Cole interview.

8. Bullock interview; Bullock could hardly help but be privy to Cole's organizational activities, owing to their kinship. In addition to Bullock's benign attitude, the views of the owner of NWA raised the pilots' ire and put them in the mood to organize for self-defense long before Behncke started his formal effort. Bullock stated: "The main reason the NWA pilots were interested in forming a union was that every time we had a discussion with management about pay or flight time, the President of NWA, Lilly, a Minneapolis banker, would say he'd quit, disband the line if he had any labor trouble. He was rich anyway he'd say, and he used to constantly tell us the air line was just a plaything for him. This was foolish, even in the early thirties. And it was our whole existence and it didn't set so good to have him sit there and tell us our livelihood was just a plaything to him. It was a pretty big air line then, as air lines went . . . and it made us more determined, I think, because we weren't afraid, we really didn't believe that. By that time it was . . . making 25 percent on the original investment, right through when the only revenue was mostly mail . . . It wasn't like a man like Lilly to pass up a profit, believe me. He didn't get to be president of the First National Bank by passing up big profits."

9. Homer F. Cole to Behncke, May 9, 1931.

10. M. D. Ator to Behncke, May 11, 1931.

11. Glenn T. Fields to Behncke, May 1931 (date obliterated).

12. R J Little to Behncke, May 12, 1931.

13. George T. Douglass to Behncke, May 14, 1931.

14. Behncke to Douglass, May 31, 1931. The relatively long intervals between answering letters are understandable when

one considers the nature of airline piloting in that day. In the event of bad weather, which was frequent in the spring, a pilot might be weathered in at an isolated emergency landing field for several days, and hence unable to get back to his home base to collect his mail. The tough tone of this letter, incidentally, indicates that Behncke had a realistic and rather unromantic view of his fellow aviators.

15. ALPA, *Proceedings of the 1932 Convention,* pp. 8–9.

16. R. L. Wagner to Behncke, June 1, 1931.

17. *The Air Line Pilot* (Apr. 5, 1932), p. 1.

18. Hal George to Behncke, June 3, 1931.

19. Ator to Behncke, June 31 [sic], 1931.

20. Behncke to "Key Men," June 30, 1931.

21. Basil L. Rowe, *Under My Wings* (New York: Bobbs Merrill, 1956), p. 130. Ormsbee once got thoroughly lost en route from Guatemala City to Brownsville, Texas, while flying a Sikorski S-38 Amphibian with ten passengers aboard. He mistook a large lake for the ocean and landed, only to find that he could not take off again because he lacked fuel. After five days he finally secured some fuel from friendly Indians in the area and resumed his trip. Airline transportation had its hazards in the 1920's, as the passengers on Ormsbee's plane would no doubt agree.

22. Frank Ormsbee to Behncke, undated, but probably written in early May 1931.

23. Ormsbee to Behncke, May 15, 1931.

24. Ormsbee to Behncke, May 18, 1931.

25. ALPA, *Proceedings of the 1932 Convention,* p. 39.

26. *Ibid.,* pp. 42–43. One reason for Behncke's dissatisfaction with Barker was that several pilots decided their wives and/or girl friends might as well have Behncke's $20 a week.

27. ALPA, "Employment Contract of Ray Brown"; Ray Brown to Behncke, June 28, 1931. On the back of Brown's telegram Behncke scribbled, "500 × 12—$6,000!" Behncke obviously felt that it was too much.

28. *The Air Line Pilot* (Apr. 20, 1932), p. 4.

29. "Anonymous Aviators" to G. W. Burbank, May 1, 1931. The letter was signed "Confidential and unsigned."

30. G. W. Burbank to Reuben Wagner, H. A. Collison, Jack O'Brien, R. J. Little, and John C. Johnston, May 5, 1931. It seems likely that Behncke talked with Burbank in Chicago either late in

April or early in May. Burbank probably discovered who the five pilots were from Behncke.

31. Little to Behncke, May 12, 1931.
32. *The Air Line Pilot* (Apr. 20, 1932), p. 4.
33. ALPA, *Proceedings of the 1932 Convention,* pp. 10–11.
34. *Ibid.,* pp. 11–12.
35. Cole interview.
36. ALPA Headquarters to all Air Line Pilots, June 15, 1931.
37. ALPA, *Proceedings of the 1932 Convention,* pp. 11–12.
38. William Green to Behncke, June 12, 1931.
39. ALPA, *Proceedings of the 1932 Convention,* pp. 37–39.
40. Cole interview.
41. *The Air Line Pilot* (Apr. 5, 1932), p. 2.
42. ALPA, "Organizational Log of the Air Line Pilots Association," Aug. 20, 1931, p. 6; ALPA, Inactive Personnel Files. A complete list of the code system and the pilot representatives of the early organizational effort leading up to the meeting of key men was:

Code	Name	Airline (Division)	Current Status (1967)
Mr. A.	Byron S. Warner	United (NAT)	Membership expired
Mr. B.	R. M. Cochran	American (Southern)	Deceased
Mr. C.	Walter Bullock	NWA	Retired, living in Lakeville, Minn.
Mr. D.	Hal George	T&WA	Deceased
Mr. E.	Marion Sterling	United (NAT)	Membership expired
Mr. F.	Frank Ormsbee	PAA	Deceased
Mr. G.	W. A. Hallgren	American (Universal)	Deceased
Mr. H.	M. D. Ator	American (Interstate)	Retired, address unknown
Mr. I.	James Burns	American (Southern)	Retired, Smyrna, Ga.
Mr. J.	John Pricer	American (Interstate)	Deceased
Mr. K.	David L. Behncke	United (Boeing)	Deceased
Mr. L.	R. L. Dobie	United (NAT)	Deceased

Code	Name	Airline (Division)	Current Status (1967)
Mr. M.	Usher Rousch	American (Interstate)	Deceased
Mr. N.	Ray Little	United (Boeing)	Deceased
Mr. O.	Ed Garbutt	United (Varney)	Deceased
Mr. P.	Reuben Wagner	United (Boeing)	Retired, address unknown
Mr. Q.	Ralph Johnson	United (Boeing)	Retired address unknown
Mr. R.	Howard Fey	United (Varney)	Deceased
Mr. S.	Homer F. Cole	NWA	Retired, Falls Church, Va.
Mr. T.	John Huber	Trans-American	Retired, Bethesda, Md.
Mr. U.	V. E. Treat	Eastern	Membership expired
Mr. V.	George Douglass	United (Varney)	Retired, San Francisco, Calif.
Mr. W.	Glenn T. Fields	American (Embry-Riddle)	Deceased
Mr. X.	G. E. Thomas	Eastern	Resigned membership

43. "Stenographic Report of Excerpts from the Proceedings of the Organizational Meeting of the Air Line Pilots Association, International, Held at the Morrison Hotel, Chicago, Illinois," Monday, July 27, 1931," p. 4.

44. *Ibid.*, p. 5.

45. *Ibid.*, p. 6.

46. *Ibid.*, pp 43–44; ALPA, *Proceedings of the 1942 Convention,* pp. 102–104. Years later, when Behncke was trying the "labor statesman" role temporarily, he secured the repeal of the racial restriction on membership. But he did so not because of any real concern with racial equality, but because he did not want to be embarrassed by the NAACP in Washington. The issue came up briefly at the 1938 convention, but the delegates were unwilling to remove the obnoxious clause, and Behncke, although

he favored elimination of the clause for tactical reasons, failed to exert real pressure (ALPA, *Proceedings of the 1938 Convention*, pp. 152–154). When he finally did get the racial restriction deleted from the by-laws in 1942, he made no secret of the fact that he believed ALPA would never have Negro members. "We all have our feelings about the colored race, and in drawing the line where colored people are concerned," he told the delegates. "Usually this is a question on which the least said the better. The point we wish to bring out is that the above quoted section is like waving a red flag about *something that should be understood without being mentioned*" (emphasis supplied). Exclusion on the local level would prevent Negroes from joining, he pointed out, and it would all be very subtle but none the less effective.

Of course it would be a bit far-fetched to say that ALPA's racial policy for the first ten years of its life accounts for the dearth of Negro airline pilots today. Lack of access to the special training which airline piloting requires, rather than the institutional racism of a single labor union, is the specific reason few American blacks have entered the profession. The more compelling explanation for the operating companies' failure to hire blacks lies in the pervasive racism of our entire society. Famed criminal lawyer F. Lee Bailey, in a nationwide telecast on NBC in February 1970, declared that there was a definite "psychological factor" which made whites feel uncomfortable when a black pilot was at the controls of an airliner. As a former Marine Aviator who now owns and flies his own jet, Bailey is committed to do something to increase the number of blacks working as airline pilots from the current fifty to a figure more closely approximating their percentage representation of the American population. He has established a "black pilot training foundation" to this end, but it seems unlikely that there will be any significant increase in the number of Negro airline pilots, given today's extremely tight pilot job market.

But ALPA's part in this sorry story aside, the operating companies, when qualified Negro pilots began to present themselves after World War II, fought with every legal tool available to avoid hiring them. Airline managers were not above arguing that white pilots would not work with black pilots, but it seems that the subtle "psychological factor" induced by rascist attitudes and exacerbated by white passengers' normal fear of flying dominated their thinking. Only after the U.S. Supreme Court ordered it to do so in 1965 did a regularly scheduled domestic passenger airline hire a Negro. Neither the union nor the industry has gained much credit in this area. Both have exhibited the same failures of mind and heart which have characterized other major industries, and especially the highly skilled craft unions. See *Time,* 81 (May 3, 1963), 24; *Ebony,* 21 (November 1965), 112–114.

47. ALPA, "Stenographic Report of Excerpts from the Proceedings of the Organizational Meeting," pp. 6–7.

48. *Ibid.,* p. 18.

49. *Ibid.,* pp. 14–16.

50. *Ibid.,* p. 19.

51. *Ibid.,* pp. 20–23.

52. *Ibid.,* pp. 51–69. Indicative of the lax and nebulous standards which prevailed in pilot licensing at the time, the key men devoted considerable time to a discussion of whether or not a prospective member should hold a certain kind of license from the Department of Commerce. Many pilots held equivalent licenses from the Federation Aeronautique Internationale (FAI), and so the delegates decided that the final criterion for membership would simply be that a man was a working airline pilot. Several of the pilots insisted that once ALPA was strong enough, it would become the primary licensing and examining agency in the country, at least for airline pilots. The Department of Commerce supposedly licensed pilots, but the process was rather haphazard. Walter Bullock stated of the late 1920's and early 1930's: "The Department of Commerce Inspector just came around from area to area licensing pilots, gave you a little check ride, and if you wanted to be a mech he gave you a little test."

53. ALPA, *Proceedings of the 1932 Convention,* pp. 13–14. Behncke later told the 1932 convention the gist of his argument. The transcript of the 1932 convention is the only reliable source, since the affiliation argument is off the record in the organizational meeting, except for a few remarks. Apparently Barker was so caught up in the excitement that he simply forgot to take notes, even when the key men were not formally off the record. There are some sketchy notes, but they are not verbatim.

54. *Ibid.,* pp. 36–37.

55. ALPA, "Stenographic Report of Excerpts from the Proceedings of the Organizational Meeting," pp. 25–42.

56. Lloyd Ulman, *The Rise of the National Trade Union: The Development and Significance of Its Structure, Governing Institutions, and Economic Policies* (Cambridge, Mass.: Harvard University Press, 1955), p. 17; Henry C. Bates, *Bricklayers' Century of Craftsmanship: A History of the Bricklayers, Masons, and Plasterers International Union of America* (Washington: 1955), pp. 1–34; Robert D. Leiter, *The Teamsters Union: A Study of Its Economic Impact* (New York: Bookman Associates, 1957), pp. 17–27.

57. Reed C. Richardson, *The Locomotive Engineers, 1863–1963: A Century of Railway Labor Relations and Work Rules,* Bureau of Industrial Relations, Graduate School of Business Administration, University of Michigan (Ann Arbor: University of Michigan Press, 1963), pp. 101–108.

58. David Brody, *The Butcher Workmen: A Study of Unionization,* Wertheim Publications in Industrial Relations (Cambridge, Mass.: Harvard University Press, 1964), pp. ix–xi, 13–33; Robert R. R. Brooks, *When Labor Organizes* (New Haven: Yale University Press, 1937), pp. 1–15; Robert D. Leiter, *The Musicians and Petrillo* (New York: Bookman Associates, 1953), pp. 3–16; Harvey J. Clermont, *Organizing the Insurance Worker: A History of the Labor Union of Insurance Employees* (Washington: Catholic University of America Press, 1966), pp. 2–4; Adolf Sturmthal, ed., *White Collar Trade Unions* (Urbana, Ill,: University of Illinois Press, 1966), pp. 305–364.

5. Internal Problems of Leadership and Policy

1. *The Air Line Pilot* (Apr. 5, 1932), p. 2.

2. Minutes of the meeting of Feb. 22, 1933, ALPA, Central Executive Council.

3. Smith, *Airways,* pp. 386–387.

4. ALPA, "Organizational Log of the Air Line Pilots Association," Aug. 20, 1931, p. 6.

5. Rickenbacker, *Rickenbacker,* pp. 178–185, 189.

6. Cole interview. Homer Cole had little respect for Rickenbacker. As a combat pilot in World War I himself, he knew that luck was the largest part of a pilot's success in fighting, and Rickenbacker's swashbuckling irritated him.

7. ALPA, *Proceedings of the 1932 Convention,* p. 39.

8. Thomas to Behncke, Sept. 23, 1931.

9. Brandon to Behncke, Sept. 18, 1931.

10. Roush to Behncke, Sept. 19, 1931.

11. Behncke to Brandon, Sept. 19, 1931.

12. Behncke to Roush, Sept. 19, 1931.

13. "Pilots Are People," *Aviation*, 34 (December 1935), 29. Commenting on recent articles in the *Saturday Evening Post* and *Esquire* about airline pilots, *Aviation* declared: "If any widespread misconception needed debunking badly, it was that hangover from the 1920's that pictured all pilots as dashing heroes with . . . a flair for recklessness . . . But there is a definite psychological value in getting across to the public that pilots, besides being highly trained professional men, are just ordinary men like themselves . . . The picture of an air line pilot returning to his home in the suburbs, picking up a snack from the family ice box, and going out for a quiet evening of bridge at 1/10 of a cent a point with his bank clerk neighbor, has in it elements that engender confidence."

14. Brown to Behncke, Sept. 19, 1931, 3:00 P.M.

15. Brown to Behncke, Sept. 19, 1931, 10:00 P.M.

16. Brown to Behncke, Sept. 20, 1931.

17. Behncke to Huber, Cole, Roush, Thomas, and Brandon, Sept. 21. 1931.

18. Thomas to Behncke, Sept. 21, 1931.

19. Behncke to Thomas, Sept. 21, 1931.

20. Behncke to James Burns, Sept. 21, 1931. Behncke declared that Brown had "spilt beans regarding AFofL. Certain others being briefed fully this time. Opinion is this is necessary as you instructed to show affiliation brief to those whom you consider trustworthy and vitally necessary . . . Am leaving this very touchy part of this proposition to you."

21. Behncke to Burns, Sept. 22, 1931.

22. Burns to Behncke, Sept. 22, 1931.

23. Brown to Behncke, Sept. 24, 1931.

24. *Ibid.* (If one can believe Brown.)

25. ALPA, *Proceedings of the 1932 Convention*, p. 39.

26. Minutes of the meeting of July 19, 1933, ALPA, Central Executive Council.

27. ALPA, *Proceedings of the 1932 Convention*, pp. 105–106.

28. Karl M. Ruppenthal, "Revolution in the Air Line Pilots Association," Ph.D. diss., Stanford University, 1959, p. 38. When Behncke was ousted from the leadership of ALPA, one of the

pilots' chief complaints was that he spent too much time on *The Air Line Pilot*. Very early, President Behncke decided Editor Behncke was the only one who could handle the newspaper, and it was his major preoccupation for many years. Behncke's journalism also irritated many pilots. As Ruppenthal put it, *The Air Line Pilot* "was frequently late in making its appearance. The May issue might, for instance, not appear until August. Thus Behncke was able to make good use of hindsight in predicting what might happen in June. Editor Behncke frequently gave sweeping commendations to President Behncke for a speech or other performance." The 1932 convention also saw considerable argument over Behncke's control of the newspaper ALPA, *Proceedings of the 1932 Convention,* pp. 690–691.

29. ALPA, *Proceedings of the 1932 Convention,* pp. 53–55.

30. *New York Times,* Nov. 1, 1931, Sec. 20, p. 7.

31. ALPA, *Proceedings of the 1932 Convention,* pp. 156–160.

32. Minutes of the meeting of Feb. 22, 1933, ALPA, Central Executive Council. Behncke presided over the first formal meeting of the council. Also present were: Sam Holbrook, First Vice-President; H. L. Knoop, proxy for J. L. Brandon of NAT; T. J. Lee, proxy for Huber; E. L. Preston, also a proxy for Huber (?); F. F. Church, proxy for Wilkins of T&WA; and Richard C. McGuire, proxy for J. A. Hamer, Vice-President for American. Hence, even the first formal meeting had a helter-skelter quality about it.

33. ALPA, "Confidential Report: Details of the Ormsbee-Barker Trouble Resulting in Their Release by a Vote of the Officers, to be Read by Chairmen of All Councils," undated mimeographed pamphlet.

34. ALPA, *Proceedings of the 1932 Convention,* pp. 129–138.

35. Ruppenthal, "Revolution in the Air Line Pilots Association," p. 34.

36. *The Air Line Pilot* (June 15, 1932), p. 1.

37. Minutes of the meeting of May 4, 1933, ALPA, Central Executive Council. During this meeting, Behncke criticized Ormsbee for failing to organize the T&WA pilots! He would seize on almost anything to belittle Ormsbee, and it apparently never occurred to him that nobody, not Hal George, nor Behncke, nor any subsequent ALPA organizer, had any success with T&WA until Congressional pressure forced that line's management to adopt a more conciliatory attitude.

38. ALPA, "Confidential Report: Details of the Ormsbee-Barker Trouble."

39. Behncke to Cole and Huber, Aug. 18, 1932. Behncke fastened the major blame for the "conspiracy" on Barker, but he declared that since Ormsbee was to replace him as ALPA President, he was equally culpable. "As far as Mr. Ormsbee is concerned, the party to whom Mr. Barker's letters were directed," Behncke wrote, "he is at fault because he did not make the matter known . . . However, at least he did not follow out the suggestion for conspiracy." Obviously, Behncke could only weakly implicate Ormsbee in Barker's and Sterling's efforts to curb his control.

40. Stuart Hayden to Central Executive Council, Sept. 1, 1932, office memorandum.

41. Ormsbee to Central Executive Council, Sept. 2, 1932.

42. Behncke, Cole, and Huber, to Ormsbee, Sept. 8, 1932.

43. ALPA, "Confidential Report: Details of the Ormsbee-Barker Trouble."

44. Ralph A. Reed to National Headquarters, Oct. 15, 1932.

45. Ralph A. Reed to Behncke, Oct. 15, 1932.

46. Huber to Behncke, Sept. 22, 1932.

47. "New York Aviators Support La Guardia," *Aerial Age Weekly*, 14 (Sept. 19, 1921), 29; Fiorello H. La Guardia, *The Making of an Insurgent: An Autobiography, 1892–1919* (New York: Macmillan, 1955), pp. 50 ff., pictures La Guardia attired in civilian clothes but with the miniature aviator's wings always in his lapel.

48. ALPA, *Proceedings of the 1932 Convention*, pp. 138–148; "Addenda, Hearing. . . ."

49. *The Air Line Pilot* (December 1932), pp. 1–5.

50. Minutes of the meetings of Apr. 7, 1933, and May 4, 1933, ALPA, Central Executive Council.

51. ALPA, Inactive Personnel Files.

6. The Century Strike

1. ALPA, *Proceedings of the 1932 Convention*, pp. 55–56; O. O. Westergaard & Associates, Public Accountants, to Behncke, Aug. 1, 1932. Behncke was deliberately vague about the total number of members, but after an audit he had prepared for the 1932 convention, the books revealed that the total receipts for the year from initiation fees and dues was $36,941.42. Assuming that

an average pilot paid $100 per year, the membership would thus have totaled between 300 and 400 pilots.

2. ALPA, *Proceedings of the 1932 Convention,* pp. 39–40. Behncke's stoutest defense of the affiliation with the AFofL came early in the 1932 convention when he discussed the Pan American yellow-dog contract. "This was the first chance we had to bring into play the power of the AFofL," he said. "We had exerted every bit of power within our organization and the result was that we were made a laughing stock by the officials of this company. Rather than cooperate with us they brought in a 'yellow dog contract' and put it before their pilots and told them to either sign it or resign from ALPA or resign from Pan American [*sic*]. We . . . called in the AFofL and three days later I was summoned to Washington to participate in a three way conference between the Pan American officials, the AFofL, and our Association for the purpose of settling the trouble." Owing to the power of the AFofL, Behncke maintained, "they withdrew the yellow dog contract and said there would be no further opposition to this Association and that their pilots had a free hand to go ahead and join this Association without any further antagonism."

3. *The Air Line Pilot* (Apr. 5, 1932), p. 1, for the best example.

4. Freudenthal, *The Aviation Business,* pp. 208–209.

5. Hugh Knowlton, *Air Transportation in the United States: Its Growth as a Business* (Chicago: University of Chicago Press, 1941), p. 5.

6. Freudenthal, *The Aviation Business,* p. 106.

7. Smith, *Airways,* pp. 199–201.

8. U.S., Bureau of Labor Statistics, "Wage and Hours of Labor in Air Transport, 1931," *Monthly Labor Review,* 35 (August 1932), 339–348. Although the report was not published until August 1932, its content was known late in 1931.

9. "Airlines and Pilots: The Pilot's Status and His Wage," *Aviation,* 31 (May 1932), 211–212.

10. Smith, *Airways,* pp. 199–200.

11. "Cord Corporation Acquiring Stinson," *Aviation,* 27 (Oct. 12, 1929), 756.

12. "E. L. Cord States His Aviation Views," *Aviation,* 28 (Mar. 22, 1930), 618.

13. Smith, *Airways,* p. 199.

14. *New York Times,* Feb. 10, 1932, p. 2.

222 / *Notes to Pages 99–101*

15. "Century Offers Frequent Trips," *Aviation*, 30 (May 1931), 265. Century offered three round trips daily between Chicago and St. Louis, with stops at Springfield, to begin, and shortly afterward it inaugurated a similar service between Chicago and Cleveland, with stops at Toledo. Cord averaged about 80 percent load factor, which is respectable even by modern standards.

16. "Luddington Line Reports a Profit," *Aviation*, 30 (November 1931), 619. Cord controlled, but did not operate, Luddington Air Lines, a nonair-mail carrier offering service between New York and Washington with stops at Philadelphia and Baltimore. Luddington was able to operate successfully for a number of years without a mail subsidy because of the density of traffic on the eastern seaboard. Luddington too paid low pilot salaries, and Cord probably derived his basic ideas about air transportation from observing its operations. Luddington eventually merged with Eastern.

17. "Century Extends," *Aviation*, 31 (January 1932), 33. American's argument before the Arizona Railroad Commission was that since it had pioneered the run between Los Angeles and Dallas via Phoenix, it was unfair for Cord to violate its rights. This business of the pioneer's right to the profits from a route it developed was a philosophy which exerted considerable influence on later federal legislation. Cord was undeterred, however. Between Los Angeles and San Francisco, Varney Air Lines was forced to reduce its fare from $25 to $18.95. Varney Air Lines was a second effort by one of the pioneer developers of airlines, who had sold his first line of that name to United and was operating without a subsidy also. Varney operated more expensive but faster Lockheed Orions at a loss in the competition with Cord's roomier but slower Stinson trimotors. It appeared that Cord was operating at a loss between Los Angeles and San Francisco also, but he was probably figuring on recovering his losses by raising prices as soon as his competitors quit.

18. "Fares Generously Cut," *Aviation*, 31 (February 1932), 85. During this period United cut its New York to San Francisco fare from $200 to $160, and the general rate slicing cut all fares from 10 to 20 percent.

19. *New York Times*, Feb. 10, 1932, p. 2.

20. ALPA, *Proceedings of the 1932 Convention*, pp. 40–41.

21. William Green to Behncke, Feb. 12, 1932.

22. ALPA, *Proceedings of the 1932 Convention,* pp. 217–221.

23. John Huber to All Members, Sept. 1, 1932. Huber as Treasurer had a tough time keeping the pilots paying their dues and strike fund assessment simultaneously. Many members thought their dues should cover the strike assessment, and while the pilots contributed nearly $5,000 in strike fund assessments, Behncke disbursed more than that amount to the strikers from the union's regular treasury. By the fall of 1932, ALPA's financial condition was desperate.

24. *New York Times,* Feb. 14, 1932, p. 22.

25. *Ibid.,* Feb. 15, 1932, p. 35.

26. ALPA, *Proceedings of the 1932 Convention,* pp. 68–71. Through the years ALPA maintained an extremely hard line toward scabs. In fact, President William Green of the AFofL counseled Behncke to go easier, but his stubbornness was clearly revealed in his refusal to do so. There was, of course, the extenuating fact that ALPA was in a better position to enforce its sanctions against scabs than other unions, owing to its relatively tight-knit structure. Still, Behncke's bulldog nature probably had something to do with the stridency of his denunciations of strikebreakers, as the following quotation from an *Air Line Pilot* (Apr. 20, 1932, p. 2) editorial reveals: "The vilest enemy of the ALPA is a SCAB! The vilest enemy of the morale of aeronautics is a SCAB! The vilest enemy to the safety, surety, and confidence for the future of air commerce is a SCAB! Those scabs recently let out by Mr. Cord . . . will now become a greater problem than when they worked for him. These scabs will start floating around the country making every possible effort to secure employment. It will be our duty to see that any one of these weak humans . . . gain [sic] no admittance to the ranks of aeronautical professions. Their plea may be that of NEED! Match that with the fact that it took GUTS, FAITH, and SACRIFICE for the CENTURY PILOTS to FIGHT AGAINST something which they knew in their hearts was wrong!"

27. ALPA, *Proceedings of the 1932 Convention,* pp. 41–42.

28. Freudenthal, *The Aviation Business,* p. 108.

29. ALPA, *Proceedings of the 1932 Convention,* pp. 33–36.

30. *New York Times,* Feb. 14, 1932, p. 27.

31. U.S., *Congressional Record,* 72nd Cong., 1st Sess., 1932, LXXV, Part 4, p. 4260.

32. *Ibid.*, Part 5, pp. 4946–4948.

33. ALPA, *Proceedings of the 1932 Convention*, pp. 73–74. The telegram was quoted verbatim during the convention.

34. *Ibid.*, p. 39; *The Aeronautical News* (October 1932), p. 1. In a box outlined in black ink on the front page, the editors of the newspaper asked the delegates the following questions:

1. How much money is coming and has gone into the treasury of ALPA?
2. Who is getting it?
3. How many more pilots are working because of the ALPA?
4. How many more pilots are *not* working because of the ALPA?
5. Why should any pilot be affiliated with the AFofL?
6. How can the AFofL improve conditions in the aeronautical industry?
7. Exactly what has the AFofL hookup done for and to you?
8. Why is the ALPA now being termed a "racket"?
9. Will you as members of ALPA be forced into contact and association with labor racketeers?
10. Why should not the American Medical Association or other high class professional men be affiliated with the AFofL?
11. How does the general public regard professional men who would affiliate themselves with the AFofL?

The editors of the newspaper hoped these questions would move the delegates to the 1932 convention to oust Behncke and terminate the affiliation. The lead editorial on page one asked why "pilots, clean cut gentlemen of education and purpose who until this AFofL hookup have been on an equal with all professional men, will make themselves part of a racket. Must we go from this to rubbing elbows with labor troubles? This newspaper certainly hopes not! The eyes of all pilots and in fact the eyes of this industry will be watching the election of new officers of the ALPA."

35. U.S., *Congressional Record*, 72nd Cong., 1st Sess., 1932, LXXV, Part 5, pp. 4946–4948.

36. *Ibid.*, pp. 4941–4942. Some idea of the extent to which most people believed that the pilot was a superman is reflected in La Guardia's description of pilots as being superior even to sea captains, an analogy which always flattered them before. He

praised the pilots as being mentally the equal of sea captains, but physically superior. Not only were they "expert in a dozen fields," La Guardia insisted, but they were "expert in judgment and reflexes" as well.

37. U.S. Congress, House Committee on the Post Office and Post Roads, *Hearings on H. R. 8390 and H. R. 9841, The Air Mail,* 72nd Cong., 1st Sess., 1932, pp. 20–155. Ormsbee was effective, and also rather devious, in refuting Manning's contention that pilot-employer relations were poor throughout the industry, and not just on Century. "We get along splendidly with most of them," Ormsbee declared. "We have no disagreements or arguments with them that have not been satisfactorily settled." Needless to say, this statement considerably distorted the conditions which then prevailed on Eastern and T&WA, although it was fairly accurate regarding American and United.

38. *New York Times,* Mar. 9, 1932, p. 5; ALPA, *Proceedings of the 1934 Convention,* pp. 556–591. One of the Century strike-breakers who was aboard the flight later applied for admission to ALPA, and during the 1934 convention he described the crash in an unsuccessful attempt to gain sympathy. "There were five of us who had to make five landings apiece at St. Louis and five apiece at Springfield, and fly the beams into Chicago before daylight. You can appreciate that that was quite a chore . . . Our ship did not come in until after one o'clock in the morning and we still had that to do. Consequently we were coming in low, setting the ship down and going around again before stopping." The aircraft struck a farmer's unlighted windmill, but the haste of training was the precipitating factor.

39. "Air Mail Hearings," *Aviation,* 31 (April 1932), 188; Smith, *Airways,* p. 200.

40. ALPA, *Proceedings of the 1944 Convention,* p. 37. At least Behncke said so, but one must keep in mind his tendency to embroider events as time passed.

41. "American Airways Moves Again," *Aviation,* 32 (February 1933), 54.

42. "Mr. Cord Capitulates," *Aviation,* 31 (May 1932), 231; Smith, *Airways,* pp. 200–201; Freudenthal, *The Aviation Business,* pp. 207–212; ALPA, *Proceedings of the 1943 Convention,* p. 40. Indicative of Cord's continuing power at American is the following story which Behncke told the tenth anniversary convention of

ALPA: "Not so long ago I was in [C. R.] Smith's office up at La
Guardia . . . Little things happen sometimes that we don't forget
. . . This day, when I was in his office, his secretary came into his
office and said, rather flustered, 'Mr. Smith, Mr. Cord is on the
phone and he wants to talk to you right away.' Out went Mr. Smith!
Prior to that incident, he had told his secretary to cut out all telephone calls."

43. Minutes of the meeting of Aug. 18, 1936, ALPA, Central
Executive Council. Many of the Century strikers never bothered
to pay ALPA back for the "loans," because they regarded them as
legitimate payments for bearing the brunt of the fight. This attitude irritated Behncke, and he actually considered expelling
some of them from ALPA because of it!

44. ALPA, *Proceedings of the 1932 Convention*, pp. 66–67.

45. ALPA, *Proceedings of the 1934 Convention*, pp. 444–445.

46. Behncke to Hugh L. Smith, Operations Manager, American
Airways, July 17, 1932.

47. ALPA, *Proceedings of the 1936 Convention*, pp. 569–571.

48. Freudenthal, *The Aviation Business*, p. 207, fn. quotation.

49. U.S., *Congressional Record*, 72nd Cong., 1st Sess., 1932,
LXXV, Part 5, pp. 4943–4944.

50. *New York Times*, Feb. 21, 1932, p. 10.

51. ALPA, *Proceedings of the 1932 Convention*, p. 73. And in
any case, Behncke never suggested that the Century Pacific pilots
were violating the code by not joining their brother Century pilots
on strike. He toyed with the idea briefly, but since the two operations were separate, and since the Century Pacific pilots agreed
in the beginning to work for low wages, he abandoned it.

52. *The Air Line Pilot* (Apr. 5, 1932), p. 1.

53. *Ibid.* (Apr. 20, 1932), p. 3.

7. The New Deal

1. Smith, *Airways*, p. 224; Knowlton, *Air Transportation in
the United States*, p. 9; Freudenthal, *The Aviation Business*, p.311.

2. "What's What Among Pilots!" *Aviation*, 32 (March 1933), 91.

3. *New York Times*, Feb. 11, 1933, Sec. 7, p. 10.

4. *The Air Line Pilot* (January 1933), p. 1.

5. James M. Mead to Behncke, Jan. 10, 1933.

6. *The Air Line Pilot* (February 1933), p. 8.

7. Milton Derber, "Growth and Expansion," *Labor and the New Deal,* ed. Milton Derber and Edwin Young (Madison: University of Wisconsin Press, 1957), pp. 3–8.

8. ALPA, *Proceedings of the 1932 Convention,* pp. 50, 127–129.

9. Behncke to All Local Chairmen, Sept. 2, 1932.

10. ALPA, *Proceedings of the 1932 Convention,* pp. 84–94.

11. Charles Frederick Roos, *N.R.A. Economic Planning,* Cowles Commission for Research in Economics, No. 2 (Bloomington, Ind.: Principia Press, 1937), pp. 28–32.

12. ALPA, *Proceedings of the 1932 Convention,* pp. 168–190.

13. Frederick C. Warnshuis, Chairman, Aeromedical Association, to Behncke, Sept. 22, 1932.

14. ALPA, *Proceedings of the 1932 Convention,* pp. 168–190.

15. *The Air Line Pilot* (February 1933), p. 1.

16. ALPA, *Proceedings of the 1934 Convention,* pp. 27–28.

17. *New York Times,* Feb. 26, 1933, p. 23.

18. *The Air Line Pilot* (February 1933), p. 6.

19. Charles A. Madison, *American Labor Leaders: Personalities and Forces in the Labor Movement* (New York: Frederick Ungar, 1950), pp. 108–135.

20. Green to Behncke, Mar. 2, 1933.

21. *The Air Line Pilot* (March 1933), p. 1.

22. Arthur M. Schlesinger, Jr., *The Coming of the New Deal,* Vol. II: *The Age of Roosevelt* (Boston: Houghton Mifflin, 1958), pp. 87–102.

23. Roos, *N.R.A. Economic Planning,* Appendix II, p. 537.

24. ALPA, *Proceedings of the 1934 Convention,* pp. 21–27.

25. Schlesinger, *The Coming of the New Deal,* Vol. II, pp. 108–109; Roos, *N.R.A. Economic Planning,* pp. 55–82.

26. Schlesinger, *The Coming of the New Deal,* Vol. II, pp. 107–108.

27. Minutes of the meeting of June 15, 1933, Central Executive Council, ALPA.

28. Minutes of the meeting of July 6, 1933, Central Executive Council, ALPA.

29. *The Air Line Pilot* (July 1933), p. 1.

30. Wallace S. Dawson to Behncke, Sept. 4, 1933.

31. *The Air Line Pilot* (July 1933), p. 1.

32. *Ibid.* (August 1933), p. 6.

33. Minutes of the meeting of Aug. 3, 1933, Central Executive

Council, ALPA; Schlesinger, *The Coming of the New Deal*, Vol.
II, p. 126; Behncke to Hugh S. Johnson, Aug. 1, 1933.

34. Green to Behncke, Aug. 15, 1933.

35. ALPA, *Proceedings of the 1934 Convention*, pp. 61–64.

36. Minutes of the meeting of Aug. 15, 1933, Central Executive
Council, ALPA.

37. Minutes of the meeting of Aug. 23, 1933, Central Executive
Council, ALPA: *The Air Line Pilot* (September 1933), p. 1.

38. ALPA, *Proceedings of the 1932 Convention*, pp. 21–22;
The Air Line Pilot (September 1933), p. 1. The pilot committee
which attended the code hearings was composed of E. Hamilton
Lee (United), Howard E. Hall (T&WA), Walter J. Hunter (Ameri-
can), Eugene Brown (Eastern), Sam Carson (Kohler), John H. Neale
(Pacific), Mal B. Freeburg (Northwest), and John H. Tilton and
C. M. Drayton (Pan American).

39 "Code for the Air Transport Industry," *Aviation*, 32 (September 1933), 290–291.

40. "Coding Air Transport," *Aviation*, 32 (October 1933), 311–
312.

41. *New York Times*, Aug. 28, 1933, p. 12.

42. *Ibid.*, Aug. 29, 1933, p. 16.

43. "Coding Air Transport," *Aviation*, 32 (October 1933), 311–
312; minutes of the meeting of Oct. 10, 1933, Central Executive
Council, ALPA.

44. ALPA, *Proceedings of the 1934 Convention*, pp. 24–26;
"Blue Eagle Takes Wing," *Aviation*, 32 (September 1933), 369–
370; *New York Times*, Sept. 12, 1933, p. 15. Muir signed the code
on Sept. 11 and passed it on to the White House for presidential
approval, which finally came on Nov. 20, 1933.

45. William Randolph Hearst to M. A. Roddy, Editor, *The
Air Line Pilot*, Dec. 8, 1933. In a letter to the nominal editor of the
union newspaper, Hearst expressed his admiration for the airline
pilots. He considered them a kind of ready reserve for the defense
of the country, since they would, in his opinion, need little or no
training before they started manning bombers. "The next war . . .
which God forbid, will be decided in the air," he said, "and some
of the brave men to whom this letter comes will determine the
decision. The nation owes them much now and may in the future
owe them many times more."

46. ALPA, *Proceedings of the 1942 Convention*, pp. 70–80;

ALPA, *Proceedings of the 1934 Convention,* p. 24.

47. ALPA, *Proceedings of the 1934 Convention,* pp. 27–28; *New York Times,* Sept. 22, 1933, p. 19. On Sept. 21, the "Big Five" finally issued a public statement declaring their intention to impose the new hourly pay system. Behncke knew about it early in September, however.

48. *New York Times,* Sept. 3, 1933, p. 7; minutes of the meeting of Oct. 10, 1933, Central Executive Council, ALPA.

49. *New York Times,* Sept. 22, 1933, p. 19; *The Air Line Pilot* (January 1934), p. 1; ALPA, *Proceedings of the 1934 Convention,* p. 76.

50. Behncke to W. M. Leiserson, Secretary, N.L.B., Sept. 20, 1933; "Truce," *Aviation,* 32 (September 1933), 297.

51. Schlesinger, *Coming of the New Deal,* Vol. II, pp. 146–147.

52. ALPA, *Proceedings of the 1934 Convention,* pp. 28–30.

53. *The Air Line Pilot* (October 1933), p. 1; minutes of the meeting of Oct. 10, 1933, Central Executive Council, ALPA.

54. *New York Times,* Sept. 3, 1933, Sec. 8, p. 7.

55. Roos, *N.R.A. Economic Planning,* pp. 33, 56–57, 221.

56. ALPA, *Proceedings of the 1934 Convention,* pp. 30–35.

57. *New York Times,* Sept. 27, 1933, p. 9; *ibid.,* Oct. 1, 1933, p. 27.

58. National Recovery Administration, National Labor Board, *In the Matter of the Hearing Between Representatives of the Air Line Pilots Association and Representatives of United Air Lines, American Airways, and North American Aviation Corporation* (abridged transcript in the ALPA archives).

59. *Ibid.*

60. *Ibid.*

61. *Ibid.;* ALPA, *Proceedings of the 1934 Convention,* pp. 37–40; *New York Times,* Oct. 3, 1933, p. 15; *ibid.,* Oct. 5, 1933, p. 1; *ibid.,* Oct. 6, 1933, p. 9; "Pilots' Debate," *Aviation,* 32 (November 1933), 354.

62. *New York Times,* Oct. 28, 1933, p. 18; *ibid.,* Oct. 29, 1933, p. 25.

63. ALPA, *Pilots' Final Brief Before a Fact Finding Committee Held by Judge Shientag, Chairman of the Committee Studying the Air Line Pilot Wage and Hour Question,* p. 1.

64. Reginald M. Cleveland, "Pilots' Pay Is Debated," New York Times, Nov. 5, 1933, Sec. 8, p. 7.

65. ALPA, *Proceedings of the 1934 Convention,* pp. 40–41.

66. *Ibid.*, pp. 41–43.

67. "Wages of Pilots," *Aviation*, 32 (December 1933), 382.

68. *Ibid.; New York Times*, Nov. 7, 1933, p. 24.

69. ALPA, *Proceedings of the 1934 Convention*, pp. 45–48; "Wages of Pilots," *Aviation*, 32 (December, 1933), 382.

70. "Wage Scale Arbitration," *Aviation*, 33 (January 1934), 26–27; ALPA, *Pilots' Report of a Conference Held at the Mayflower Hotel, December 15, 1933, Between the Pilots' Subcommittee and the Operators in Compliance with a Suggestion of the National Labor Board at the Hearing of December 14, 1933*. The Pilots present at the meeting were Behncke and Jack O'Brien for United, Eugene Brown for Eastern, Alexis Klotz for Western Air Express, and Clyde Holbrook for American. The officials representing the operators were W. A. Patterson for United, Harris M. "Pop" Hanshue for North American Aviation (which by this time controlled Eastern, T&WA, and Western), and Lester D. "Bing" Seymour for American.

71. "No Quarter in Wage War," *Aviation*, 33 (February 1934), 54–55; *The Air Line Pilot* (January 1934), p. 1; minutes of the meeting of Jan. 16, 1934, Central Executive Council, ALPA.

72. John M. Baitsell, *Airline Industrial Relations: Pilots and Flight Engineers* (Cambridge, Mass.: Harvard University Press, 1966), p. 32.

73. Mark L. Kahn, *Pay Practices for Flight Employees on U.S. Airlines* (University of Michigan–Wayne State University, Institute of Labor and Industrial Relations, No. 23, 1961), p. 12. Reprinted from U.S., President's Railroad Commission, *Report of the Presidential Railroad Commission*, Appendix, Vol. IV (Washington: U.S. Government Printing Office, 1962), pp. 1–38.

8. Victory in Washington

1. U.S., Department of Labor, Bureau of Labor Statistics, "Wages and Hours in Air Transport in 1933," *Monthly Labor Review*, 38 (March 1934), 647–665; "For Want of a Horsehoe Nail," *Aviation*, 32 (December 1933), 380.

2. Herbert Hoover, *The Memoirs of Herbert Hoover: The Cabinet and the Presidency, 1920–1923* (New York: Macmillan, 1952), pp. 132–135, 243–245; Schlesinger, *The Coming of the New Deal*, Vol. II, pp. 446–450; Smith, *Airways*, pp. 228–238.

3. Smith, *Airways,* pp. 239–251; Schlesinger, *The Coming of the New Deal,* Vol. II, pp. 450–451; "Air Mail Investigation," *Aviation,* 33 (March 1934), 91–92.

4. Minutes of the meeting of Jan. 10, 1934, Central Executive Council, ALPA.

5. *New York Times,* Feb. 11, 1934, p. 38; ALPA, *Proceedings of the 1934 Convention,* pp. 50–51.

6. Walter S. Ross, *The Last Hero: Charles A. Lindbergh* (New York: Harper & Row, 1968), pp. 254–260.

7. *The Air Line Pilot* (February 1934), p. 3.

8. Schlesinger, *The Coming of the New Deal,* Vol. II, p. 452.

9. Robert L. Scott, Jr., *Runway to the Sun* (New York: Charles Scribner's & Son, 1945), pp. 82–89.

10. "Mail Moratorium," *Aviation,* 33 (April 1934), 117–118; Smith, *Airways,* pp. 249–255; U.S., Federal Aviation Commission, *Report of the Federal Aviation Commission,* p. 4. The report declared that the Army's inability to fly the mail when its leaders said it could indicated "serious internal problems." To correct these problems, the commission urged that a high-level study of Army training practices and operations be undertaken.

11. Schlesinger, *The Coming of the New Deal,* Vol. II, pp. 452–455.

12. Harold L. Ickes, *The Secret Diary of Harold L. Ickes: The First 1000 Days, 1933–36* (New York: Simon & Schuster, 1953), pp. 146–147.

13. *New York Times,* Mar. 9, 1934, p. 1.

14. ALPA, *Proceedings of the 1934 Convention,* pp. 50–51.

15. "Reconstruction," *Aviation,* 33 (April 1934), 118.

16. Behncke to Roosevelt, Mar. 9, 1934.

17. ALPA, *Proceedings of the 1934 Convention,* pp. 51–53; *The Air Line Pilot* (April 1934), p. 2.

18. ALPA, *Proceedings of the 1934 Convention,* pp. 48–49; "Martial Mail," *Aviation,* 33 (March 1934), 92; U.S. Congress, House Committee on the Post Office and Post Roads, *Hearing on H. R. 73 and H. R. 8578 and Other Air Mail Bills,* 73rd Cong., 2nd Sess., 1934, p. 157.

19. Minutes of the meeting of Mar. 2, 1934, Central Executive Council, ALPA.

20. Minutes of the meeting of Mar. 8, 1934, Central Executive Council, ALPA.

21. Minutes of the meeting of Jan. 10, 1934, Central Executive Council, ALPA.

22. *The Air Line Pilot* (February 1934), p. 3.

23. Ross, *The Last Hero*, p. 90.

24. "The Army Flies the Mail," *Aviation,* 33 (March 1934), 114–115.

25. ALPA, *Proceedings of the 1934 Convention,* pp. 89–90.

26. Smith, *Airways,* pp. 278–279.

27. Schlesinger, *The Coming of the New Deal,* Vol. II, pp. 148–149.

28. ALPA, *Proceedings of the 1934 Convention,* pp. 48–49.

29. Smith, *Airways,* pp. 282–285; "A New Law for Air Transport," *Aviation,* 33 (July 1934), 205–207.

30. Minutes of the meeting of Mar. 30, 1934, Central Executive Council, ALPA. The council designated fifty pilots who, whenever they were temporarily in Washington, were to make themselves available for duty with Behncke.

31. ALPA, *Proceedings of the 1934 Convention,* pp. 50–51.

32. *Ibid.,* pp. 90–91; U.S., *Congressional Record,* 73rd Cong., 2nd Sess., 1934, LXXVIII, Part 8, p. 8550. Behncke's suspicious attitude toward Rickenbacker was shared by some Congressmen. Representative Michael J. Hart of Michigan criticized Rickenbacker's use of the term "legalized murder" in describing the Administration's use of the Army to fly the air mail. He wondered why the World War I ace would stoop to defending "these pirates" if he did not have some financial interest in doing so. He pointed out that Rickenbacker was not really a flier anymore, but rather a "promoter." He cited a long list of shaky business deals Rickenbacker had supported. "His name was attached to a car . . . The car and the company have both disappeared."

33. U.S. Congress, House Committee on the Post Office and Post Roads, *Hearing on H. R. 3 and H. R. 8578 and Other Air Mail Bills,* pp. 74–78, 157–158, 245–248, 270–273.

34. ALPA, *Proceedings of the 1934 Convention,* pp. 55–57.

35. *Ibid.,* p. 55; U.S., *Congressional Record,* 73rd Cong., 2nd Sess., 1934, LXXVIII, Part 4, pp. 4040–4042.

36. Behncke to McKellar, Mar. 8, 1934.

37. U.S. *Congressional Record,* 73rd Cong., 2nd Sess., 1934, LXXVIII, Part 6, p. 6724; *The Air Line Pilot* (March 1934), p. 1.

38. U.S., *Congressional Record,* 73rd Cong., 2nd Sess., 1934, LXXVIII, Part 7, pp. 6983, 7123–7124, 7622.

39. William Green to Behncke, Apr. 23, 1934.

40. *The Air Line Pilot* (March 1934), p. 3.

41. *Ibid.* (March 1935), p. 5.

42. "A New Law for Air Transport," *Aviation,* 33 (July 1934), 205–207; Smith, *Airways,* pp. 286–287.

9. Ceiling and Visibility Unlimited

1. *The Air Line Pilot* (June 1934), p. 1; ALPA, *Proceedings of the 1934 Convention,* pp. 29–30, 93, 178–180, 210, 331, 741–780, 892.

2. Jack Barbash, *Labor's Grass Roots: A Study of Local Unionism* (New York: Harper & Brothers, 1961), pp. 131–134.

3. ALPA, *Proceedings of the 1934 Convention,* pp. 142–150, 593–623, 920.

4. *Ibid.,* pp. 81, 287–296, 407, 987–989; ALPA, *Proceedings of the 1936 Convention,* pp. 129–136, 332–334, 374–375; Baitsell, *Airline Industrial Relations,* pp. 94–96.

5. Minutes of the meeting of Apr. 17, 1935, Central Executive Council, ALPA.

6. ALPA, *Proceedings of the 1934 Convention,* pp. 78–80, 261–274, 318–337, 346, 928.

7. ALPA, *Proceedings of the 1932 Convention,* p. 164.

8. Behncke to All Members, June 25, 1934; ALPA, *Proceedings of the 1934 Convention,* pp. 103–104; minutes of the meeting of Mar. 8, 1934, Central Executive Council, ALPA.

9. ALPA, *Proceedings of the 1934 Convention,* pp. 412–439; *The Air Line Pilot* (November 1934), p. 7. The other vice-presidents were: Audrey Durst, American; Roy Keeler, Pan American; James Ingram, American; Duncan McCallum, American; R. Lee Smith, Northwest; Ralph Johnson, United; Tom Hardin, American; Vernon Powers, Braniff; and Frank Andre, Eastern.

10. ALPA, *Proceedings of the 1934 Convention,* p. 230.

11. *Ibid.,* pp. 416–423.

12. ALPA, *Proceedings of the 1936 Convention,* p. 8; minutes of the meeting of Oct. 7, 1935, Central Executive Council, ALPA; Behncke to All Members, (notarized public statement dated Jan 1, 1936); Behncke to W. A. Patterson, Dec. 2, 1935; Wesley Price, "Labor's Biggest Wind," *Saturday Evening Post,* 220 (Aug. 2, 1947), 117–118. Needless to say, *The Air Line Pilot* described the crash in heroic terms, omitting the part about Behncke slipping

off the wing. It also quoted a telegram from William Randolph Hearst which concluded by saying: "This telegram should be signed by the whole American people" (*The Air Line Pilot* [December 1934], p. 1).

13. U.S., Federal Aviation Commission, *Report of the Federal Aviation Commission,* pp. 11, 13, 27–50; "Air Policy Board," *Aviation,* 33 (August 1934), 262; Smith, *Airways,* pp. 286–290.

14. Minutes of the meeting of Oct. 14, 1935, Central Executive Council, ALPA; ALPA, *Proceedings of the 1934 Convention,* pp. 371–373.

15. Smith, *Airways,* pp. 291–300.

16. ALPA, *Proceedings of the 1936 Convention,* pp. 3, 573–574.

17. Edward Hamilton to Representative D. C. Dobbins, Aug. 27, 1934.

18. D. C. Dobbins to Hamilton, Aug. 29, 1934.

19. James M. Mead to Behncke, Aug. 31, 1934.

20. *The Air Line Pilot* (September 1934), p. 1.

21. *Ibid.,* p. 3; *The Air Line Pilot* (December 1934), p. 1; *New York Times,* Oct. 17, 1934, p. 20; *ibid.,* Dec. 16, 1934, p. 27; "Wages and Rates," *Aviation,* 33 (November 1934), 370; "The Transport Month," *Aviation,* 35 (March 1936), 94.

22. *The Air Line Pilot* (February 1935), p. 1; ALPA, *Proceedings of the 1936 Convention,* pp. 575–578.

23. Smith, *Airways,* pp. 288–290; ALPA, *Proceedings of the 1938 Convention,* pp. 81–82; minutes of the meeting of Mar. 8, 1935, Central Executive Council, ALPA; *The Air Line Pilot* (September 1934), p. 1.

24. U.S., *Congressional Record,* 74th Cong., 2nd Sess., 1936, LXXX, Part 10, pp. 10349–10359 (Senate Report No. 2455); "Tragedy in Missouri," *Aviation,* 34 (June 1935), 56–58.

25. ALPA, *Proceedings of the 1932 Convention,* pp. 121–122.

26. "Commerce Department Crash Findings to Senate," *Aviation,* 27 (Nov. 9, 1929), 949.

27. *The Air Line Pilot* (January 1933), p. 2.

28. U.S., Federal Aviation Commission, *Report of the Federal Aviation Commission,* pp. 27–50; *The Air Line Pilot* (November 1934), p. 6; U.S., *Congressional Record,* 74th Cong., 2nd Sess., 1936, LXXX, Part 10, pp. 10354–10355.

29. Irving Bernstein, *The Lean Years: A History of the American*

Worker 1920–1933 (Boston: Houghton Mifflin, 1961), pp. 215–220; Gerald G. Eggert, *Railroad Labor Disputes: The Beginning of Federal Strike Policy* (Ann Arbor: University of Michigan Press, 1967), *passim;* see also Robert H. Zieger, *Republicans and Labor: 1919–1929* (Lexington: University of Kentucky Press, 1969), pp. 190–215, for a fine analysis of the political background of the 1926 law's passage.

30. U.S. *Congressional Record,* 72nd Cong., 1st Sess., 1932, LXXV, Part 7, p. 7344; A. O. Wharton, President of the International Association of Machinists and member of the Executive Council of the AFofL, to Behncke, July 10, 1932. The energetic Ormsbee had also won the approval of the Association of Railway Labor Executives for the amendment. Wharton had only praise for Ormsbee, and this fact alone may have been enough to light the initial fires of jealousy in Behncke.

31. ALPA, *Proceedings of the 1932 Convention,* pp. 49–50.

32. ALPA, *Proceedings of the 1936 Convention,* pp. 17–18, 33–36; *The Air Line Pilot* (May 1935), p. 1; ibid. (June 1, 1932), p. 1.

33. ALPA, *Proceedings of the 1938 Convention,* p. 125.

34. U.S. Congress, House Committee on the Post Office and Post Roads, *Hearings on H. Res. 344, A Resolution for the Investigation of the Air Mail Contractors from the Standpoint of Safety and for Other Purposes,* 74th Cong., 2nd Sess., 1936, pp. 132–133; U.S. Congress, Senate Committee on Interstate Commerce, *Hearing Before a Subcommittee of the Committee on Interstate Commerce on S2996, A Bill to Amend the Railway Labor Act,* 74th Cong., 1st Sess., 1935, pp. 4–29.

35. U.S., *Congressional Record,* 74th Cong., 1st Sess., 1935, LXXVIX, Part 5, p. 4900, Part 9, pp. 9414, 10058; *ibid.,* 74th Cong., 2nd Sess., 1936, LXXX, Part 5, pp. 5034–5040.

36. U.S., Bureau of Labor Statistics, *Monthly Labor Review,* 43 (August 1936), 373–380.

37. Baitsell, *Airline Industrial Relations,* p. 33.

38. ALPA, *Proceedings of the 1936 Convention,* p. 522; minutes of the meeting of May 15, 1936, Central Executive Council, ALPA. Ironically, one reason for the long delay in making a direct employment agreement with an operating company was that Behncke feared he had outsmarted himself in seeking to amend the Railway Labor Act. As he later explained to the Senate Interstate Commerce Subcommittee, he was reluctant to sign an employment agree-

ment until after the pilot provisions of the Air Mail Act of 1934 had been incorporated in permanent legislation because he feared that the courts might rule that the terms agreed upon in the contract superseded the protective provisions in law. Under the Railway Labor Act, Behncke felt, the operators could break the contract following a specified procedure, and then ALPA would be back where it started from without protection either in a contract or in law. It was a far-fetched and fuzzy notion, but it illustrates Behncke's cautiousness and inveterate suspiciousness. U.S. Congress, Senate Subcommittee of the Committee on Interstate Commerce, *Hearing on S3659, A Bill to Promote the Development of Safety and to Provide for the Regulation of Civil Aviation and Air Transport*, 75th Cong., 3rd Sess., 1938, pp. 90–91.

39. ALPA, *Proceedings of the 1936 Convention*, pp. 542–553.

40. *Ibid.*, pp. 453, 525–526.

41. Minutes of the meeting of May 2, 1935, Central Executive Council, ALPA; minutes of the meeting of June 6, 1936, Central Executive Council, ALPA.

42. ALPA, *Proceedings of the 1936 Convention*, pp. 87, 633, 668, 712. The new Secretary was Laurance W. Harris of American and the Treasurer was Cameron T. Robertson of United. The First Vice-President was Thomas O. Hardin of American, and the regional vice-presidents were Charles H. Dolson (EAL-Atlanta), Audrey Durst (PAA-Brownsville), Walter Effsen (UAL-Portland), Ray Elsmore (National Parks-Salt Lake City), Mal B. Freeburg (NWA-Minneapolis), Fred W. Kelley (WAE-Los Angeles), Fred B. Kern (PAA-Miami), Emery J. Martin (UAL-Newark), Jack O'Brien (UAL-San Francisco), Vernon I. Powers (Braniff-Kansas City), Sanis E. Robbins (Pacific Alaska-Alaska), Warren B. Smith (PAA-Santiago, Chile), and Stephen J. Williamson (PAA-Caribbean). *The Air Line Pilot* (October 1936), p. 1.

43. ALPA, *Proceedings of the 1936 Convention*, p. 53.

44. *Ibid.*, pp. 19–20; Smith, *Airways*, pp. 351–352; "Between the Lines," *Aviation*, 35 (January 1936), 46; James P. Vines, "Activities of the Aeronautical Chamber of Commerce," *Aviation*, 26 (Mar. 2, 1929), 630–631. Gorrell was a West Point graduate who had served as a pilot in World War I and also as Chief of Staff for Air Operations to Pershing. During the 1920s he had represented various aviation businesses in Washington, and he had, on occasion, represented the United States at international air shows and the like. "Airline Coordinator," *Aviation*, 35 (February 1936), 60.

45. U.S. Congress, Senate Subcommittee of the Committee on Interstate Commerce, *Hearings on S3659, A Bill to Promote the Development of Safety and to Provide for the Regulation of Civil Aviation and Air Transport,* 75th Cong., 3rd Sess., 1938, pp. 37–38, 48–98.

46. *The Air Line Pilot* (June 1938), p. 1; minutes of the meeting of July 19, 1938, Central Executive Council, ALPA. The pilots who missed work to help Behncke in the summer of 1938 were later fully reimbursed for lost time, an indication of the union's growing affluence.

47. *The Air Line Pilot* (August 1937), p. 1.

48. U.S., Federal Aviation Commission, *Report of the Federal Aviation Commission,* pp. iii–iv; U.S., *Congressional Record,* 74th Cong., 1st Sess., 1935 LXXIX, Part 2, p. 1310.

49. Minutes of the meeting of May 28, 1937, Central Executive Council, ALPA.

50. ALPA, *Proceedings of the 1938 Convention,* pp. 26–35; Smith, *Airways,* pp. 300–305.

51. ALPA, *Proceedings of the 1938 Convention,* pp. 116–117; Smith, *Airways,* pp. 303–306; National Advisory Committee for Aeronautics, *Twenty-Fourth Annual Report* (Washington: U.S. Government Printing Office, 1938), pp. 1–3; "Meet the CAA," *Aviation,* 37 (August 1938), 56–57.

52. U.S., *Congressional Record,* 75th Cong., 3rd Sess., 1938, LXXXIII, Part 6, p. 6409.

Epilogue

1. ALPA, *Proceedings of the 1942 Convention,* pp. 24–27; "Jobs for Fliers," *Business Week* (Feb. 24, 1946), pp. 102–103; "Labor Union up in the Air," *Nation's Business,* 34 (June 1946), 47–49.

2. Minutes of the meeting of June 21, 1943, Central Executive Council, ALPA.

3. "Golden Boys," *Time,* 47 (Feb. 4, 1946), 22; "Peace Between Capitalists," *Time,* 48 (July 22, 1946), 82.

4. The information in this section comes from a variety of sources, among them interviews with Wallace Anderson, R. L. Oakman, Homer Cole, Walter Bullock, and Mrs. Clarence N. Sayen, and Ruppenthal, "Revolution in the Air Line Pilots Association," pp. iv–x.

Index

Aeromedical Association, 118, 125
Aeronautical Chamber of Commerce, 124, 180
Aeronautical News, The, 104
Air Line Pilot, The: mentioned, 85; on AFofL benefits, 96; Behncke's editorship of, 218n28
Airline pilots: salaries, 1, 18, 39–40, 42–43, 142; status, 13; the press on, 15, 126–127, 218n13; titles for, 16–17; during depression, 40–41; unionization criticized, 49; Negro, 71, 214–216n46; Cord on, 98; surplus in 1933, 113; maximum hours, 116, 172; managerial mentality, 117; unemployed during air mail controversy, 151–152; praised by Will Rogers and Charles Lindbergh, 152; Roosevelt calls for federal protection of, 156–157
Air Line Pilots Association: named, 65–66, 70; meeting of organizers, 68–76; racial restriction on membership, 71; existence disclosed, 85–86; 1932 convention, 92–94; denounced as a racket, 104, 141, 224n34; and maximum hour issue, 116–118; seniority issue, 117; NRA code conferences, 122–128; and Hearst, 128, 161; in air mail controversy, 147, 151, 152; financial condition in 1934, 151–152; 1934 convention,
161; and Will Rogers, 161; status by 1934, 162–164; and status of co-pilots, 163–164, 182; and Long and Harmon, 169–171; and safety issue, 176–178; status by 1936, 182–183; and politicians, 184; office building, 193
Airlines: passenger service, 16; mergers, 38; reorganized, 152–153
Air mail: background, 6; contracts denounced, 107; contract cancellations, 109–110, 142–160; investigated by Senator Black, 112
Air Mail Act of 1934: origin, 153–160; inadequacies, 168–171; amended, 171
Air Mail Pilot Medal of Honor, 125
Air Mail Pilot of America, The, 29
Air Mail Pilots of America, 28–29, 207n27
Air Mail Service: Post Office, 11–13, 19–29; Roosevelt considers reestablishing, 150
Air Mail Strike of 1919, 19–29
Air Transport Association, 184–185
Allison, Earnest M., 32
American Airlines, 107–108
American Federation of Labor: mentioned, 17, 54; and ALPA affiliation, 62–67, 68–76, 96; and Pan American dispute, 221n2
American Medical Association, 63